Buffy
the vampire slayer

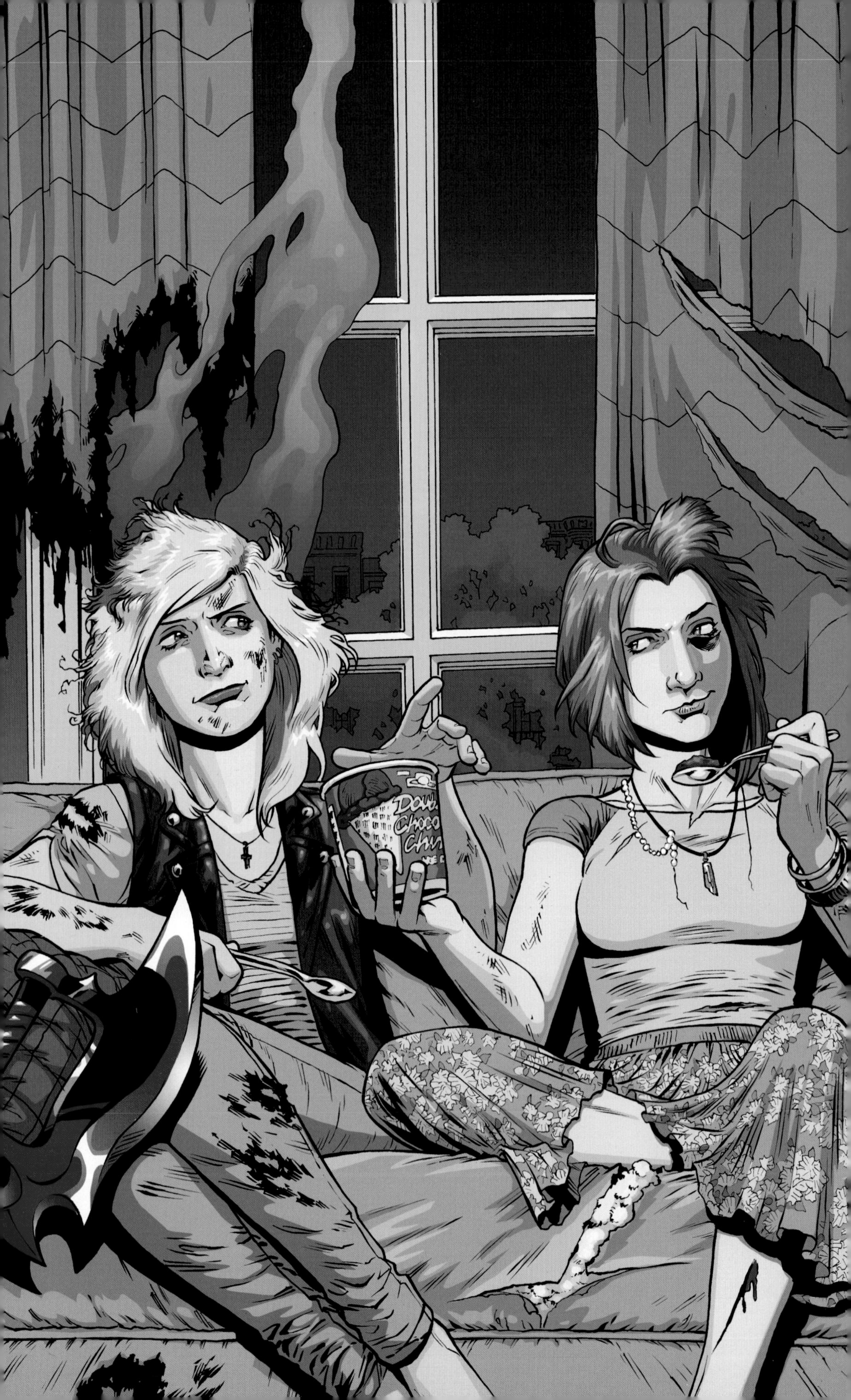

Buffy the Vampire Slayer

SEASON 10 · VOLUME 5

IN PIECES ON THE GROUND

SCRIPT
CHRISTOS GAGE

ART · CHAPTERS 1–2
REBEKAH ISAACS

ART · CHAPTERS 3–5
MEGAN LEVENS

COLORS DAN JACKSON

LETTERS RICHARD STARKINGS & COMICRAFT'S JIMMY BETANCOURT

COVER AND CHAPTER BREAK ART STEVE MORRIS

EXECUTIVE PRODUCER JOSS WHEDON

DARK HORSE BOOKS

PRESIDENT & PUBLISHER: MIKE RICHARDSON · EDITORS: SIERRA HAHN,
JIM GIBBONS & FREDDYE MILLER · ASSISTANT EDITORS: BEKAH CADEN & SPENCER CUSHING ·
COLLECTION DESIGNER: JUSTIN COUCH · DIGITAL ART TECHNICIAN: CHRISTIANNE GOUDREAU

Special thanks to NICOLE SPIEGEL *and* JOSH IZZO *at Twentieth Century Fox,*
DANIEL KAMINSKY, *and* CARDNER CLARK *and* HANNAH MEANS-SHANNON.

The art on page 2 is the variant cover for *Buffy* Season 10 #22, by Rebekah Isaacs with Dan Jackson.

This story takes place after the events in *Buffy the Vampire Slayer* Season 9, created by Joss Whedon.

DARKHORSE.COM

First edition: July 2016
ISBN 978-1-61655-944-1

1 3 5 7 9 10 8 6 4 2
Printed in China

Published by Dark Horse Books, a division of Dark Horse Comics, Inc.
10956 SE Main Street, Milwaukie, OR 97222

BUFFY THE VAMPIRE SLAYER SEASON 10 VOLUME 5: IN PIECES ON THE GROUND

This volume reprints the comic book series *Buffy the Vampire Slayer* Season 10 #21–#25, from
Dark Horse Comics.

Neil Hankerson, Executive Vice President · Tom Weddle, Chief Financial Officer · Randy
Stradley, Vice President of Publishing · Michael Martens, Vice President of Book Trade Sales
· Matt Parkinson, Vice President of Marketing · David Scroggy, Vice President of Product
Development · Dale LaFountain, Vice President of Information Technology · Cara Niece, Vice
President of Production and Scheduling · Nick McWhorter, Vice President of Media Licensing ·
Ken Lizzi, General Counsel · Dave Marshall, Editor in Chief · Davey Estrada, Editorial Director
· Scott Allie, Executive Senior Editor · Chris Warner, Senior Books Editor · Cary Grazzini,
Director of Print and Development · Lia Ribacchi, Art Director · Mark Bernardi, Director of
Digital Publishing · Michael Gombos, Director of International Publishing and Licensing

To find a comics shop in your area, call the Comic Shop Locator Service toll-free at
(888) 266-4226. International Licensing: 503-905-2377.

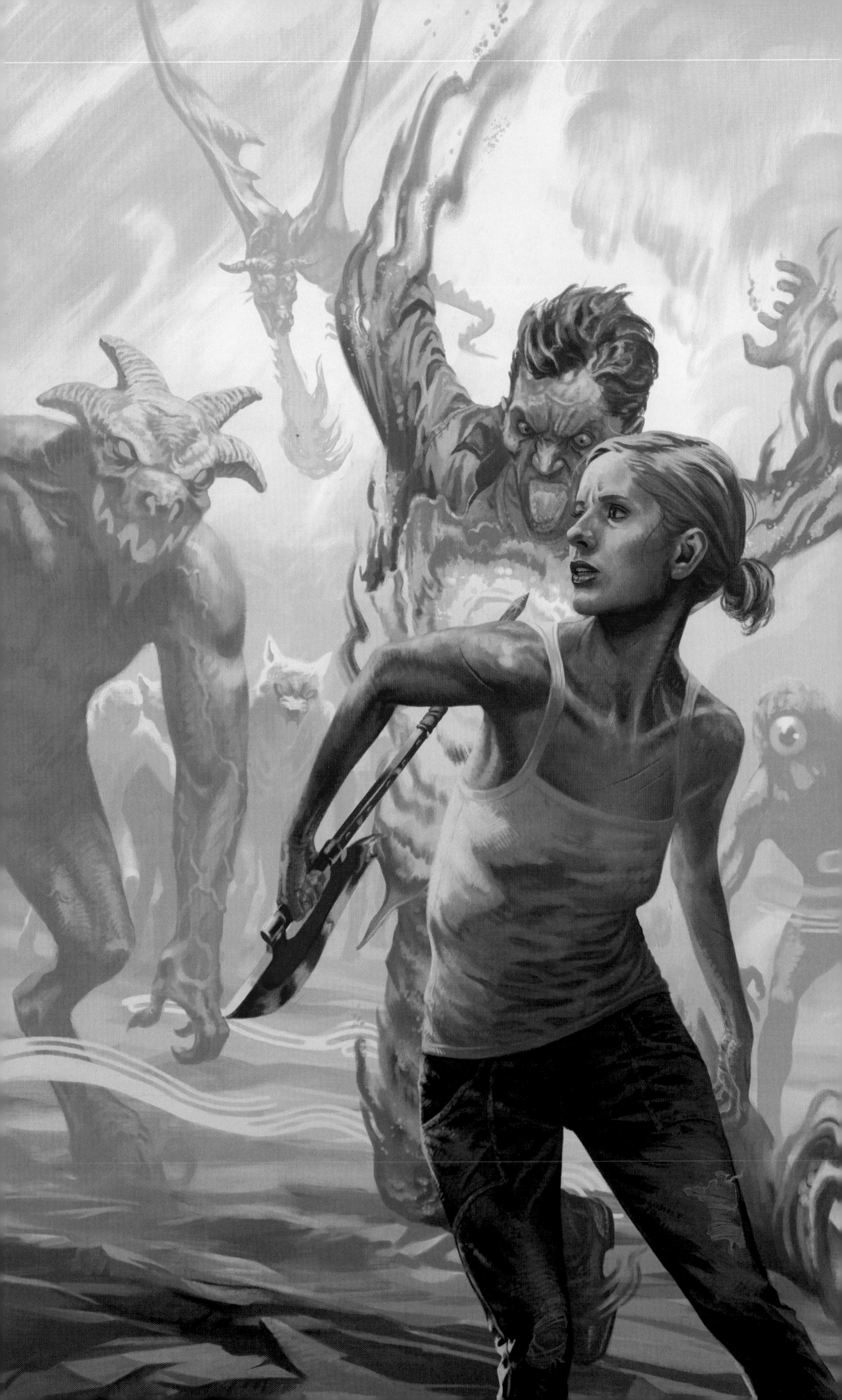

IN PIECES ON THE GROUND

PART ONE

LIVE

MONSTER SIGHTINGS

...JOINT U.S./ARGENTINIAN AIR FORCE STRIKE SEEMS TO HAVE KILLED THE GIGANTIC HORNED GORILLA TERRORIZING THE CITY OF BUENOS AIRES.

OUR EXPERT SUPERNATURAL ANALYST, GRAHAM MILLER, SAYS IT'S NOT YOUR IMAGINATION: WE *ARE* EXPERIENCING AN UPTICK IN EXTRADIMENSIONAL ATTACKS.

THAT'S TRUE, CHUCK. AND WHAT'S DISTURBING IS THAT THEY'RE HAPPENING WHERE YOU WOULDN'T EXPECT IT. THE ICE DEMONS IN ONTARIO, THE FLYING CENTIPEDES IN ITALY...

...SOMEHOW THESE CREATURES ARE INVADING OUR WORLD IN THE ABSENCE OF *HELLMOUTHS* OR OTHER PREEXISTING GATEWAYS. WE NEED TO FIND OUT HOW.

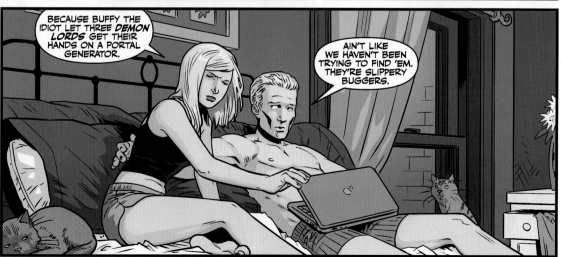

BECAUSE BUFFY THE IDIOT LET THREE *DEMON LORDS* GET THEIR HANDS ON A PORTAL GENERATOR.

AIN'T LIKE WE HAVEN'T BEEN TRYING TO FIND 'EM. THEY'RE SLIPPERY BUGGERS.

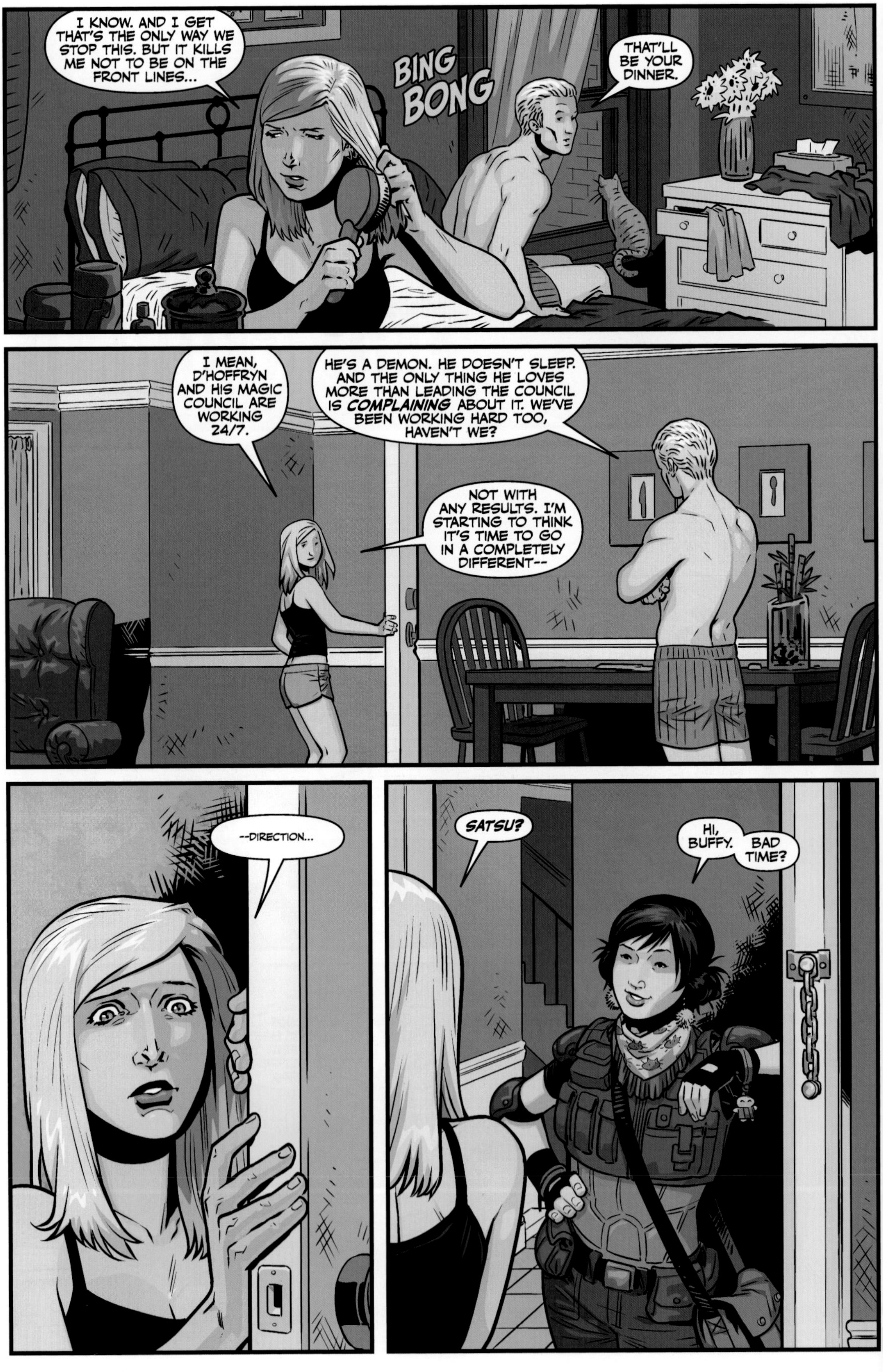
I KNOW. AND I GET THAT'S THE ONLY WAY WE STOP THIS. BUT IT KILLS ME NOT TO BE ON THE FRONT LINES...
BING BONG
THAT'LL BE YOUR DINNER.
I MEAN, D'HOFFRYN AND HIS MAGIC COUNCIL ARE WORKING 24/7.
HE'S A DEMON. HE DOESN'T SLEEP. AND THE ONLY THING HE LOVES MORE THAN LEADING THE COUNCIL IS COMPLAINING ABOUT IT. WE'VE BEEN WORKING HARD TOO, HAVEN'T WE?
NOT WITH ANY RESULTS. I'M STARTING TO THINK IT'S TIME TO GO IN A COMPLETELY DIFFERENT--
--DIRECTION...
SATSU?
HI, BUFFY.
BAD TIME?

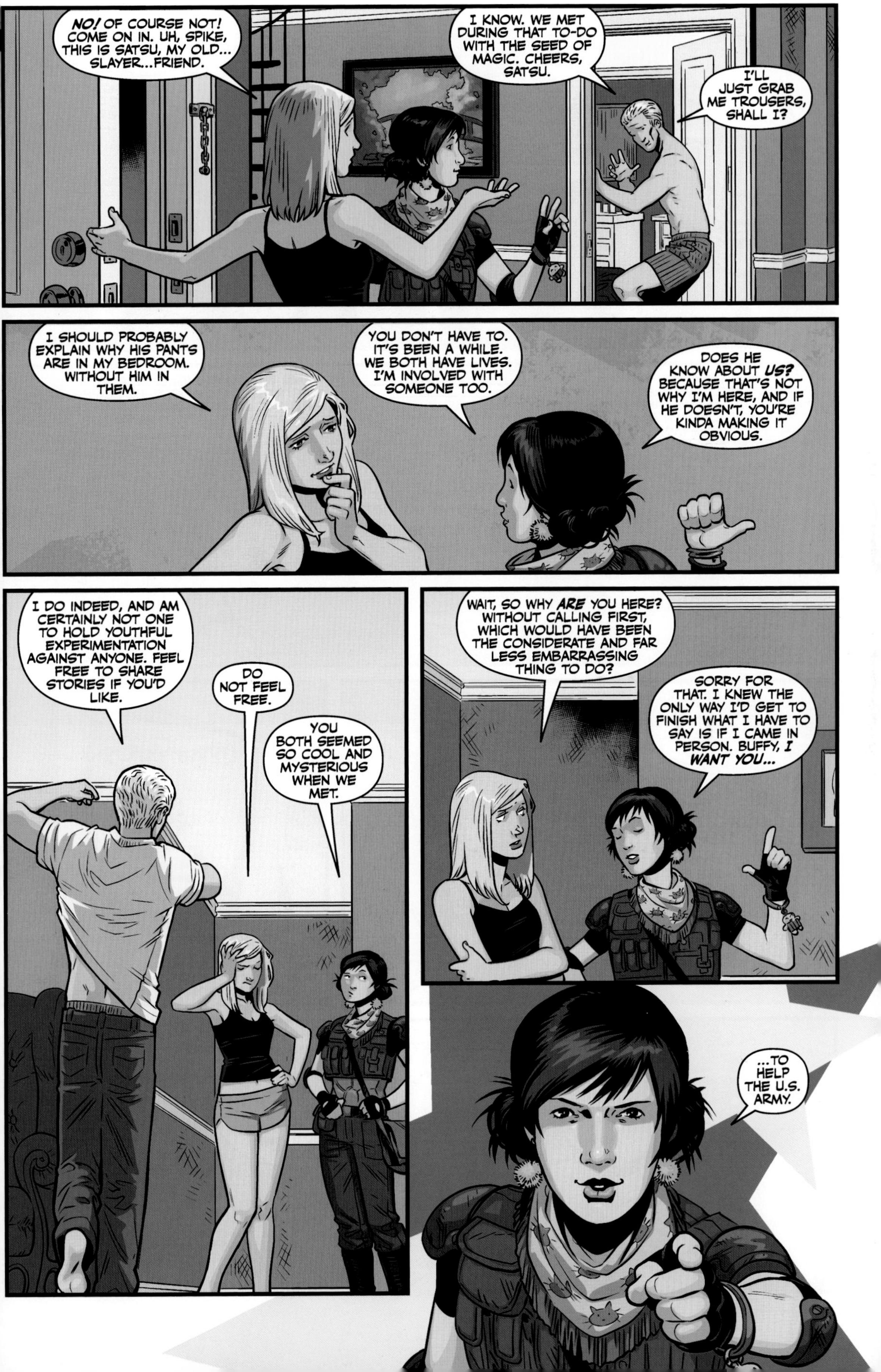

NO! OF COURSE NOT! COME ON IN. UH, SPIKE, THIS IS SATSU, MY OLD... SLAYER...FRIEND.
I KNOW. WE MET DURING THAT TO-DO WITH THE SEED OF MAGIC. CHEERS, SATSU.
I'LL JUST GRAB ME TROUSERS, SHALL I?
I SHOULD PROBABLY EXPLAIN WHY HIS PANTS ARE IN MY BEDROOM. WITHOUT HIM IN THEM.
YOU DON'T HAVE TO. IT'S BEEN A WHILE. WE BOTH HAVE LIVES. I'M INVOLVED WITH SOMEONE TOO.
DOES HE KNOW ABOUT US? BECAUSE THAT'S NOT WHY I'M HERE, AND IF HE DOESN'T, YOU'RE KINDA MAKING IT OBVIOUS.
I DO INDEED, AND AM CERTAINLY NOT ONE TO HOLD YOUTHFUL EXPERIMENTATION AGAINST ANYONE. FEEL FREE TO SHARE STORIES IF YOU'D LIKE.
DO NOT FEEL FREE.
YOU BOTH SEEMED SO COOL AND MYSTERIOUS WHEN WE MET.
WAIT, SO WHY ARE YOU HERE? WITHOUT CALLING FIRST, WHICH WOULD HAVE BEEN THE CONSIDERATE AND FAR LESS EMBARRASSING THING TO DO?
SORRY FOR THAT. I KNEW THE ONLY WAY I'D GET TO FINISH WHAT I HAVE TO SAY IS IF I CAME IN PERSON. BUFFY, I WANT YOU...
...TO HELP THE U.S. ARMY.

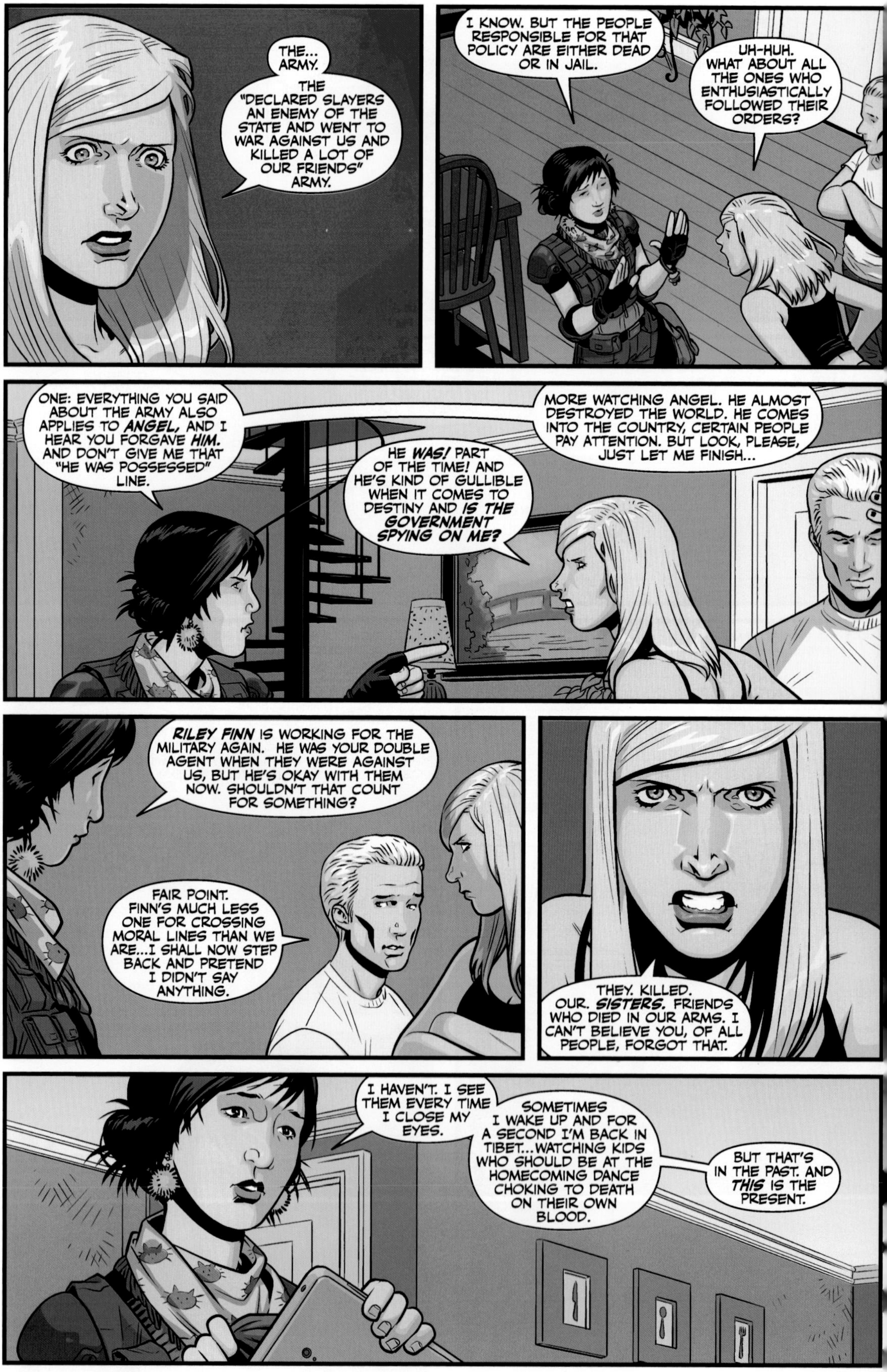
THE... ARMY.
THE "DECLARED SLAYERS AN ENEMY OF THE STATE AND WENT TO WAR AGAINST US AND KILLED A LOT OF OUR FRIENDS" ARMY.
I KNOW. BUT THE PEOPLE RESPONSIBLE FOR THAT POLICY ARE EITHER DEAD OR IN JAIL.
UH-HUH. WHAT ABOUT ALL THE ONES WHO ENTHUSIASTICALLY FOLLOWED THEIR ORDERS?
ONE: EVERYTHING YOU SAID ABOUT THE ARMY ALSO APPLIES TO ANGEL, AND I HEAR YOU FORGAVE HIM. AND DON'T GIVE ME THAT "HE WAS POSSESSED" LINE.
HE WAS! PART OF THE TIME! AND HE'S KIND OF GULLIBLE WHEN IT COMES TO DESTINY AND IS THE GOVERNMENT SPYING ON ME?
MORE WATCHING ANGEL. HE ALMOST DESTROYED THE WORLD. HE COMES INTO THE COUNTRY, CERTAIN PEOPLE PAY ATTENTION. BUT LOOK, PLEASE, JUST LET ME FINISH...
RILEY FINN IS WORKING FOR THE MILITARY AGAIN. HE WAS YOUR DOUBLE AGENT WHEN THEY WERE AGAINST US, BUT HE'S OKAY WITH THEM NOW. SHOULDN'T THAT COUNT FOR SOMETHING?
FAIR POINT. FINN'S MUCH LESS ONE FOR CROSSING MORAL LINES THAN WE ARE...I SHALL NOW STEP BACK AND PRETEND I DIDN'T SAY ANYTHING.
THEY. KILLED. OUR. SISTERS. FRIENDS WHO DIED IN OUR ARMS. I CAN'T BELIEVE YOU, OF ALL PEOPLE, FORGOT THAT.
I HAVEN'T. I SEE THEM EVERY TIME I CLOSE MY EYES.
SOMETIMES I WAKE UP AND FOR A SECOND I'M BACK IN TIBET...WATCHING KIDS WHO SHOULD BE AT THE HOMECOMING DANCE CHOKING TO DEATH ON THEIR OWN BLOOD.
BUT THAT'S IN THE PAST. AND THIS IS THE PRESENT.

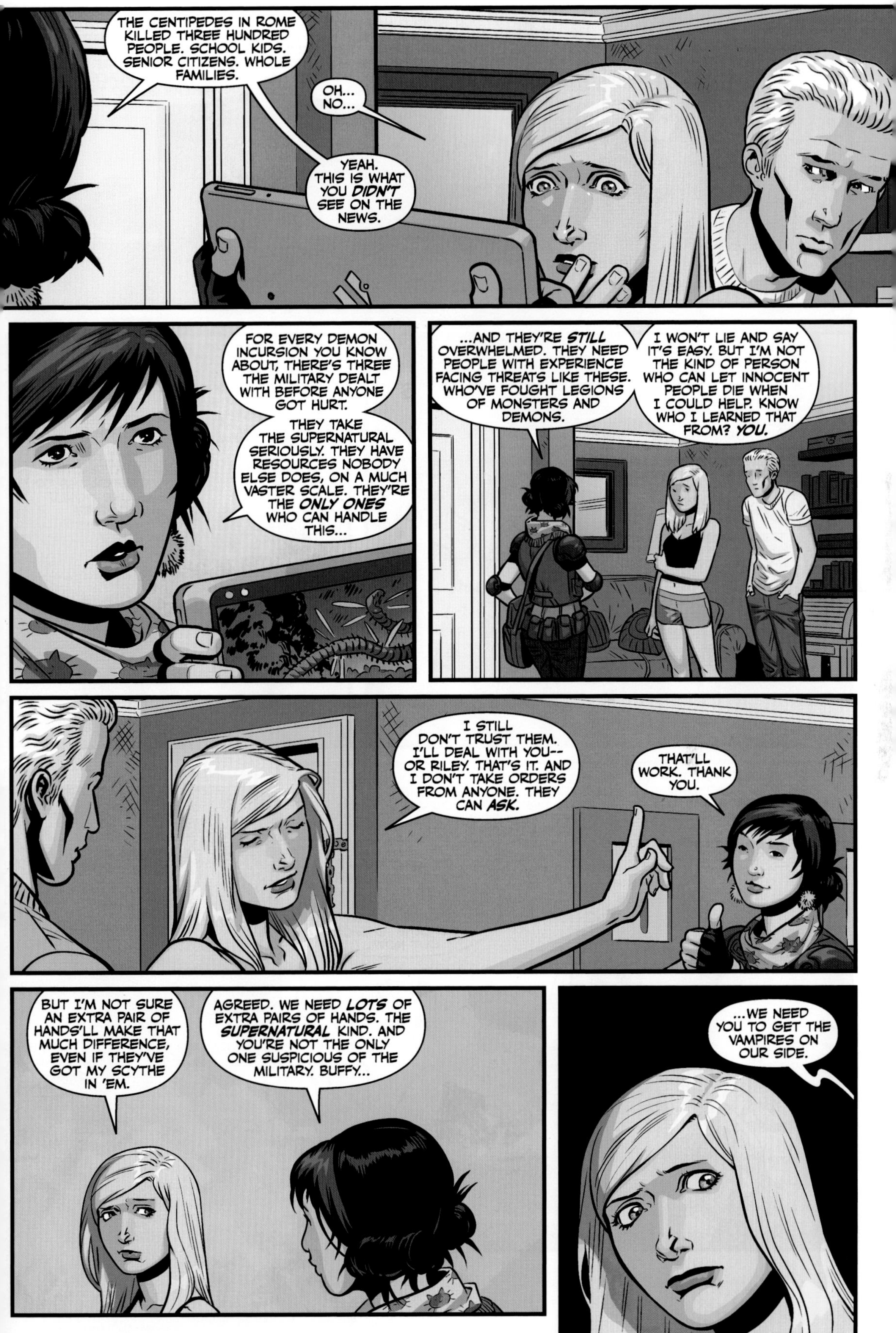

THE CENTIPEDES IN ROME KILLED THREE HUNDRED PEOPLE. SCHOOL KIDS. SENIOR CITIZENS. WHOLE FAMILIES.
OH... NO...
YEAH. THIS IS WHAT YOU DIDN'T SEE ON THE NEWS.
FOR EVERY DEMON INCURSION YOU KNOW ABOUT, THERE'S THREE THE MILITARY DEALT WITH BEFORE ANYONE GOT HURT.
THEY TAKE THE SUPERNATURAL SERIOUSLY. THEY HAVE RESOURCES NOBODY ELSE DOES, ON A MUCH VASTER SCALE. THEY'RE THE ONLY ONES WHO CAN HANDLE THIS...
...AND THEY'RE STILL OVERWHELMED. THEY NEED PEOPLE WITH EXPERIENCE FACING THREATS LIKE THESE. WHO'VE FOUGHT LEGIONS OF MONSTERS AND DEMONS.
I WON'T LIE AND SAY IT'S EASY. BUT I'M NOT THE KIND OF PERSON WHO CAN LET INNOCENT PEOPLE DIE WHEN I COULD HELP. KNOW WHO I LEARNED THAT FROM? YOU.
I STILL DON'T TRUST THEM. I'LL DEAL WITH YOU-- OR RILEY. THAT'S IT. AND I DON'T TAKE ORDERS FROM ANYONE. THEY CAN ASK.
THAT'LL WORK. THANK YOU.
BUT I'M NOT SURE AN EXTRA PAIR OF HANDS'LL MAKE THAT MUCH DIFFERENCE, EVEN IF THEY'VE GOT MY SCYTHE IN 'EM.
AGREED. WE NEED LOTS OF EXTRA PAIRS OF HANDS. THE SUPERNATURAL KIND. AND YOU'RE NOT THE ONLY ONE SUSPICIOUS OF THE MILITARY. BUFFY...
...WE NEED YOU TO GET THE VAMPIRES ON OUR SIDE.

LATER, UPSTAIRS.

OUR WORLD HAS NATURALLY OCCURRING PORTALS IN FIXED LOCATIONS, WHERE THE BARRIER TO HELL DIMENSIONS IS WEAKER. HELLMOUTHS BEING THE PRIME EXAMPLE.

EVEN THERE, ONE REQUIRES A TOOL--A SPELL OR OTHER SOURCE OF MYSTIC ENERGY--TO PIERCE THE BARRIER. AND BECAUSE WE KNOW WHERE THESE PLACES ARE, WE CAN GUARD THEM.

THE *RESTLESS DOOR* IS OF CONCERN BECAUSE IT CAN OPEN PORTALS ANYWHERE. BETWEEN ANY TWO DIMENSIONS, IN ANY LOCATION.

BECAUSE THE RESTLESS DOOR WAS *CREATED* IN A HELL DIMENSION, IT IS NOT BOUND BY THE LAWS OF OUR REALITY.

OUR DEMON TRIUMVIRATE IS FILLING EARTH WITH CREATURES WHO OWE THEM A DEBT FOR MAKING THE JOURNEY POSSIBLE. THEY ARE SOLIDIFYING A VAST POWER BASE.

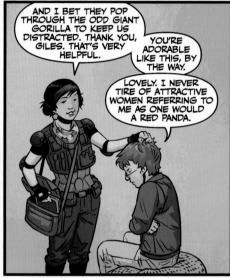

AND I BET THEY POP THROUGH THE ODD GIANT GORILLA TO KEEP US DISTRACTED. THANK YOU, GILES. THAT'S VERY HELPFUL.

YOU'RE ADORABLE LIKE THIS, BY THE WAY.

LOVELY. I NEVER TIRE OF ATTRACTIVE WOMEN REFERRING TO ME AS ONE WOULD A RED PANDA.

LOOK, I GET THAT THE VAMPIRES DON'T LIKE G.I.'S, BUT I'M BUFFY THE *VAMPIRE SLAYER.* NOT EVEN CLOSE TO MAKING THEIR "WOMEN WE LOVE" LIST.

BELIEVE IT OR NOT, THEY *ASKED* FOR YOU. YOU'RE THE DEVIL THEY KNOW...YOU'VE SEALED TREATIES WITH THEM BEFORE, WHICH IS MORE THAN THE ARMY CAN SAY.

WE NEED THEM ON OUR SIDE. THEIR MANPOWER AND DURABILITY WOULD MAKE A HUGE DIFFERENCE. ANYWAY, IT'S TOO LATE TO BACK OUT NOW...

WHUP WHUP WHUP

WHUP W

...OUR RIDE'S HERE.

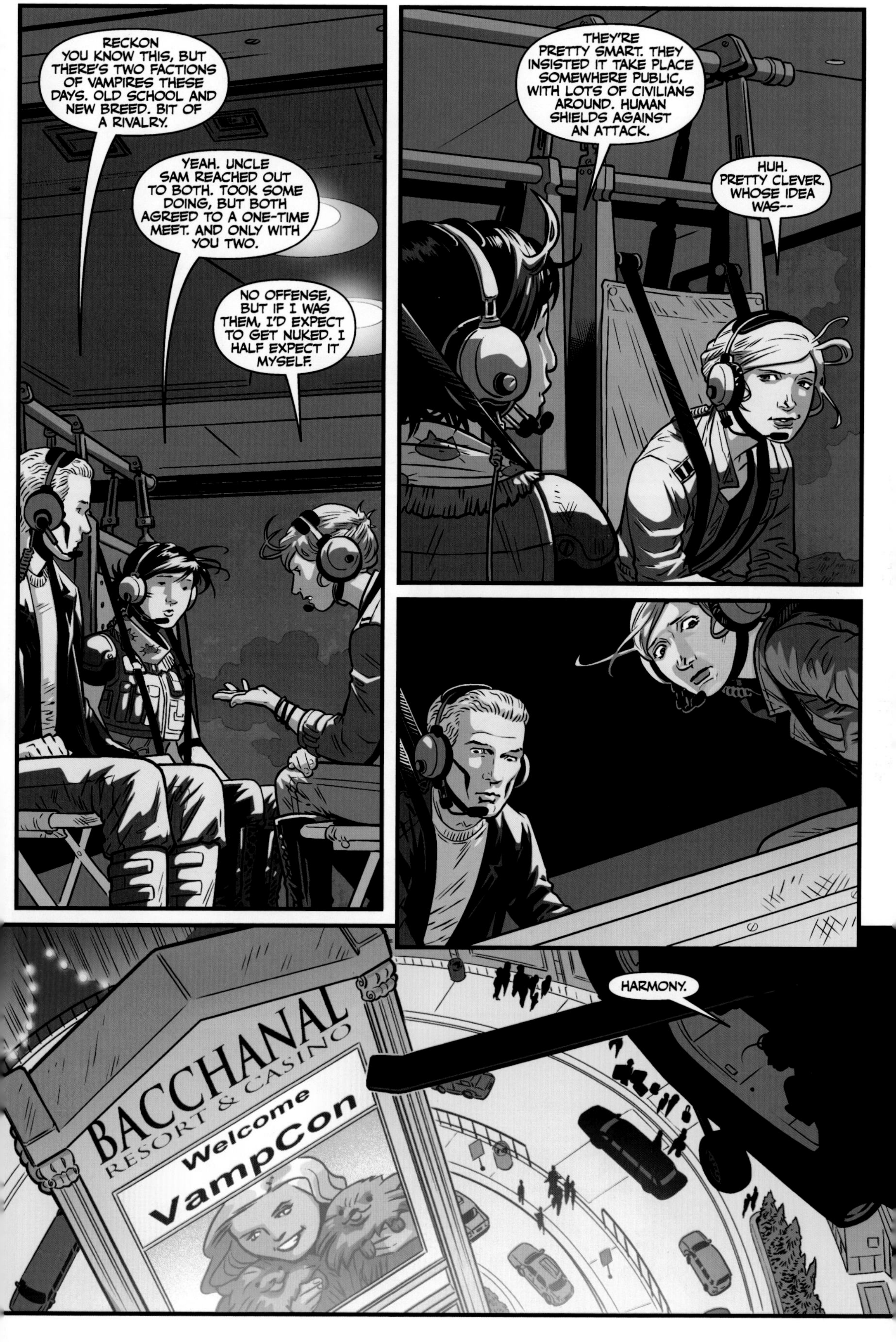

RECKON YOU KNOW THIS, BUT THERE'S TWO FACTIONS OF VAMPIRES THESE DAYS. OLD SCHOOL AND NEW BREED. BIT OF A RIVALRY.
YEAH. UNCLE SAM REACHED OUT TO BOTH. TOOK SOME DOING, BUT BOTH AGREED TO A ONE-TIME MEET. AND ONLY WITH YOU TWO.
NO OFFENSE, BUT IF I WAS THEM, I'D EXPECT TO GET NUKED. I HALF EXPECT IT MYSELF.
THEY'RE PRETTY SMART. THEY INSISTED IT TAKE PLACE SOMEWHERE PUBLIC, WITH LOTS OF CIVILIANS AROUND. HUMAN SHIELDS AGAINST AN ATTACK.
HUH. PRETTY CLEVER. WHOSE IDEA WAS--
HARMONY.
BACCHANAL
RESORT & CASINO
Welcome
VampCon

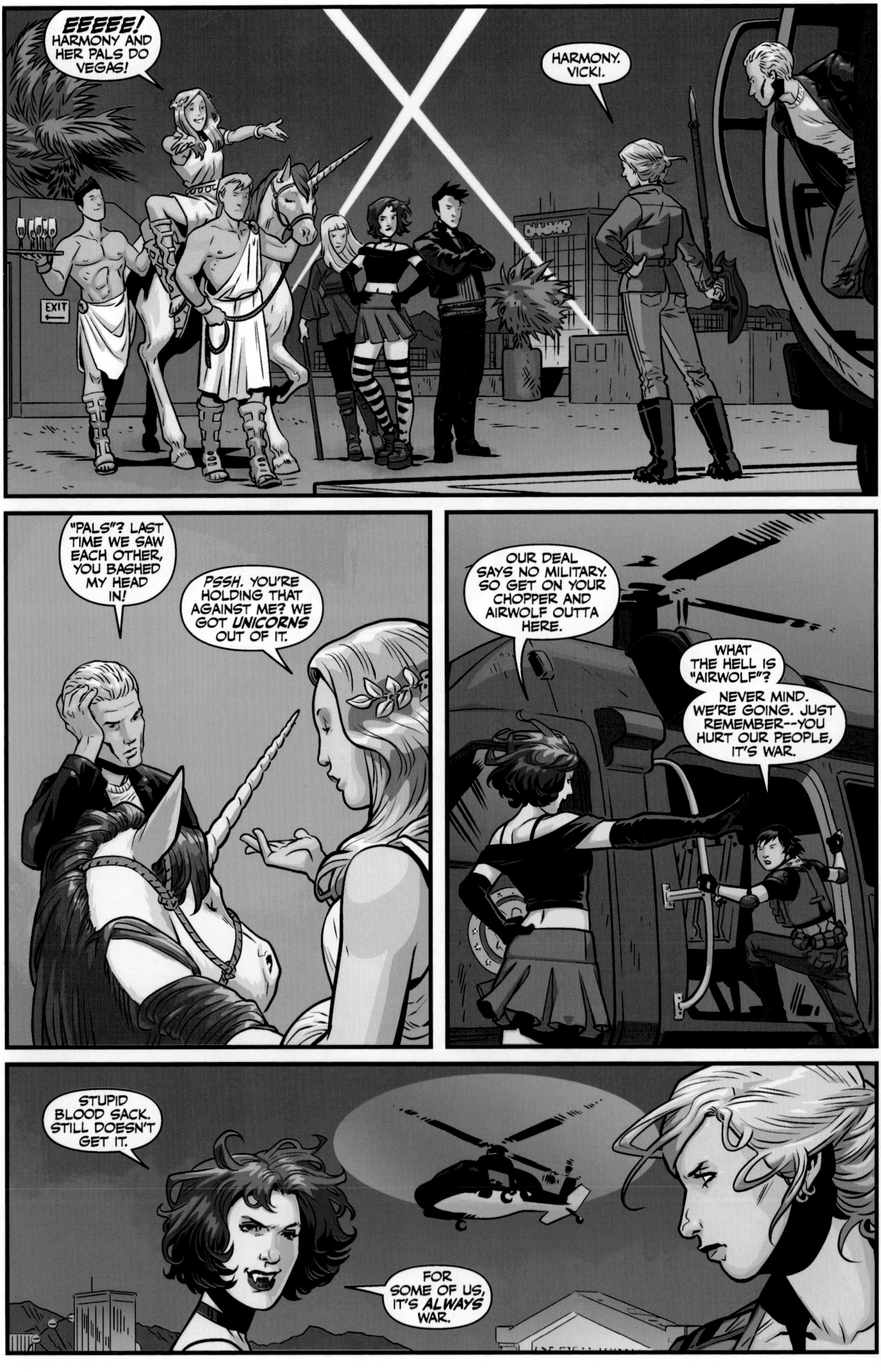
EEEEE! HARMONY AND HER PALS DO VEGAS!
HARMONY. VICKI.
EXIT
"PALS"? LAST TIME WE SAW EACH OTHER, YOU BASHED MY HEAD IN!
PSSH. YOU'RE HOLDING THAT AGAINST ME? WE GOT UNICORNS OUT OF IT.
OUR DEAL SAYS NO MILITARY. SO GET ON YOUR CHOPPER AND AIRWOLF OUTTA HERE.
WHAT THE HELL IS "AIRWOLF"?
NEVER MIND. WE'RE GOING. JUST REMEMBER--YOU HURT OUR PEOPLE, IT'S WAR.
STUPID BLOOD SACK. STILL DOESN'T GET IT.
FOR SOME OF US, IT'S ALWAYS WAR.

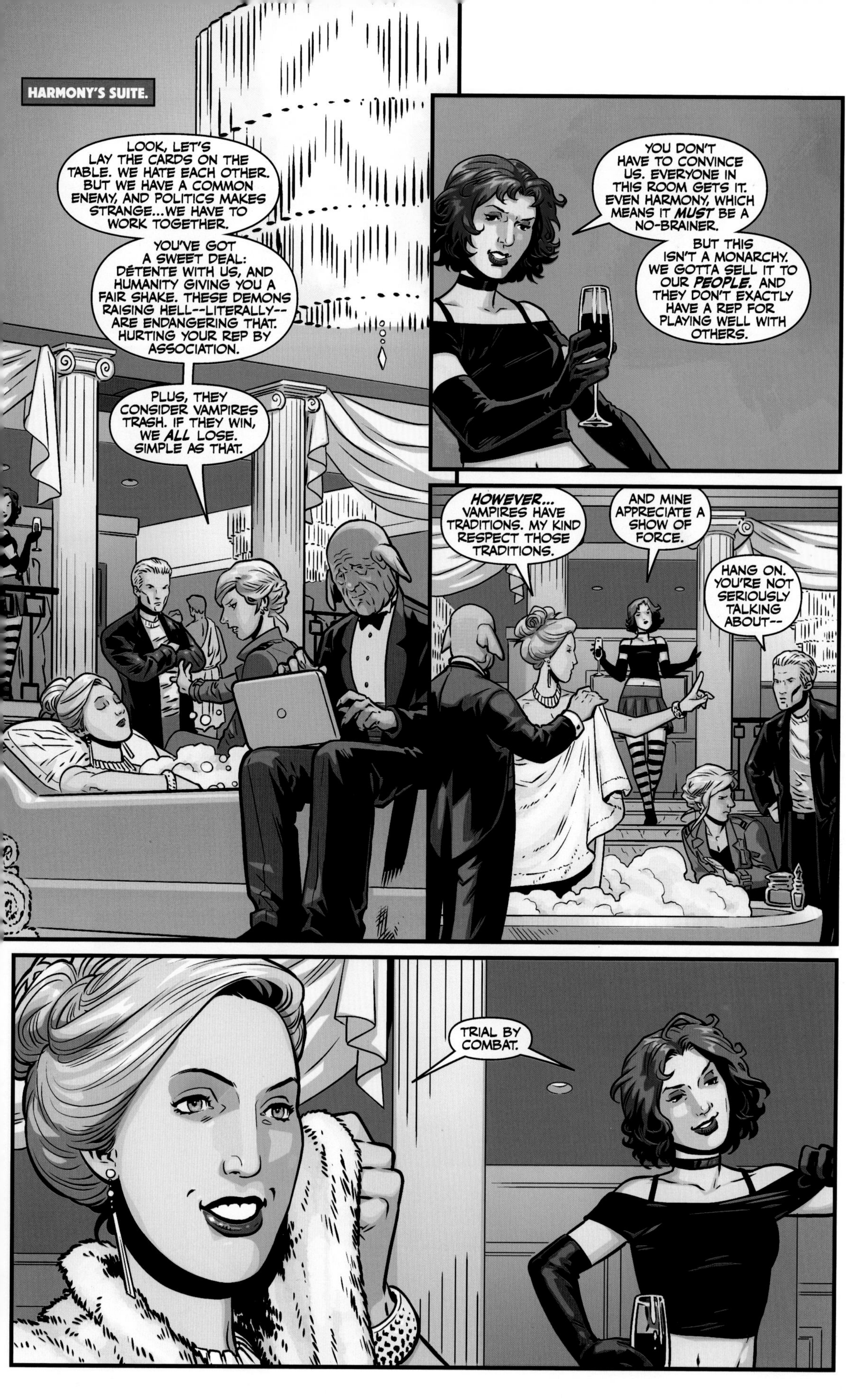
HARMONY'S SUITE.
LOOK, LET'S LAY THE CARDS ON THE TABLE. WE HATE EACH OTHER. BUT WE HAVE A COMMON ENEMY, AND POLITICS MAKES STRANGE...WE HAVE TO WORK TOGETHER.
YOU'VE GOT A SWEET DEAL: DÉTENTE WITH US, AND HUMANITY GIVING YOU A FAIR SHAKE. THESE DEMONS RAISING HELL--LITERALLY--ARE ENDANGERING THAT. HURTING YOUR REP BY ASSOCIATION.
PLUS, THEY CONSIDER VAMPIRES TRASH. IF THEY WIN, WE ALL LOSE. SIMPLE AS THAT.
YOU DON'T HAVE TO CONVINCE US. EVERYONE IN THIS ROOM GETS IT. EVEN HARMONY, WHICH MEANS IT MUST BE A NO-BRAINER.
BUT THIS ISN'T A MONARCHY. WE GOTTA SELL IT TO OUR PEOPLE. AND THEY DON'T EXACTLY HAVE A REP FOR PLAYING WELL WITH OTHERS.
HOWEVER... VAMPIRES HAVE TRADITIONS. MY KIND RESPECT THOSE TRADITIONS.
AND MINE APPRECIATE A SHOW OF FORCE.
HANG ON. YOU'RE NOT SERIOUSLY TALKING ABOUT--
TRIAL BY COMBAT.

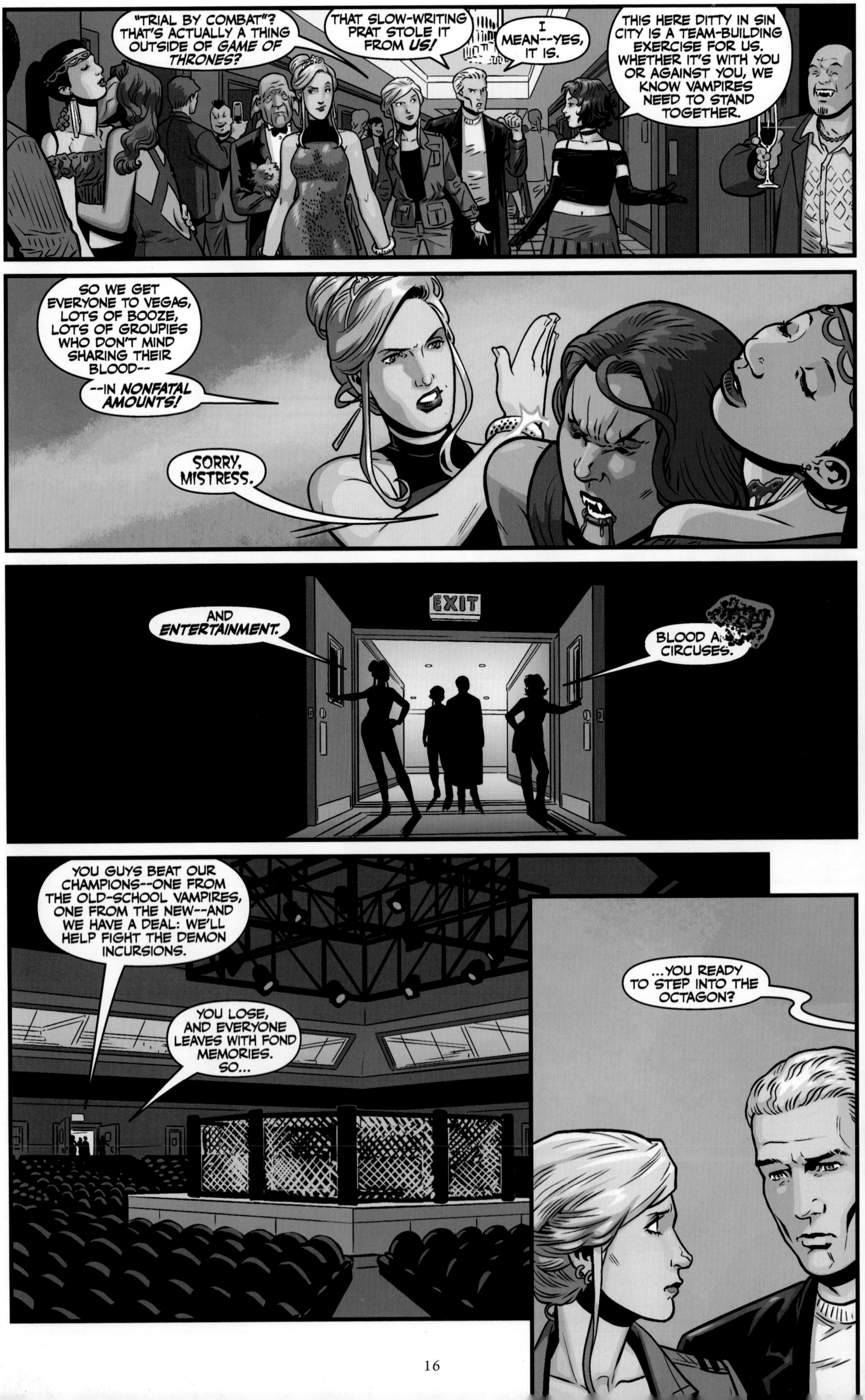
"TRIAL BY COMBAT"? THAT'S ACTUALLY A THING OUTSIDE OF *GAME OF THRONES*?
THAT SLOW-WRITING PRAT STOLE IT FROM *US!*
I MEAN--YES, IT IS.
THIS HERE DITTY IN SIN CITY IS A TEAM-BUILDING EXERCISE FOR US. WHETHER IT'S WITH YOU OR AGAINST YOU, WE KNOW VAMPIRES NEED TO STAND TOGETHER.
SO WE GET EVERYONE TO VEGAS, LOTS OF BOOZE, LOTS OF GROUPIES WHO DON'T MIND SHARING THEIR BLOOD--
--IN *NONFATAL AMOUNTS!*
SORRY, MISTRESS.
EXIT
AND *ENTERTAINMENT.*
BLOOD A CIRCUSES.
YOU GUYS BEAT OUR CHAMPIONS--ONE FROM THE OLD-SCHOOL VAMPIRES, ONE FROM THE NEW--AND WE HAVE A DEAL: WE'LL HELP FIGHT THE DEMON INCURSIONS.
YOU LOSE, AND EVERYONE LEAVES WITH FOND MEMORIES. SO...
...YOU READY TO STEP INTO THE OCTAGON?

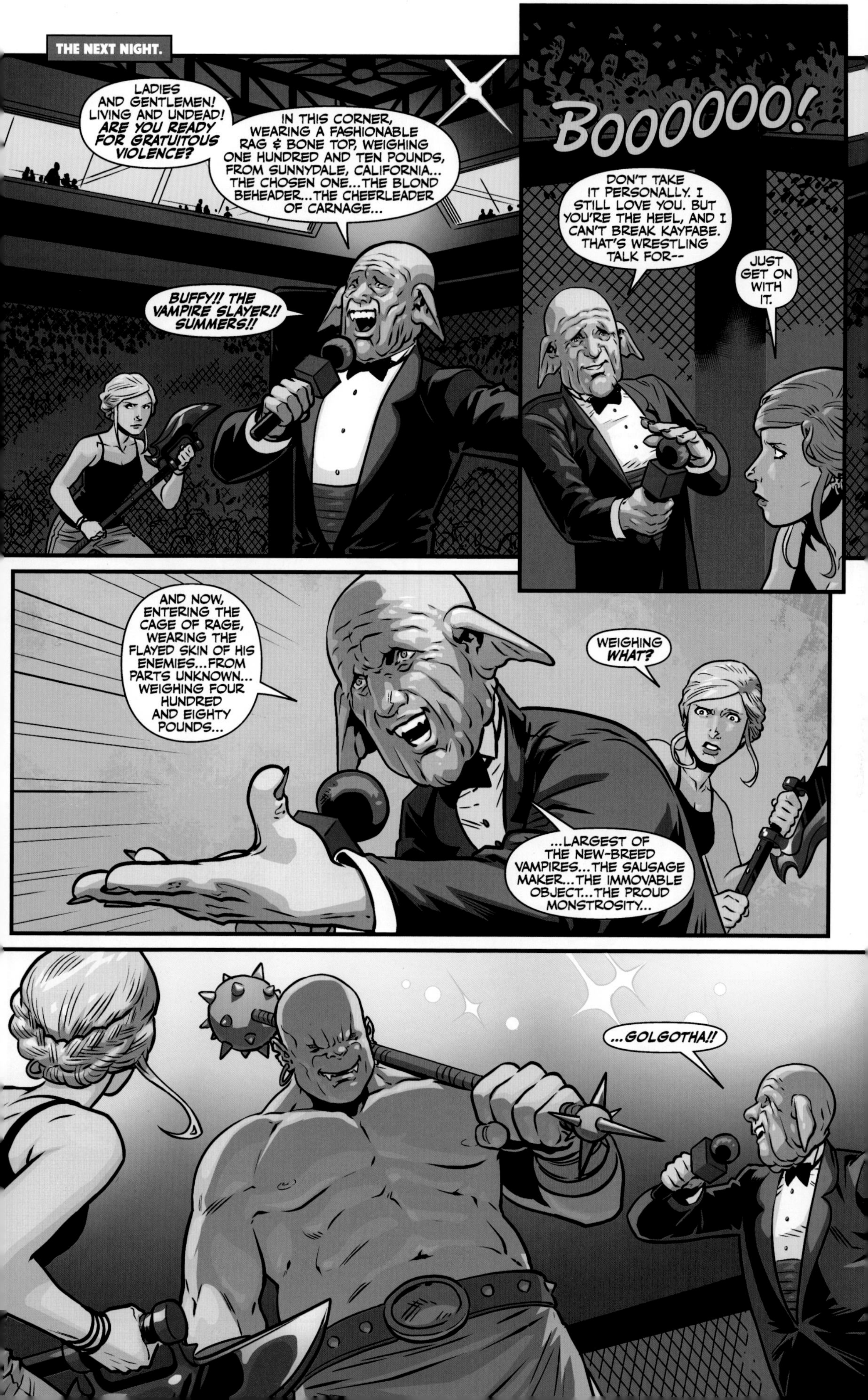
THE NEXT NIGHT.
LADIES AND GENTLEMEN! LIVING AND UNDEAD! ARE YOU READY FOR GRATUITOUS VIOLENCE?
IN THIS CORNER, WEARING A FASHIONABLE RAG & BONE TOP, WEIGHING ONE HUNDRED AND TEN POUNDS, FROM SUNNYDALE, CALIFORNIA... THE CHOSEN ONE...THE BLOND BEHEADER...THE CHEERLEADER OF CARNAGE...
BUFFY!! THE VAMPIRE SLAYER!! SUMMERS!!
BOOOOOO!
DON'T TAKE IT PERSONALLY. I STILL LOVE YOU. BUT YOU'RE THE HEEL, AND I CAN'T BREAK KAYFABE. THAT'S WRESTLING TALK FOR--
JUST GET ON WITH IT.
AND NOW, ENTERING THE CAGE OF RAGE, WEARING THE FLAYED SKIN OF HIS ENEMIES...FROM PARTS UNKNOWN... WEIGHING FOUR HUNDRED AND EIGHTY POUNDS...
WEIGHING WHAT?
...LARGEST OF THE NEW-BREED VAMPIRES...THE SAUSAGE MAKER...THE IMMOVABLE OBJECT...THE PROUD MONSTROSITY...
...GOLGOTHA!!

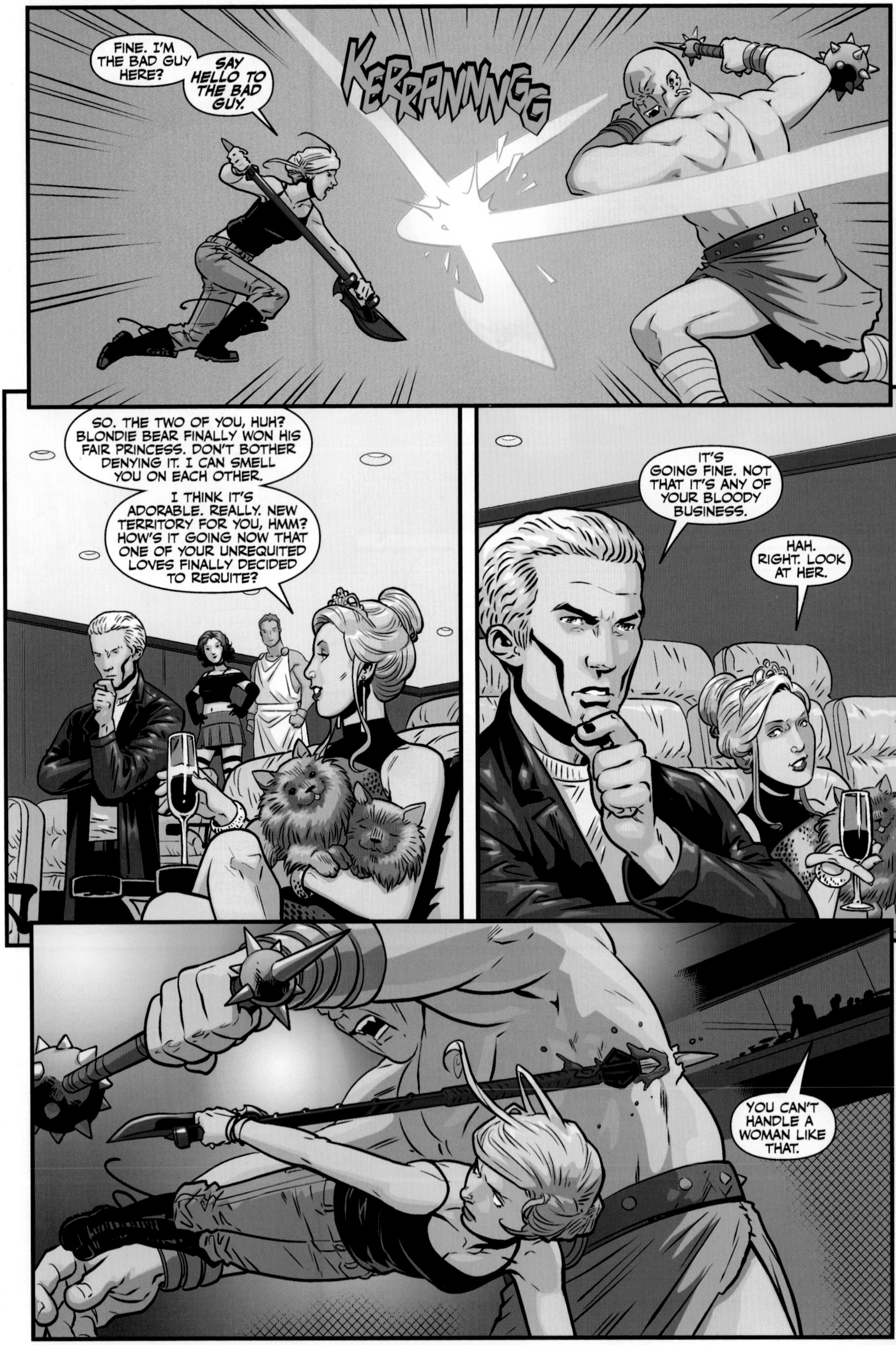
FINE. I'M THE BAD GUY HERE?
SAY HELLO TO THE BAD GUY.
KERRANNNGG
SO. THE TWO OF YOU, HUH? BLONDIE BEAR FINALLY WON HIS FAIR PRINCESS. DON'T BOTHER DENYING IT. I CAN SMELL YOU ON EACH OTHER.
I THINK IT'S ADORABLE. REALLY. NEW TERRITORY FOR YOU, HMM? HOW'S IT GOING NOW THAT ONE OF YOUR UNREQUITED LOVES FINALLY DECIDED TO REQUITE?
IT'S GOING FINE. NOT THAT IT'S ANY OF YOUR BLOODY BUSINESS.
HAH. RIGHT. LOOK AT HER.
YOU CAN'T HANDLE A WOMAN LIKE THAT.

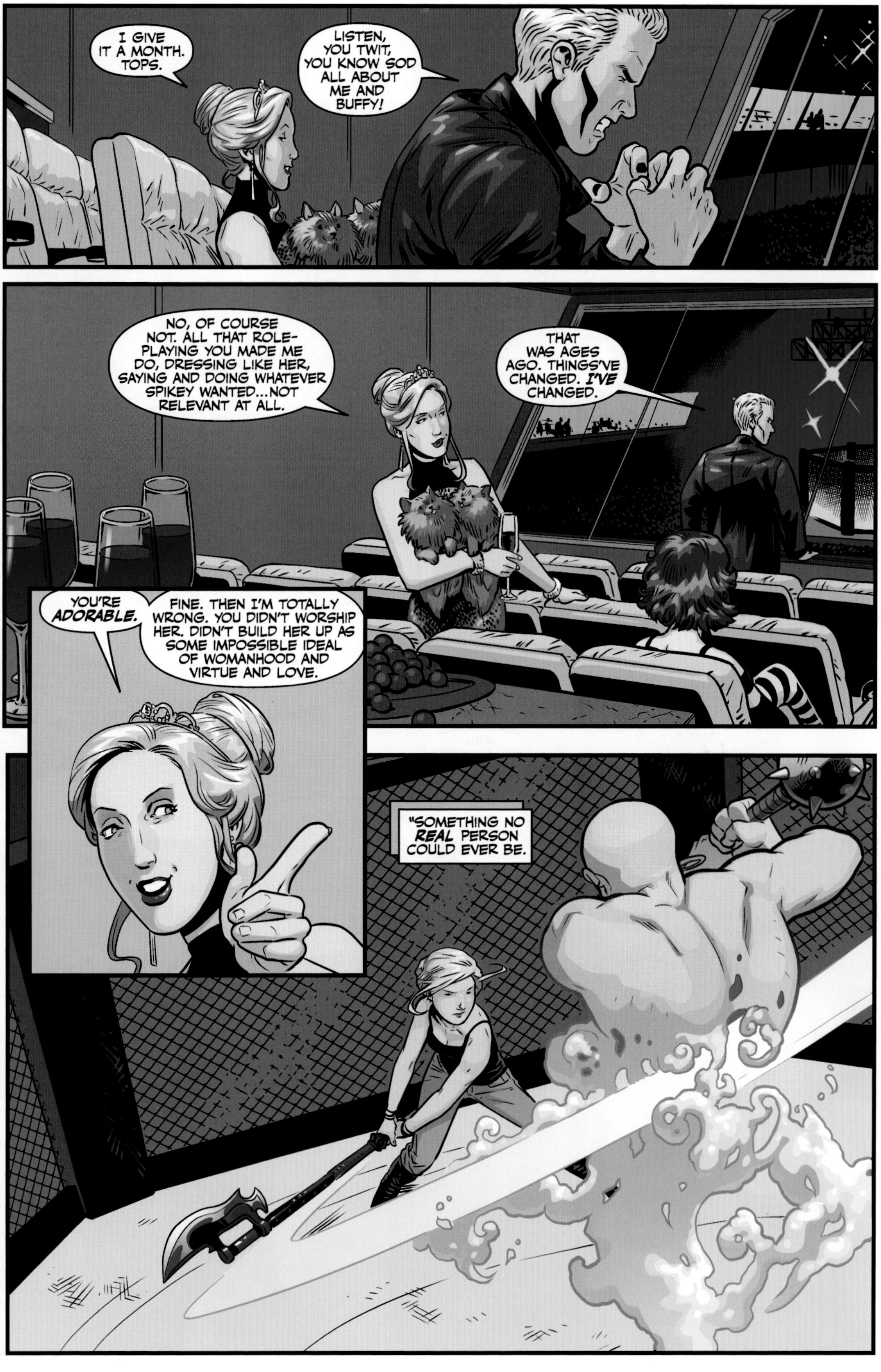
I GIVE IT A MONTH. TOPS.
LISTEN, YOU TWIT, YOU KNOW SOD ALL ABOUT ME AND BUFFY!
NO, OF COURSE NOT. ALL THAT ROLE-PLAYING YOU MADE ME DO, DRESSING LIKE HER, SAYING AND DOING WHATEVER SPIKEY WANTED...NOT RELEVANT AT ALL.
THAT WAS AGES AGO. THINGS'VE CHANGED. *I'VE* CHANGED.
FINE. THEN I'M TOTALLY WRONG. YOU DIDN'T WORSHIP HER. DIDN'T BUILD HER UP AS SOME IMPOSSIBLE IDEAL OF WOMANHOOD AND VIRTUE AND LOVE.
YOU'RE *ADORABLE.*
"SOMETHING NO *REAL* PERSON COULD EVER BE.

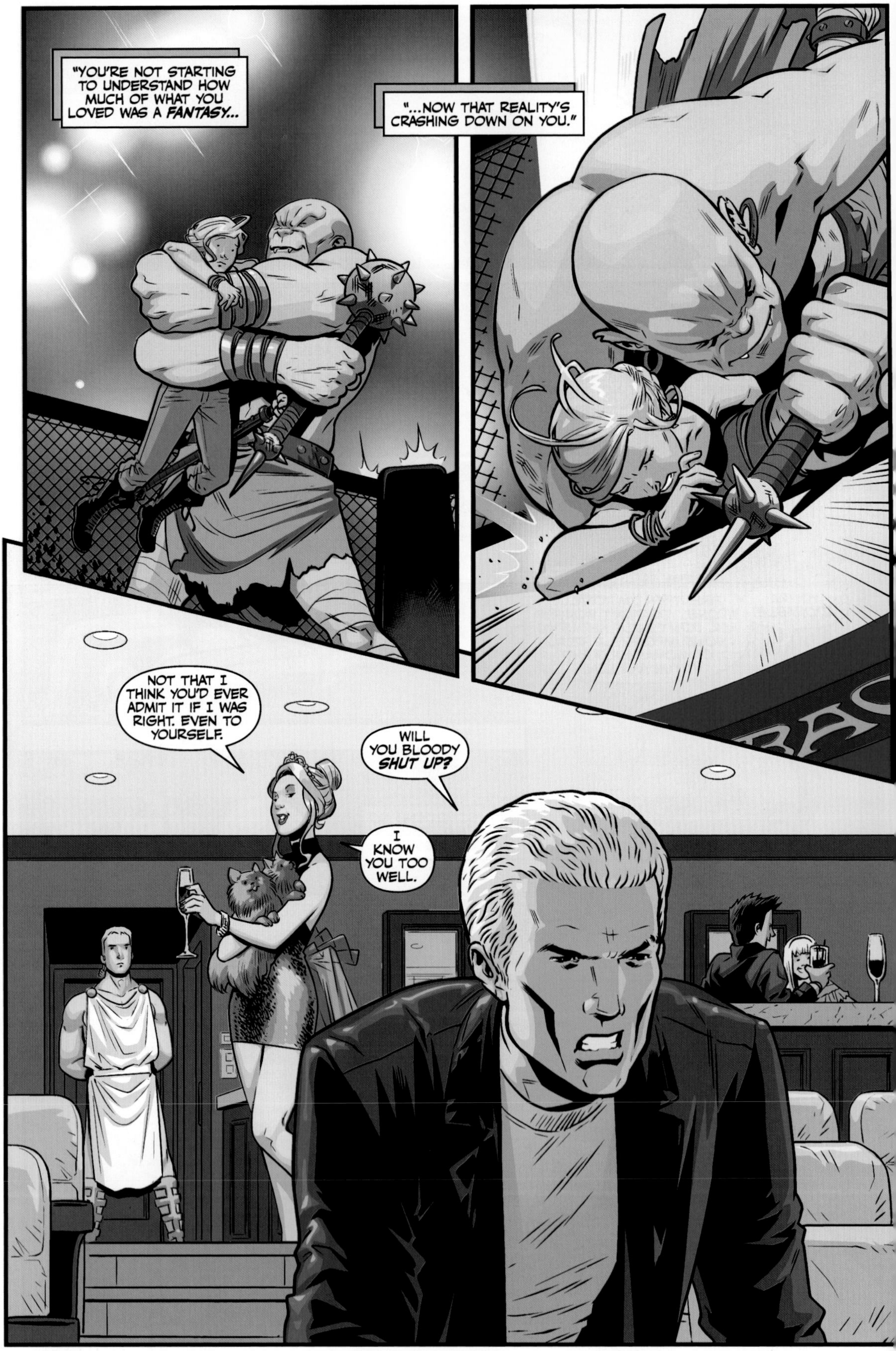
"YOU'RE NOT STARTING TO UNDERSTAND HOW MUCH OF WHAT YOU LOVED WAS A *FANTASY*...
"...NOW THAT REALITY'S CRASHING DOWN ON YOU."
NOT THAT I THINK YOU'D EVER ADMIT IT IF I WAS RIGHT. EVEN TO YOURSELF.
WILL YOU BLOODY *SHUT UP?*
I KNOW YOU TOO WELL.

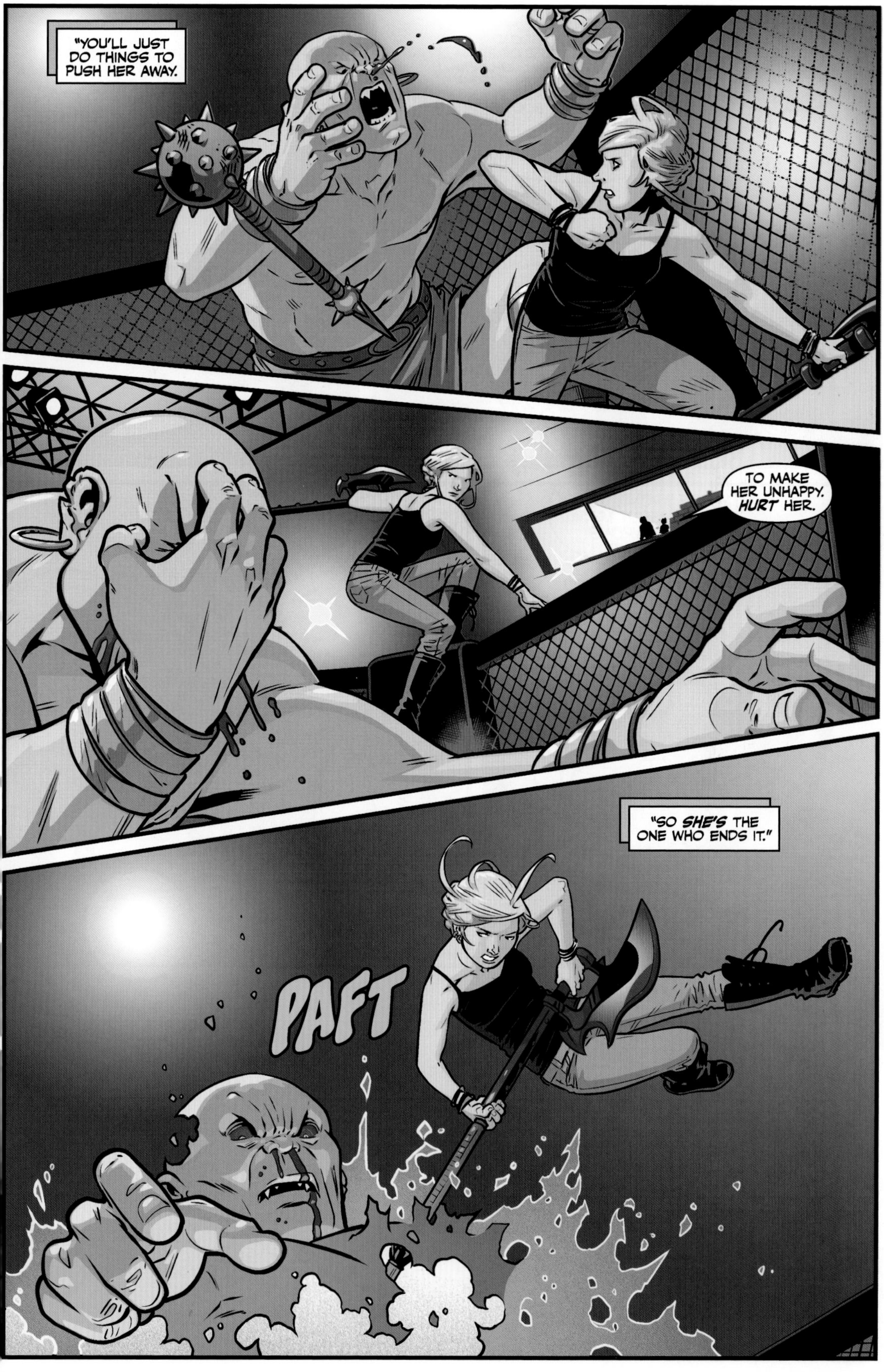
"YOU'LL JUST DO THINGS TO PUSH HER AWAY.
TO MAKE HER UNHAPPY. HURT HER.
"SO SHE'S THE ONE WHO ENDS IT."
PAFT

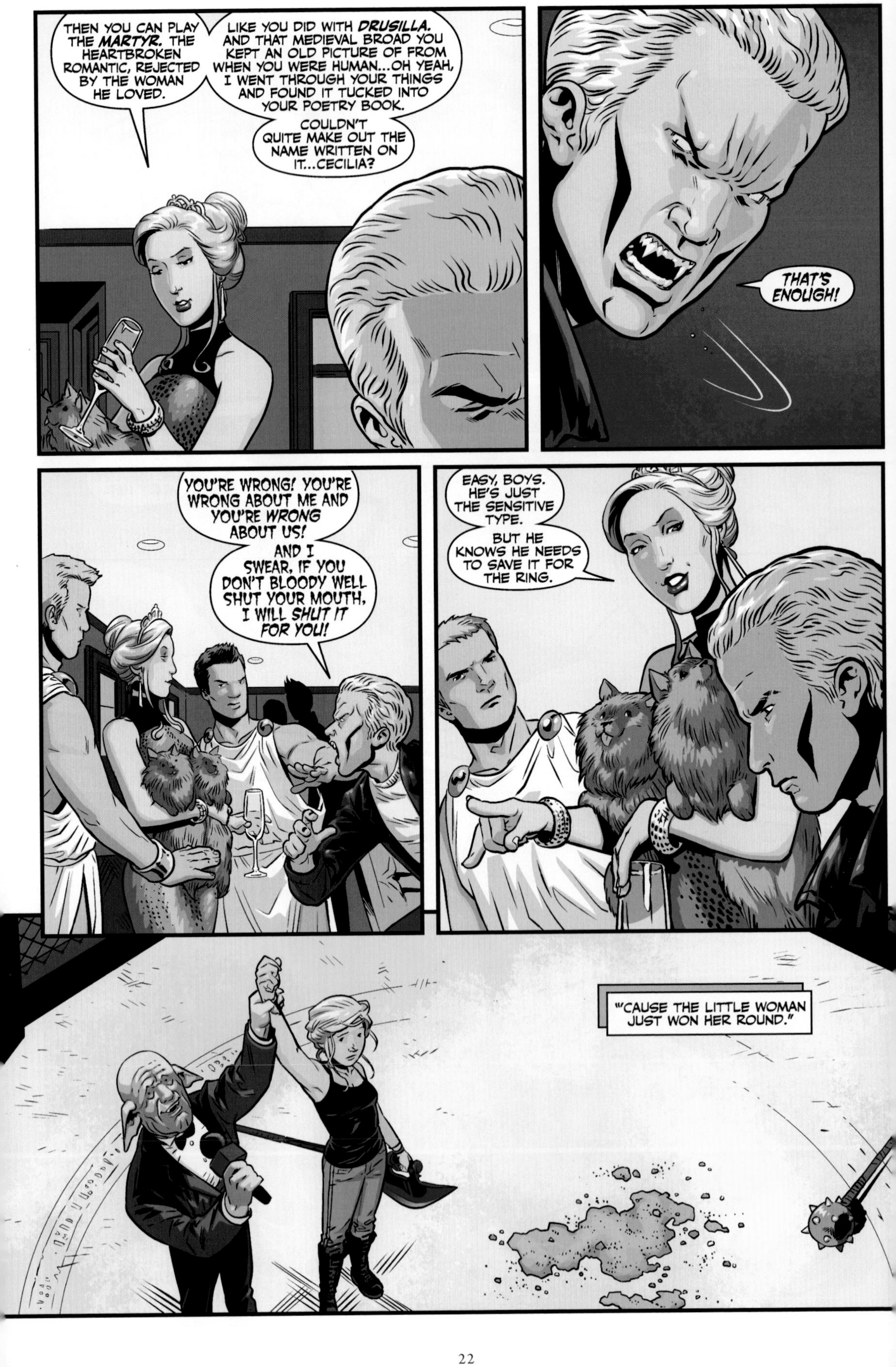
THEN YOU CAN PLAY THE MARTYR. THE HEARTBROKEN ROMANTIC, REJECTED BY THE WOMAN HE LOVED.
LIKE YOU DID WITH DRUSILLA. AND THAT MEDIEVAL BROAD YOU KEPT AN OLD PICTURE OF FROM WHEN YOU WERE HUMAN...OH YEAH, I WENT THROUGH YOUR THINGS AND FOUND IT TUCKED INTO YOUR POETRY BOOK.
COULDN'T QUITE MAKE OUT THE NAME WRITTEN ON IT...CECILIA?
THAT'S ENOUGH!
YOU'RE WRONG! YOU'RE WRONG ABOUT ME AND YOU'RE WRONG ABOUT US!
AND I SWEAR, IF YOU DON'T BLOODY WELL SHUT YOUR MOUTH, I WILL SHUT IT FOR YOU!
EASY, BOYS. HE'S JUST THE SENSITIVE TYPE.
BUT HE KNOWS HE NEEDS TO SAVE IT FOR THE RING.
"CAUSE THE LITTLE WOMAN JUST WON HER ROUND."

NICE ONE.

THANKS. BIGGEST PILE OF DUST I EVER SAW.

BE CAREFUL.

NO WORRIES THERE.

NOT BAD. NOW ALL IT TAKES IS FOR YOUR BOY TOY TO HOLD UP HIS END.

I'M NOT WORRIED ABOUT HIM.

OVERCONFIDENT MUCH?

IT'S NOT THAT.

OBVIOUSLY YOU IDIOTS COULDN'T KEEP YOUR MOUTHS SHUT IN HERE.

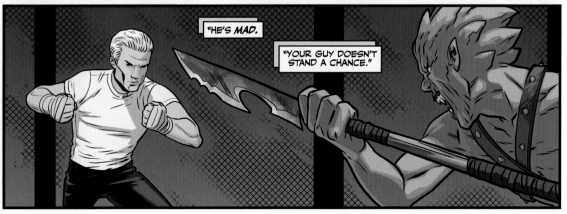

"HE'S MAD.

"YOUR GUY DOESN'T STAND A CHANCE."

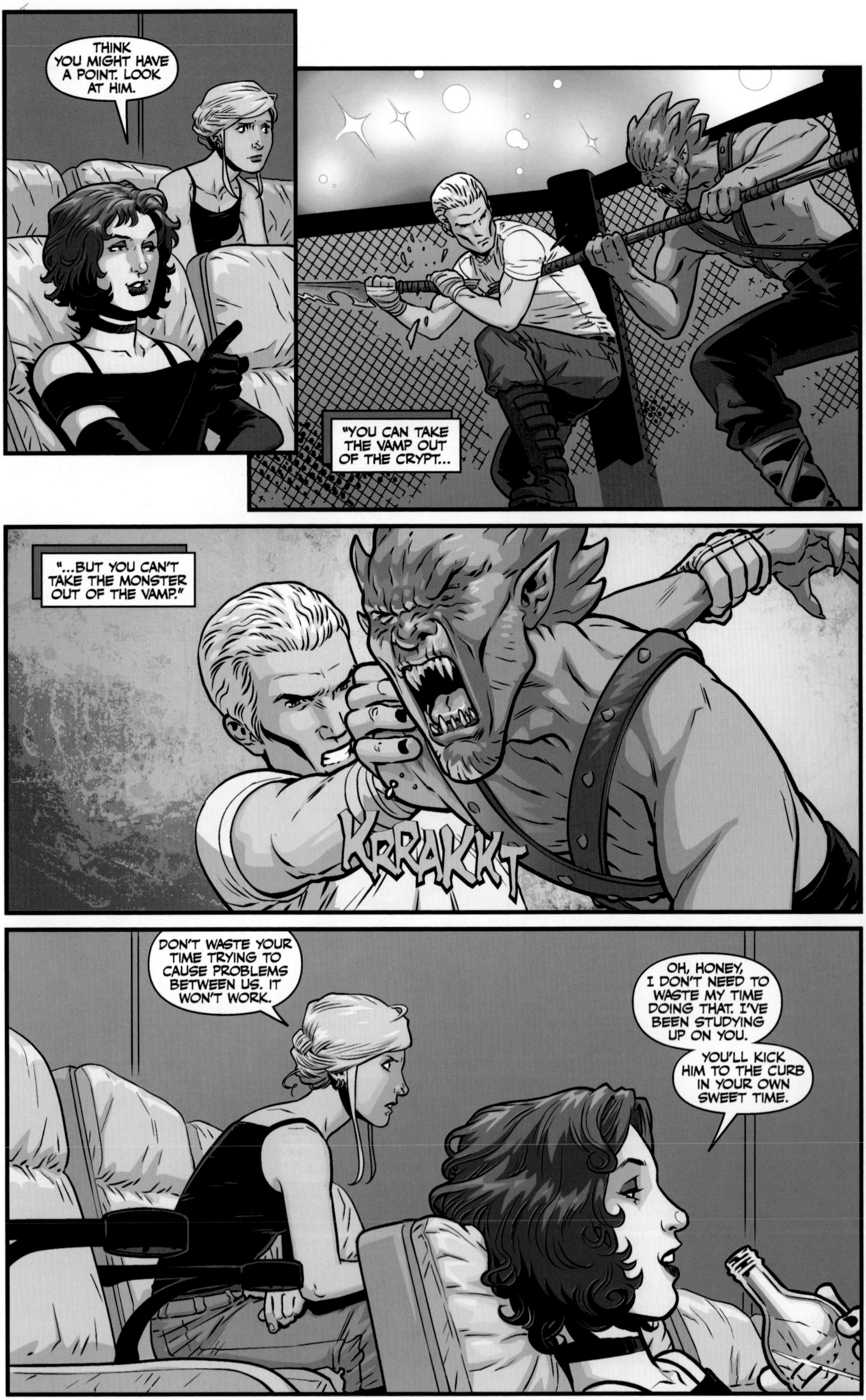
THINK YOU MIGHT HAVE A POINT. LOOK AT HIM.
"YOU CAN TAKE THE VAMP OUT OF THE CRYPT...
"...BUT YOU CAN'T TAKE THE MONSTER OUT OF THE VAMP."
KRRAKKT
DON'T WASTE YOUR TIME TRYING TO CAUSE PROBLEMS BETWEEN US. IT WON'T WORK.
OH, HONEY, I DON'T NEED TO WASTE MY TIME DOING THAT. I'VE BEEN STUDYING UP ON YOU.
YOU'LL KICK HIM TO THE CURB IN YOUR OWN SWEET TIME.

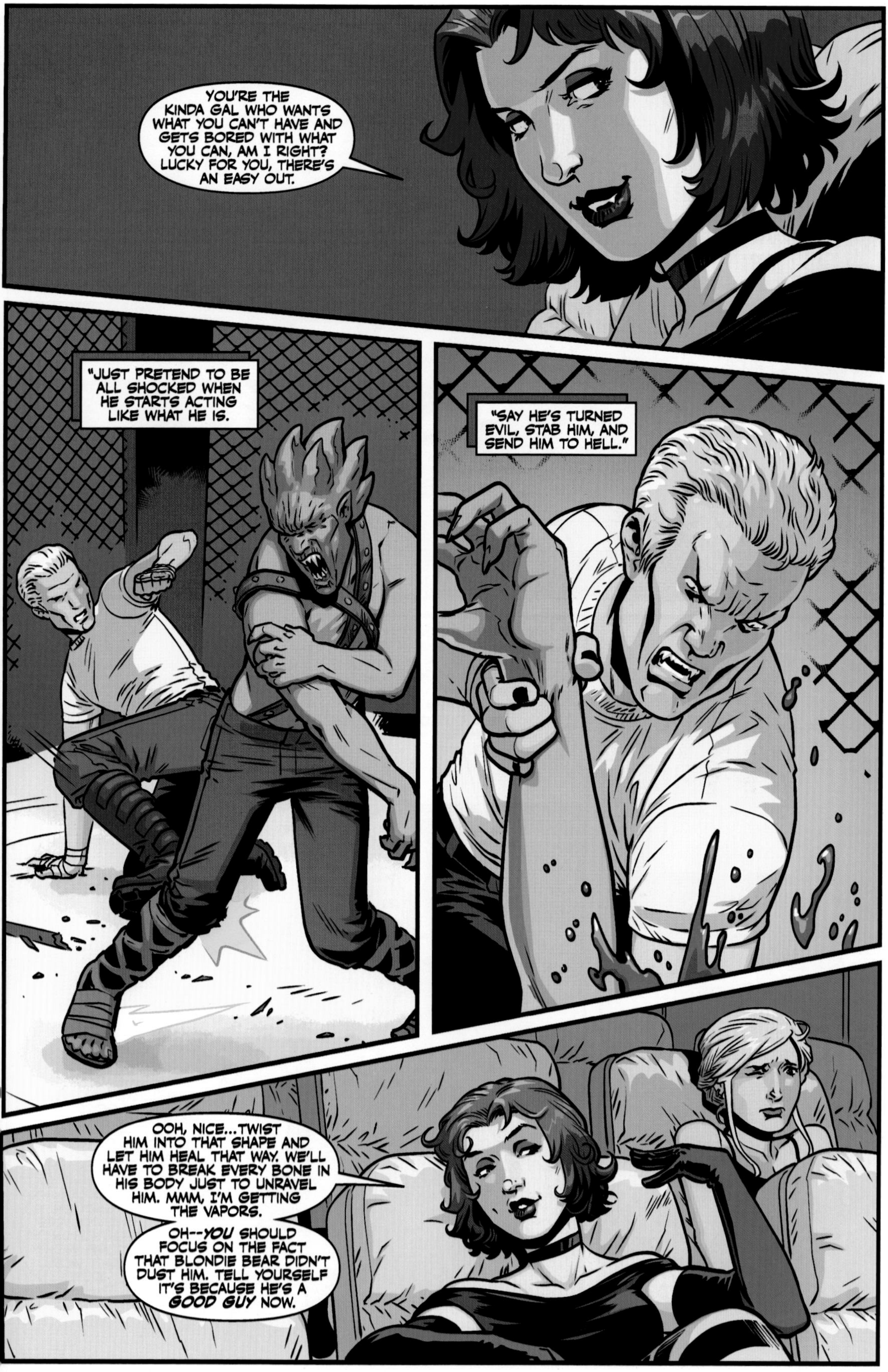
YOU'RE THE KINDA GAL WHO WANTS WHAT YOU CAN'T HAVE AND GETS BORED WITH WHAT YOU CAN, AM I RIGHT? LUCKY FOR YOU, THERE'S AN EASY OUT.
"JUST PRETEND TO BE ALL SHOCKED WHEN HE STARTS ACTING LIKE WHAT HE IS.
"SAY HE'S TURNED EVIL, STAB HIM, AND SEND HIM TO HELL."
OOH, NICE...TWIST HIM INTO THAT SHAPE AND LET HIM HEAL THAT WAY. WE'LL HAVE TO BREAK EVERY BONE IN HIS BODY JUST TO UNRAVEL HIM. MMM, I'M GETTING THE VAPORS.
OH--*YOU* SHOULD FOCUS ON THE FACT THAT BLONDIE BEAR DIDN'T DUST HIM. TELL YOURSELF IT'S BECAUSE HE'S A *GOOD GUY* NOW.

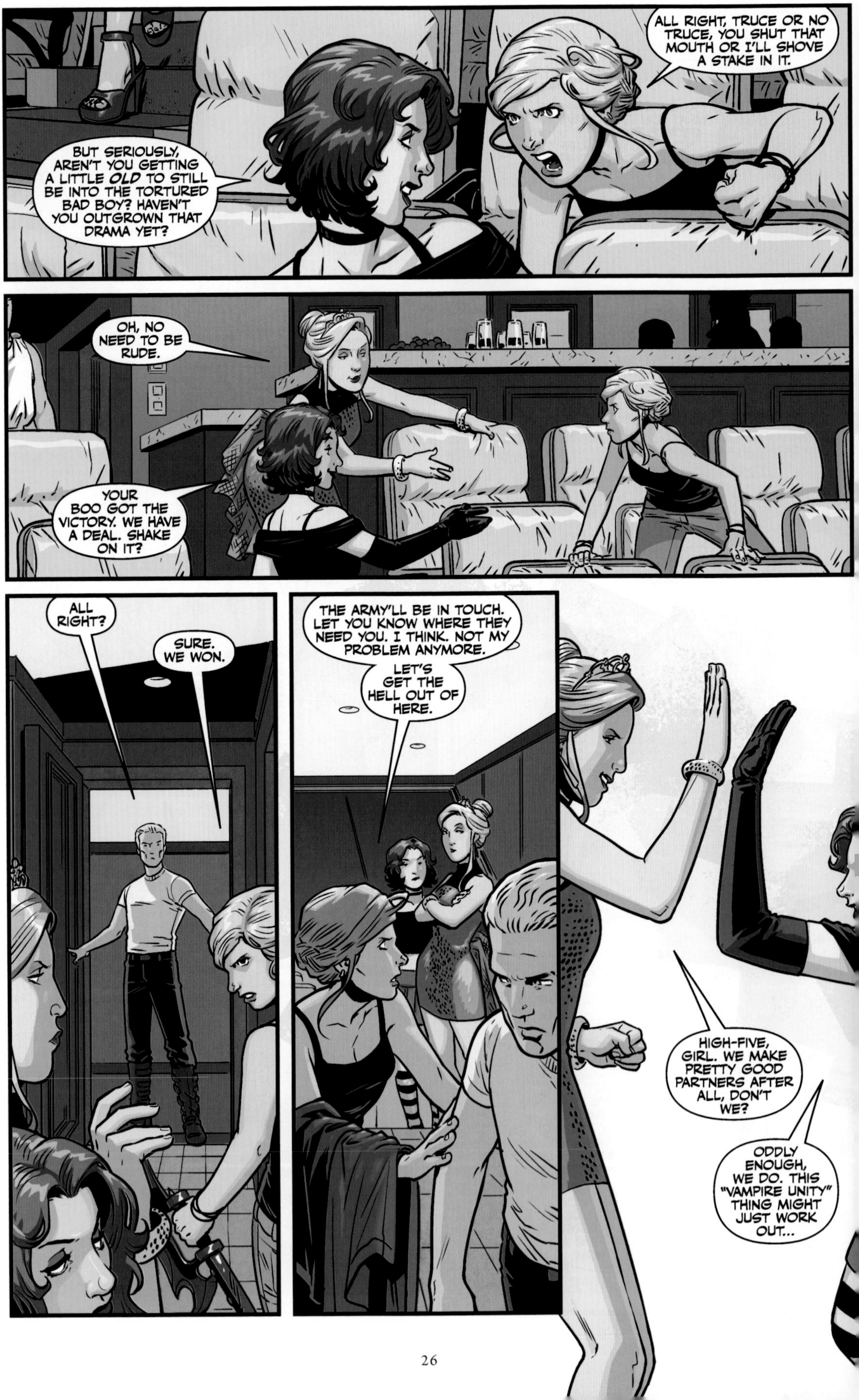
ALL RIGHT, TRUCE OR NO TRUCE, YOU SHUT THAT MOUTH OR I'LL SHOVE A STAKE IN IT.
BUT SERIOUSLY, AREN'T YOU GETTING A LITTLE *OLD* TO STILL BE INTO THE TORTURED BAD BOY? HAVEN'T YOU OUTGROWN THAT DRAMA YET?
OH, NO NEED TO BE RUDE.
YOUR BOO GOT THE VICTORY. WE HAVE A DEAL. SHAKE ON IT?
ALL RIGHT?
SURE. WE WON.
THE ARMY'LL BE IN TOUCH. LET YOU KNOW WHERE THEY NEED YOU. I THINK. NOT MY PROBLEM ANYMORE.
LET'S GET THE HELL OUT OF HERE.
HIGH-FIVE, GIRL. WE MAKE PRETTY GOOD PARTNERS AFTER ALL, DON'T WE?
ODDLY ENOUGH, WE DO. THIS "VAMPIRE UNITY" THING MIGHT JUST WORK OUT...

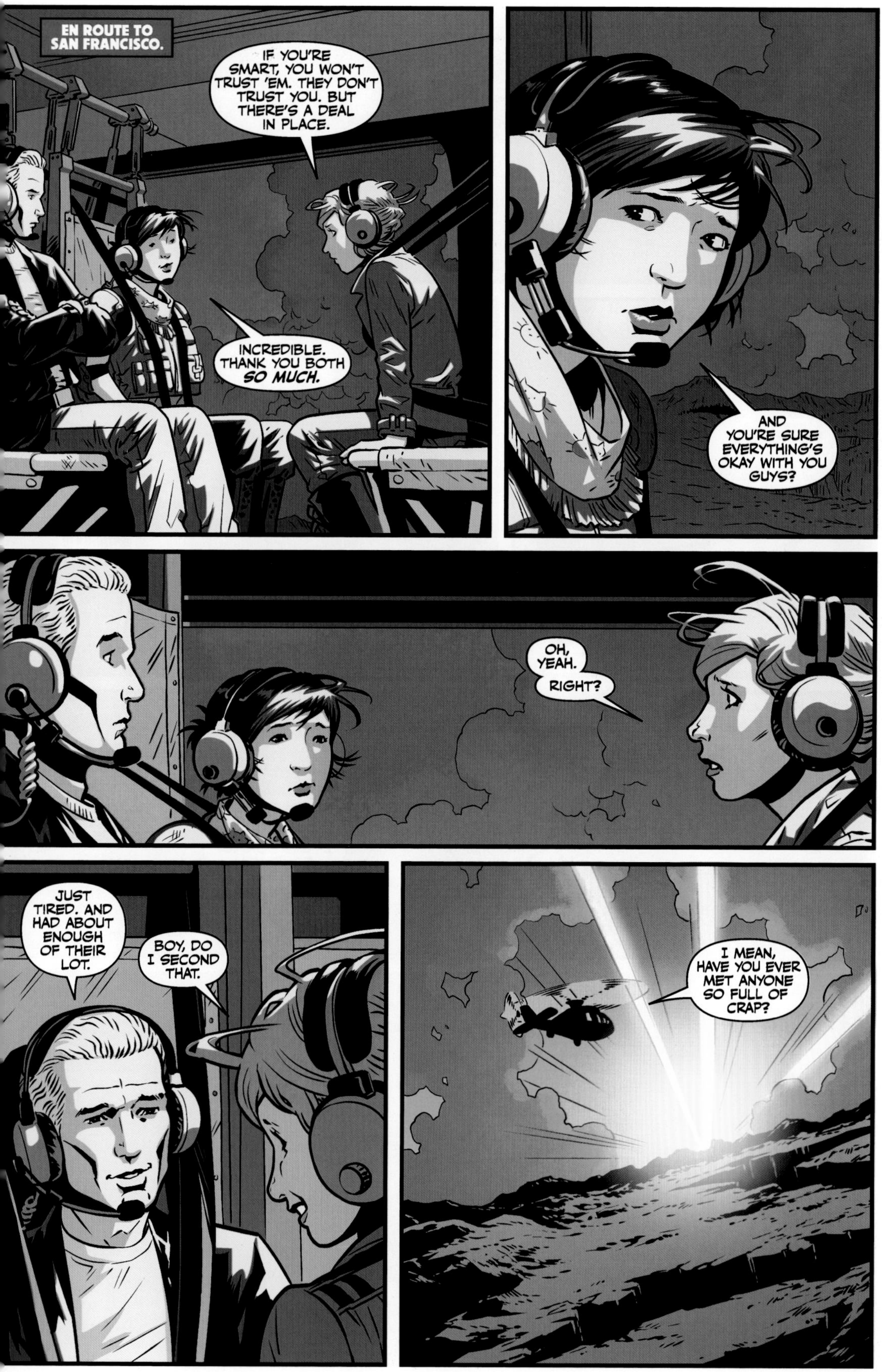
EN ROUTE TO SAN FRANCISCO.
IF YOU'RE SMART, YOU WON'T TRUST 'EM. THEY DON'T TRUST YOU. BUT THERE'S A DEAL IN PLACE.
INCREDIBLE. THANK YOU BOTH SO MUCH.
AND YOU'RE SURE EVERYTHING'S OKAY WITH YOU GUYS?
OH, YEAH.
RIGHT?
JUST TIRED. AND HAD ABOUT ENOUGH OF THEIR LOT.
BOY, DO I SECOND THAT.
I MEAN, HAVE YOU EVER MET ANYONE SO FULL OF CRAP?

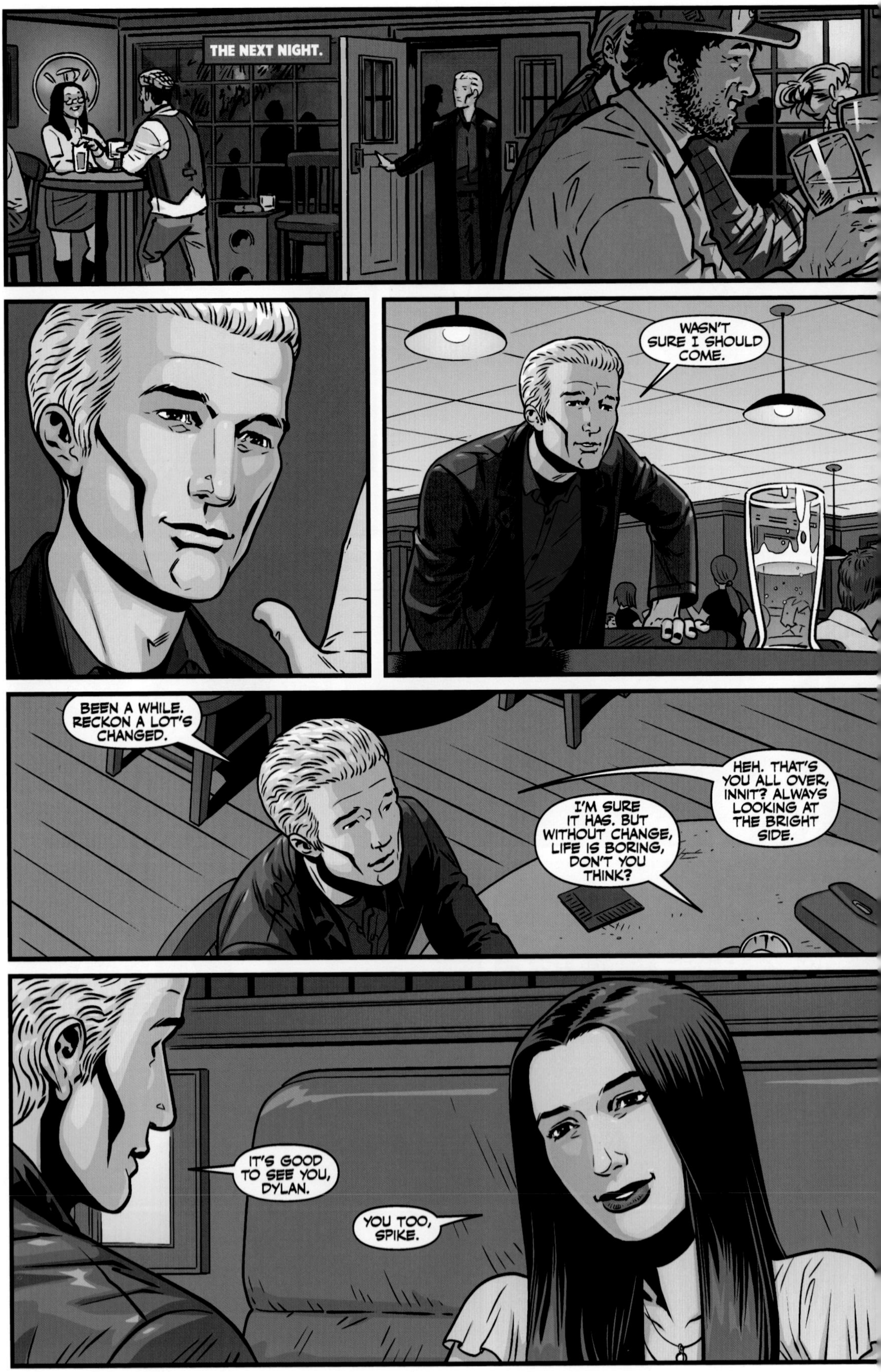
THE NEXT NIGHT.
WASN'T SURE I SHOULD COME.
BEEN A WHILE. RECKON A LOT'S CHANGED.
I'M SURE IT HAS. BUT WITHOUT CHANGE, LIFE IS BORING, DON'T YOU THINK?
HEH. THAT'S YOU ALL OVER, INNIT? ALWAYS LOOKING AT THE BRIGHT SIDE.
IT'S GOOD TO SEE YOU, DYLAN.
YOU TOO, SPIKE.

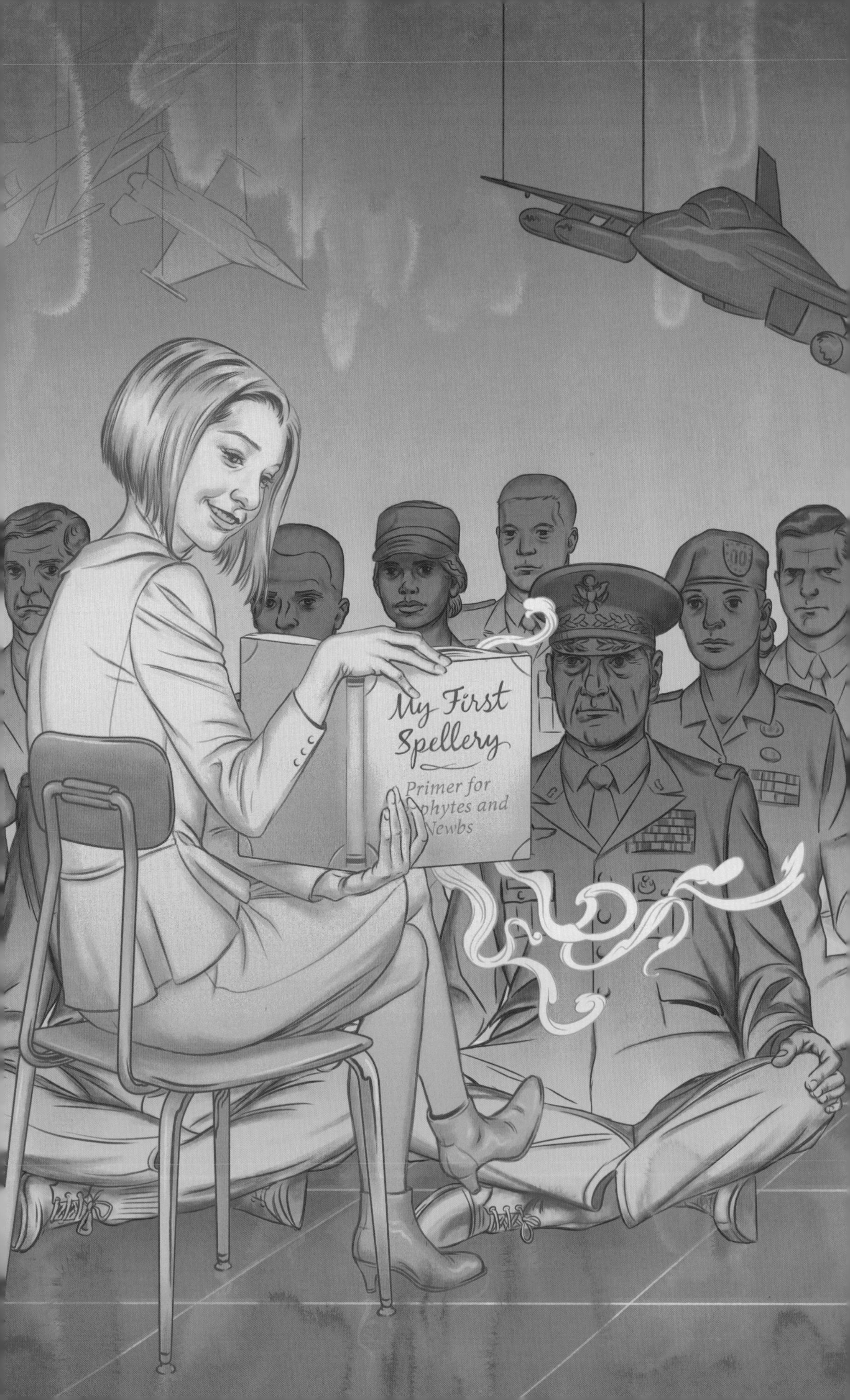
My First Spellery
Primer for
phytes and
Newbs

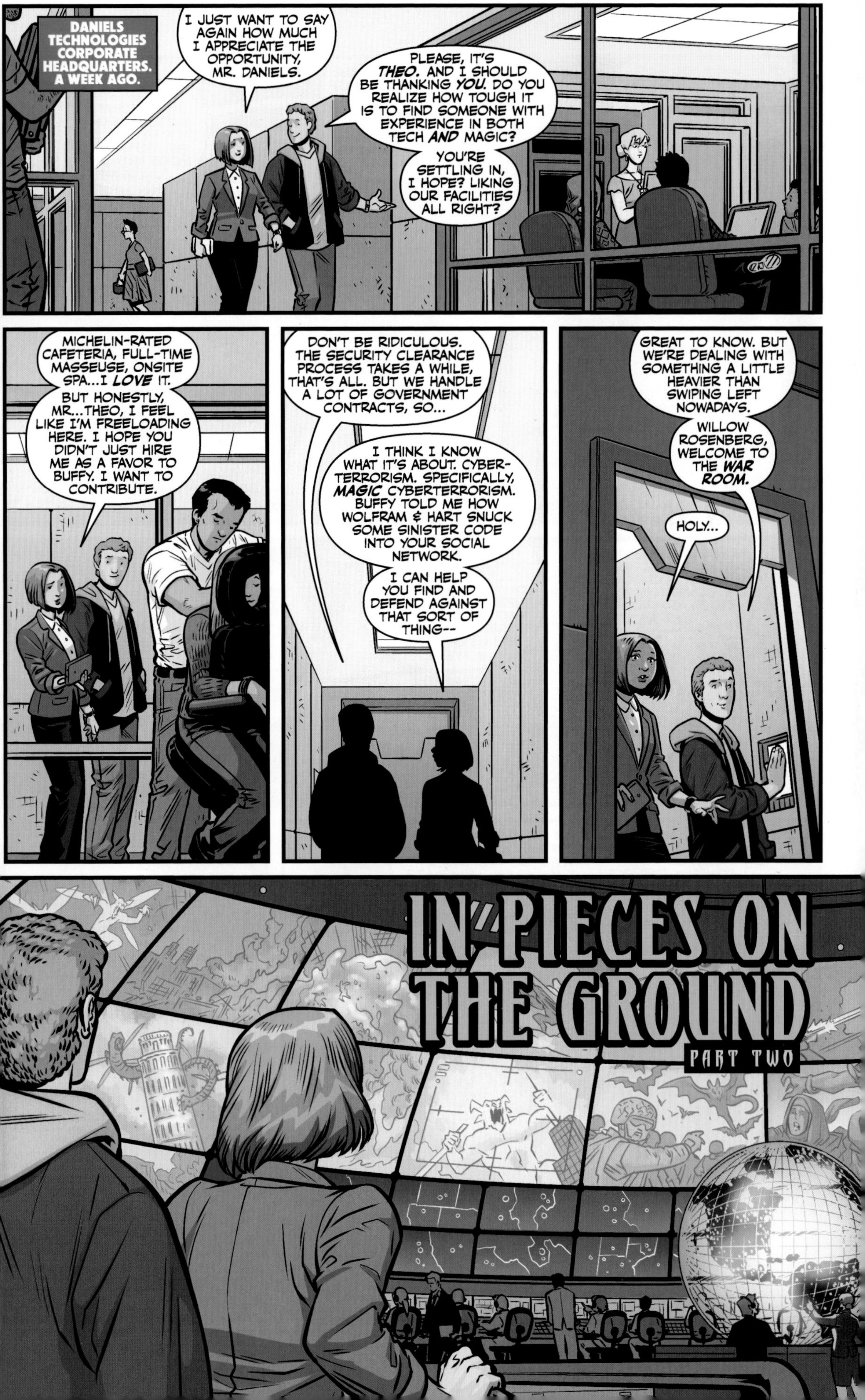
DANIELS TECHNOLOGIES CORPORATE HEADQUARTERS. A WEEK AGO.
I JUST WANT TO SAY AGAIN HOW MUCH I APPRECIATE THE OPPORTUNITY, MR. DANIELS.
PLEASE, IT'S THEO. AND I SHOULD BE THANKING YOU. DO YOU REALIZE HOW TOUGH IT IS TO FIND SOMEONE WITH EXPERIENCE IN BOTH TECH AND MAGIC?
YOU'RE SETTLING IN, I HOPE? LIKING OUR FACILITIES ALL RIGHT?
MICHELIN-RATED CAFETERIA, FULL-TIME MASSEUSE, ONSITE SPA...I LOVE IT.
BUT HONESTLY, MR...THEO, I FEEL LIKE I'M FREELOADING HERE. I HOPE YOU DIDN'T JUST HIRE ME AS A FAVOR TO BUFFY. I WANT TO CONTRIBUTE.
DON'T BE RIDICULOUS. THE SECURITY CLEARANCE PROCESS TAKES A WHILE, THAT'S ALL. BUT WE HANDLE A LOT OF GOVERNMENT CONTRACTS, SO...
I THINK I KNOW WHAT IT'S ABOUT. CYBER-TERRORISM. SPECIFICALLY, MAGIC CYBERTERRORISM. BUFFY TOLD ME HOW WOLFRAM & HART SNUCK SOME SINISTER CODE INTO YOUR SOCIAL NETWORK.
I CAN HELP YOU FIND AND DEFEND AGAINST THAT SORT OF THING--
GREAT TO KNOW. BUT WE'RE DEALING WITH SOMETHING A LITTLE HEAVIER THAN SWIPING LEFT NOWADAYS.
WILLOW ROSENBERG, WELCOME TO THE WAR ROOM.
HOLY...
IN PIECES ON THE GROUND
PART TWO

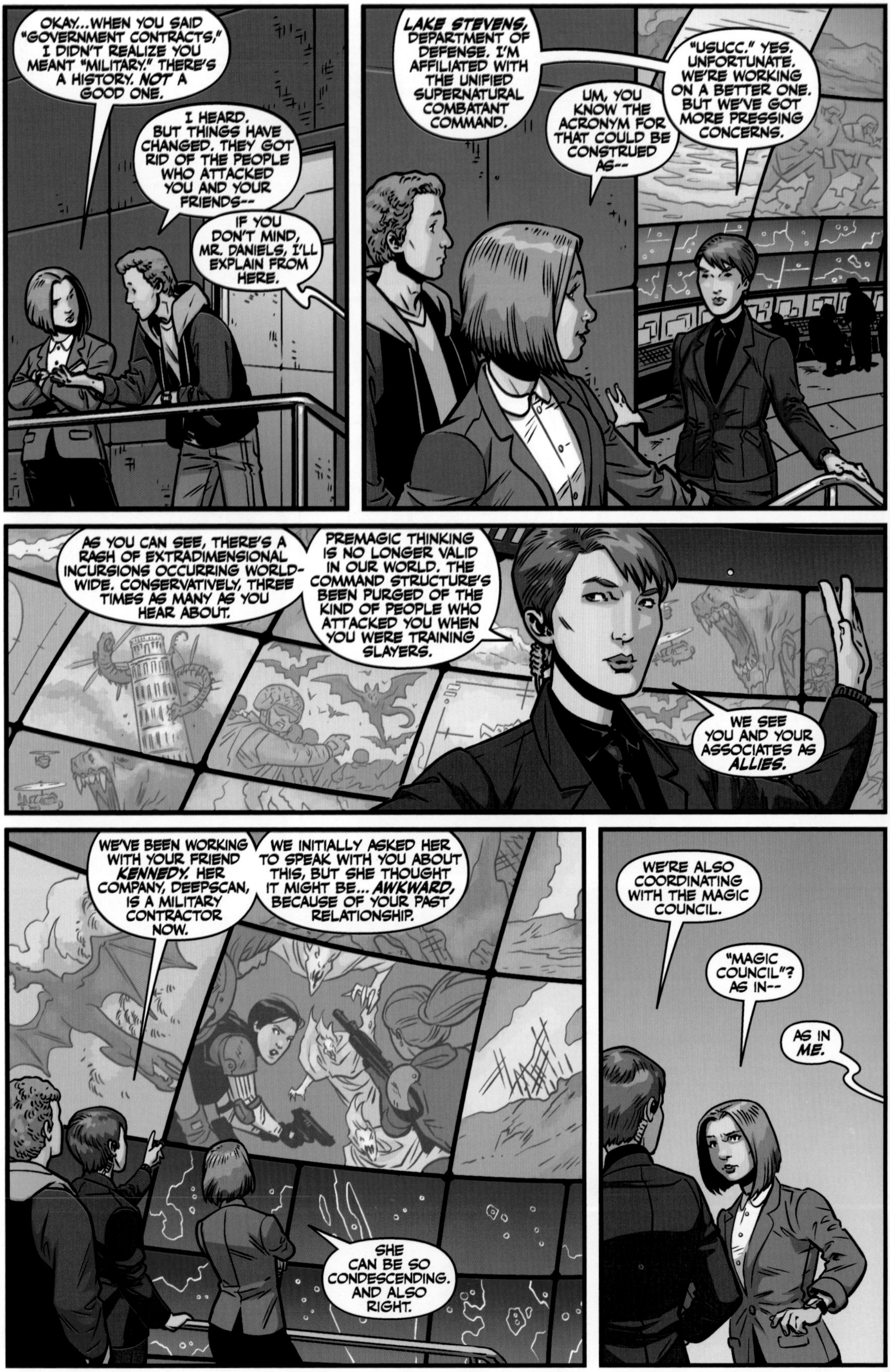

OKAY...WHEN YOU SAID "GOVERNMENT CONTRACTS," I DIDN'T REALIZE YOU MEANT "MILITARY." THERE'S A HISTORY. *NOT* A GOOD ONE.
I HEARD. BUT THINGS HAVE CHANGED. THEY GOT RID OF THE PEOPLE WHO ATTACKED YOU AND YOUR FRIENDS--
IF YOU DON'T MIND, MR. DANIELS, I'LL EXPLAIN FROM HERE.
LAKE STEVENS, DEPARTMENT OF DEFENSE. I'M AFFILIATED WITH THE UNIFIED SUPERNATURAL COMBATANT COMMAND.
UM, YOU KNOW THE ACRONYM FOR THAT COULD BE CONSTRUED AS--
"USUCC." YES. UNFORTUNATE. WE'RE WORKING ON A BETTER ONE. BUT WE'VE GOT MORE PRESSING CONCERNS.
AS YOU CAN SEE, THERE'S A RASH OF EXTRADIMENSIONAL INCURSIONS OCCURRING WORLD-WIDE. CONSERVATIVELY, THREE TIMES AS MANY AS YOU HEAR ABOUT.
PREMAGIC THINKING IS NO LONGER VALID IN OUR WORLD. THE COMMAND STRUCTURE'S BEEN PURGED OF THE KIND OF PEOPLE WHO ATTACKED YOU WHEN YOU WERE TRAINING SLAYERS.
WE SEE YOU AND YOUR ASSOCIATES AS *ALLIES.*
WE'VE BEEN WORKING WITH YOUR FRIEND *KENNEDY.* HER COMPANY, DEEPSCAN, IS A MILITARY CONTRACTOR NOW.
WE INITIALLY ASKED HER TO SPEAK WITH YOU ABOUT THIS, BUT SHE THOUGHT IT MIGHT BE... *AWKWARD,* BECAUSE OF YOUR PAST RELATIONSHIP.
SHE CAN BE SO CONDESCENDING. AND ALSO RIGHT.
WE'RE ALSO COORDINATING WITH THE MAGIC COUNCIL.
"MAGIC COUNCIL"? AS IN--
AS IN *ME.*

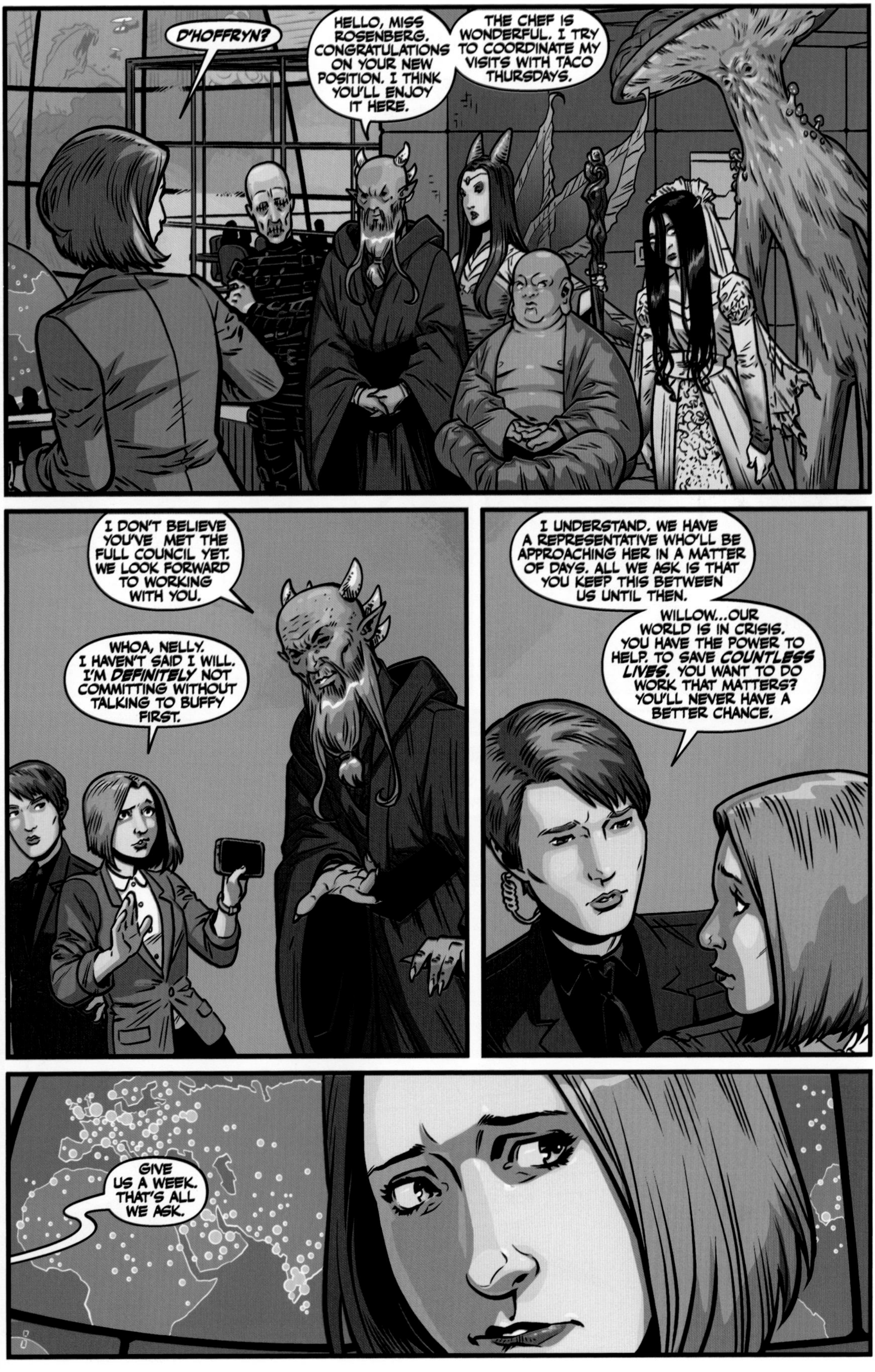
D'HOFFRYN?
HELLO, MISS ROSENBERG. CONGRATULATIONS ON YOUR NEW POSITION. I THINK YOU'LL ENJOY IT HERE.
THE CHEF IS WONDERFUL. I TRY TO COORDINATE MY VISITS WITH TACO THURSDAYS.
I DON'T BELIEVE YOU'VE MET THE FULL COUNCIL YET. WE LOOK FORWARD TO WORKING WITH YOU.
WHOA, NELLY. I HAVEN'T SAID I WILL. I'M DEFINITELY NOT COMMITTING WITHOUT TALKING TO BUFFY FIRST.
I UNDERSTAND. WE HAVE A REPRESENTATIVE WHO'LL BE APPROACHING HER IN A MATTER OF DAYS. ALL WE ASK IS THAT YOU KEEP THIS BETWEEN US UNTIL THEN.
WILLOW...OUR WORLD IS IN CRISIS. YOU HAVE THE POWER TO HELP. TO SAVE COUNTLESS LIVES. YOU WANT TO DO WORK THAT MATTERS? YOU'LL NEVER HAVE A BETTER CHANCE.
GIVE US A WEEK. THAT'S ALL WE ASK.

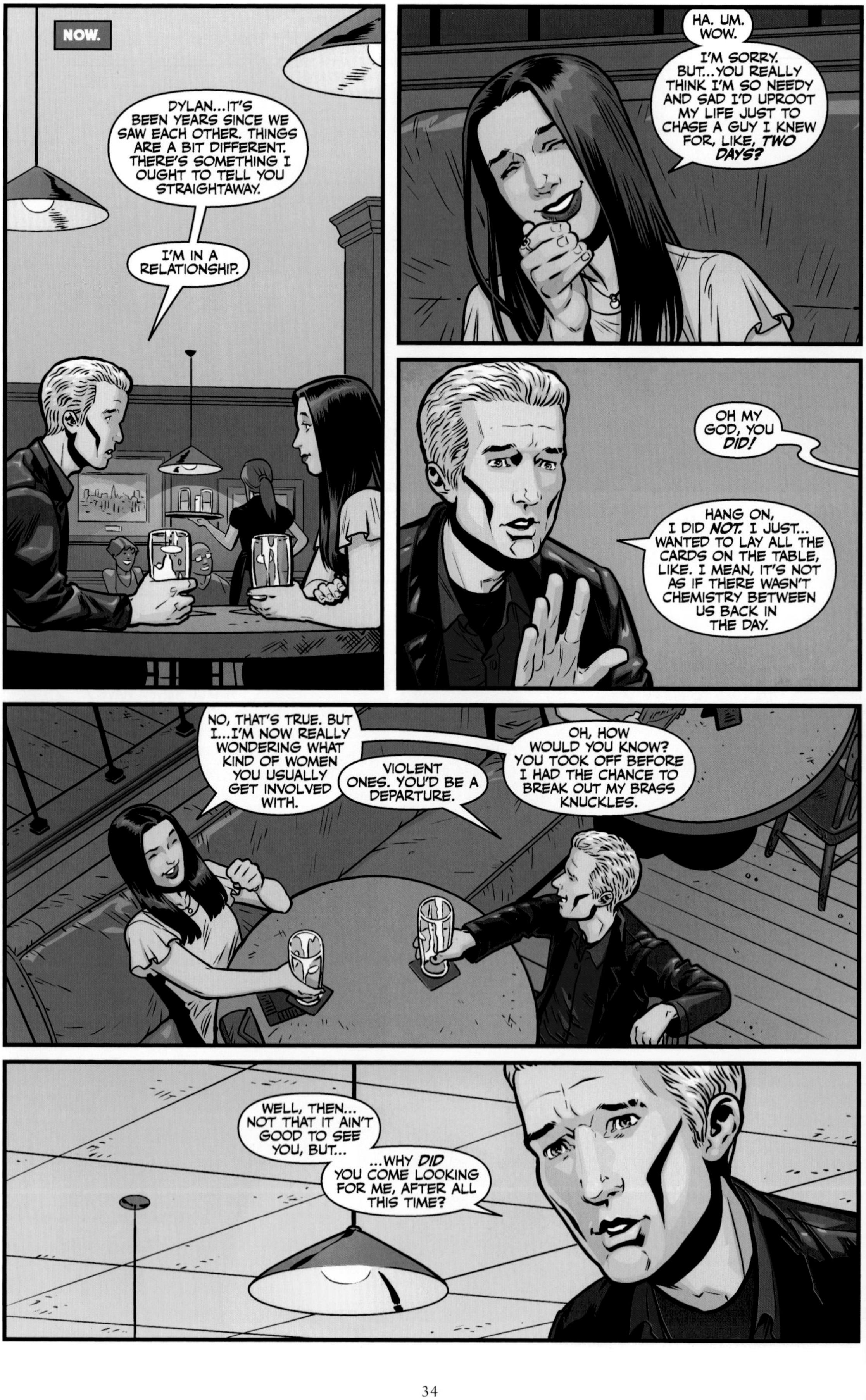
NOW.
DYLAN...IT'S BEEN YEARS SINCE WE SAW EACH OTHER. THINGS ARE A BIT DIFFERENT. THERE'S SOMETHING I OUGHT TO TELL YOU STRAIGHTAWAY.
I'M IN A RELATIONSHIP.
HA. UM. WOW.
I'M SORRY. BUT...YOU REALLY THINK I'M SO NEEDY AND SAD I'D UPROOT MY LIFE JUST TO CHASE A GUY I KNEW FOR, LIKE, TWO DAYS?
OH MY GOD, YOU DID!
HANG ON, I DID NOT. I JUST... WANTED TO LAY ALL THE CARDS ON THE TABLE, LIKE. I MEAN, IT'S NOT AS IF THERE WASN'T CHEMISTRY BETWEEN US BACK IN THE DAY.
NO, THAT'S TRUE. BUT I...I'M NOW REALLY WONDERING WHAT KIND OF WOMEN YOU USUALLY GET INVOLVED WITH.
VIOLENT ONES. YOU'D BE A DEPARTURE.
OH, HOW WOULD YOU KNOW? YOU TOOK OFF BEFORE I HAD THE CHANCE TO BREAK OUT MY BRASS KNUCKLES.
WELL, THEN... NOT THAT IT AIN'T GOOD TO SEE YOU, BUT...
...WHY DID YOU COME LOOKING FOR ME, AFTER ALL THIS TIME?

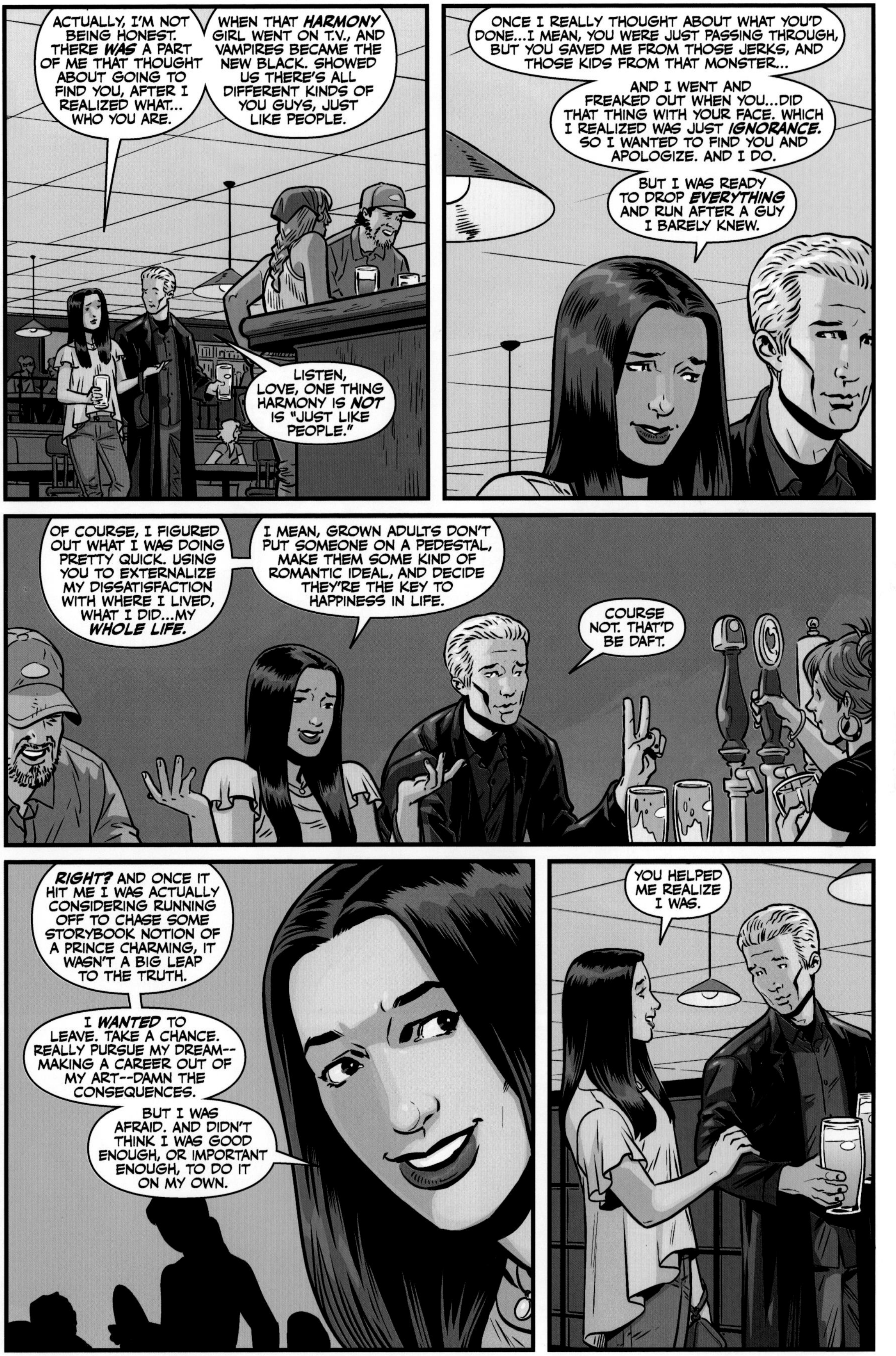
ACTUALLY, I'M NOT BEING HONEST. THERE WAS A PART OF ME THAT THOUGHT ABOUT GOING TO FIND YOU, AFTER I REALIZED WHAT... WHO YOU ARE.
WHEN THAT HARMONY GIRL WENT ON T.V., AND VAMPIRES BECAME THE NEW BLACK. SHOWED US THERE'S ALL DIFFERENT KINDS OF YOU GUYS, JUST LIKE PEOPLE.
LISTEN, LOVE, ONE THING HARMONY IS NOT IS "JUST LIKE PEOPLE."
ONCE I REALLY THOUGHT ABOUT WHAT YOU'D DONE...I MEAN, YOU WERE JUST PASSING THROUGH, BUT YOU SAVED ME FROM THOSE JERKS, AND THOSE KIDS FROM THAT MONSTER...
AND I WENT AND FREAKED OUT WHEN YOU...DID THAT THING WITH YOUR FACE. WHICH I REALIZED WAS JUST IGNORANCE. SO I WANTED TO FIND YOU AND APOLOGIZE. AND I DO.
BUT I WAS READY TO DROP EVERYTHING AND RUN AFTER A GUY I BARELY KNEW.
OF COURSE, I FIGURED OUT WHAT I WAS DOING PRETTY QUICK. USING YOU TO EXTERNALIZE MY DISSATISFACTION WITH WHERE I LIVED, WHAT I DID...MY WHOLE LIFE.
I MEAN, GROWN ADULTS DON'T PUT SOMEONE ON A PEDESTAL, MAKE THEM SOME KIND OF ROMANTIC IDEAL, AND DECIDE THEY'RE THE KEY TO HAPPINESS IN LIFE.
COURSE NOT. THAT'D BE DAFT.
RIGHT? AND ONCE IT HIT ME I WAS ACTUALLY CONSIDERING RUNNING OFF TO CHASE SOME STORYBOOK NOTION OF A PRINCE CHARMING, IT WASN'T A BIG LEAP TO THE TRUTH.
I WANTED TO LEAVE. TAKE A CHANCE. REALLY PURSUE MY DREAM--MAKING A CAREER OUT OF MY ART--DAMN THE CONSEQUENCES.
BUT I WAS AFRAID. AND DIDN'T THINK I WAS GOOD ENOUGH, OR IMPORTANT ENOUGH, TO DO IT ON MY OWN.
YOU HELPED ME REALIZE I WAS.

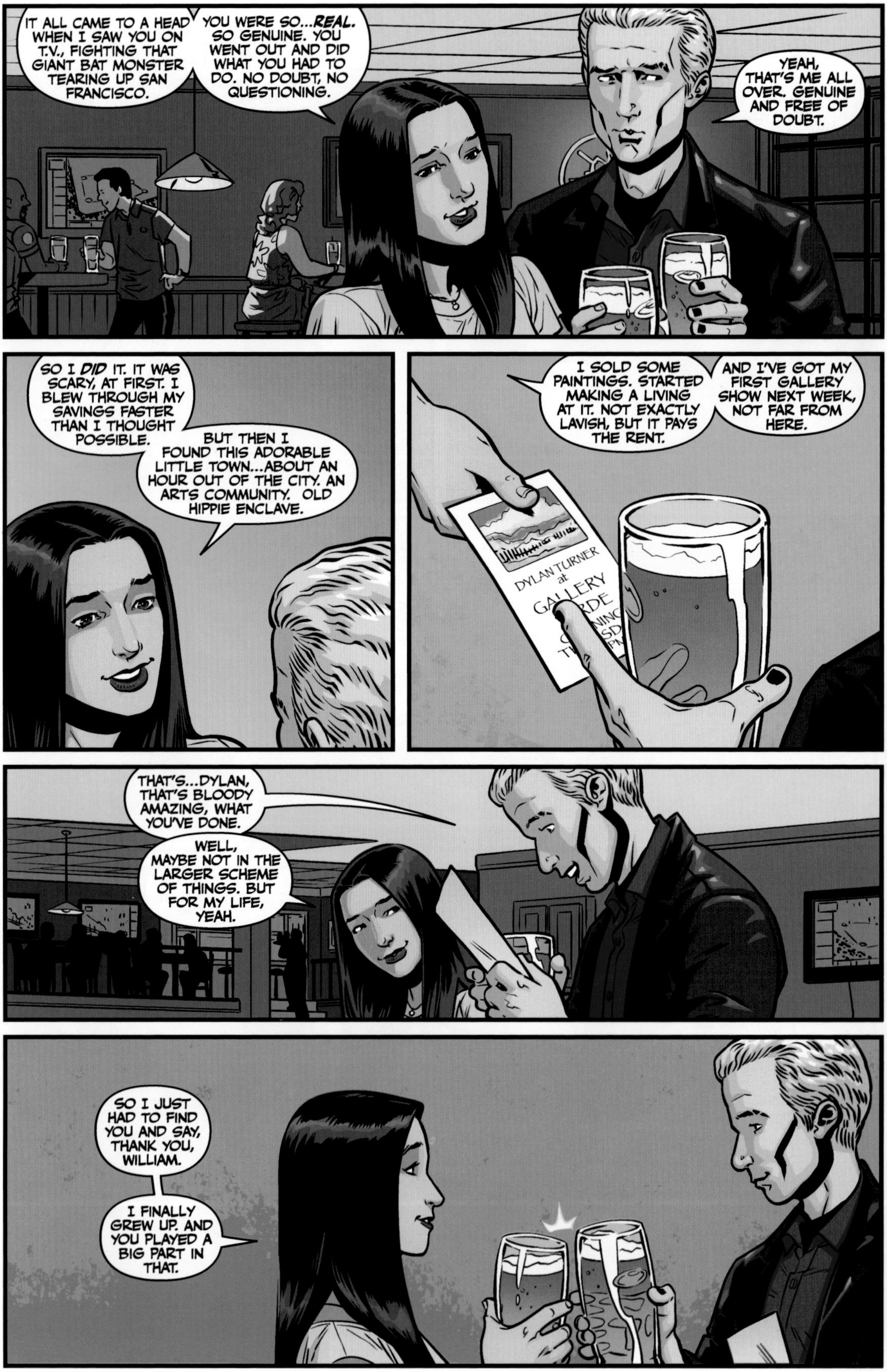
IT ALL CAME TO A HEAD WHEN I SAW YOU ON T.V., FIGHTING THAT GIANT BAT MONSTER TEARING UP SAN FRANCISCO.
YOU WERE SO...REAL. SO GENUINE. YOU WENT OUT AND DID WHAT YOU HAD TO DO. NO DOUBT, NO QUESTIONING.
YEAH, THAT'S ME ALL OVER. GENUINE AND FREE OF DOUBT.
SO I DID IT. IT WAS SCARY, AT FIRST. I BLEW THROUGH MY SAVINGS FASTER THAN I THOUGHT POSSIBLE.
BUT THEN I FOUND THIS ADORABLE LITTLE TOWN...ABOUT AN HOUR OUT OF THE CITY. AN ARTS COMMUNITY. OLD HIPPIE ENCLAVE.
I SOLD SOME PAINTINGS. STARTED MAKING A LIVING AT IT. NOT EXACTLY LAVISH, BUT IT PAYS THE RENT.
AND I'VE GOT MY FIRST GALLERY SHOW NEXT WEEK, NOT FAR FROM HERE.
DYLAN TURNER
at
GALLERY
THAT'S...DYLAN, THAT'S BLOODY AMAZING, WHAT YOU'VE DONE.
WELL, MAYBE NOT IN THE LARGER SCHEME OF THINGS. BUT FOR MY LIFE, YEAH.
SO I JUST HAD TO FIND YOU AND SAY, THANK YOU, WILLIAM.
I FINALLY GREW UP. AND YOU PLAYED A BIG PART IN THAT.

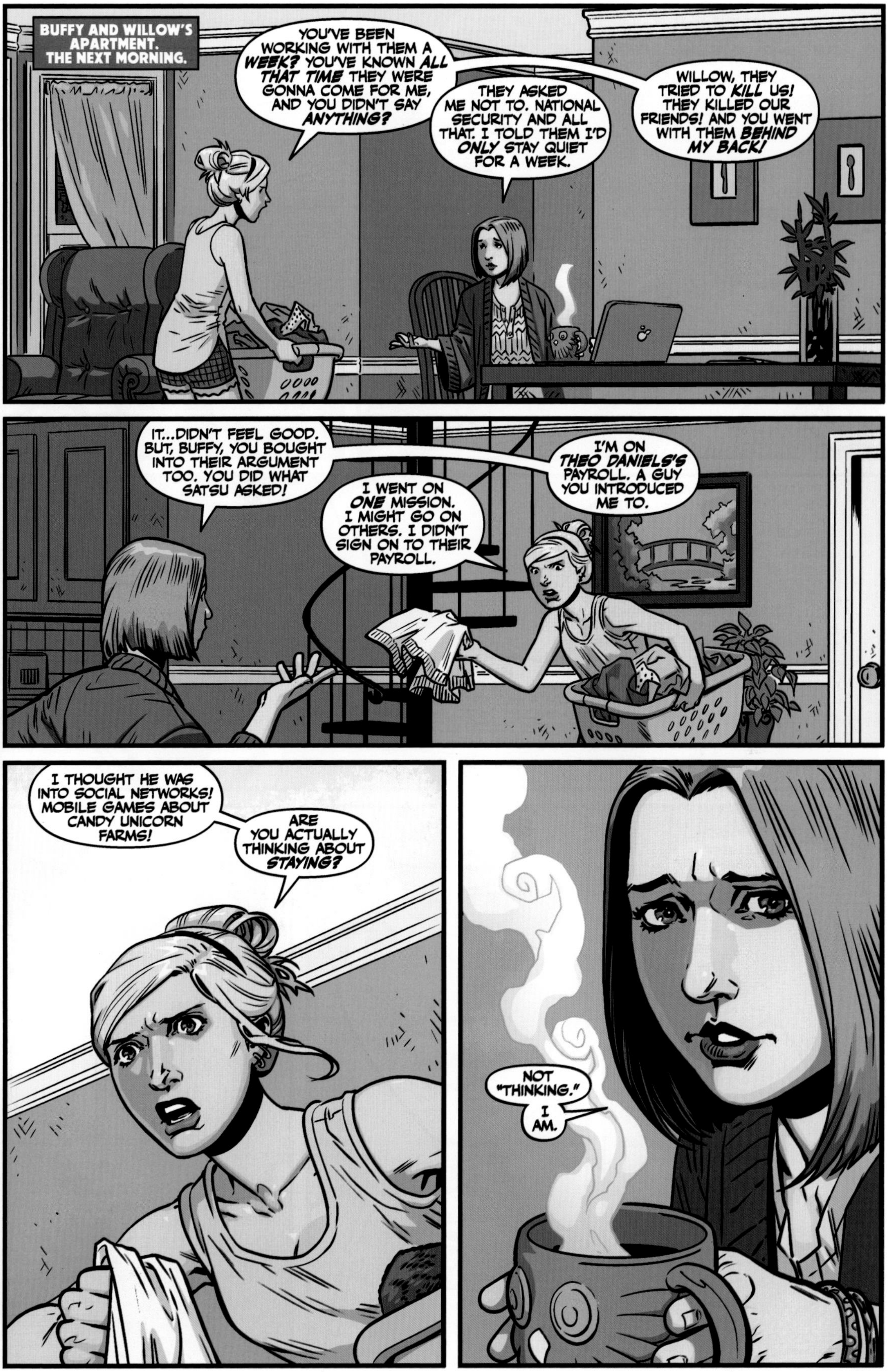
BUFFY AND WILLOW'S APARTMENT. THE NEXT MORNING.
YOU'VE BEEN WORKING WITH THEM A WEEK? YOU'VE KNOWN ALL THAT TIME THEY WERE GONNA COME FOR ME, AND YOU DIDN'T SAY ANYTHING?
THEY ASKED ME NOT TO. NATIONAL SECURITY AND ALL THAT. I TOLD THEM I'D ONLY STAY QUIET FOR A WEEK.
WILLOW, THEY TRIED TO KILL US! THEY KILLED OUR FRIENDS! AND YOU WENT WITH THEM BEHIND MY BACK!
IT...DIDN'T FEEL GOOD. BUT, BUFFY, YOU BOUGHT INTO THEIR ARGUMENT TOO. YOU DID WHAT SATSU ASKED!
I WENT ON ONE MISSION. I MIGHT GO ON OTHERS. I DIDN'T SIGN ON TO THEIR PAYROLL.
I'M ON THEO DANIELS'S PAYROLL. A GUY YOU INTRODUCED ME TO.
I THOUGHT HE WAS INTO SOCIAL NETWORKS! MOBILE GAMES ABOUT CANDY UNICORN FARMS!
ARE YOU ACTUALLY THINKING ABOUT STAYING?
NOT "THINKING."
I AM.

BUFFY, IN JUST THE PAST WEEK I HELPED PUT DOWN FOUR DEMON INVASIONS. SAVED WHO KNOWS HOW MANY LIVES.

AND THE ONE WE DIDN'T GET TO IN TIME? *SIXTEEN PEOPLE* DIED. EATEN ALIVE BY A SNAKE THE SIZE OF A SUBWAY TRAIN.

WE CAN FIGHT ALL THAT OURSELVES! WITH THE MAGIC COUNCIL, OR KENNEDY--

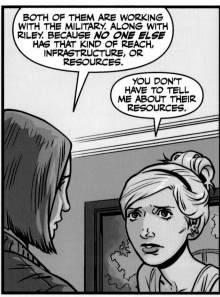

BOTH OF THEM ARE WORKING WITH THE MILITARY. ALONG WITH RILEY. BECAUSE *NO ONE ELSE* HAS THAT KIND OF REACH, INFRASTRUCTURE, OR RESOURCES.

YOU DON'T HAVE TO TELL ME ABOUT THEIR RESOURCES.

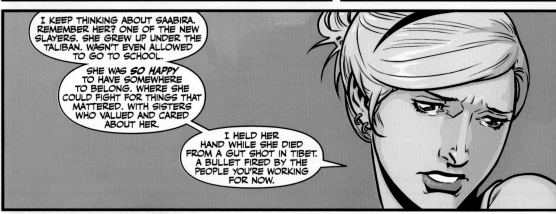

I KEEP THINKING ABOUT SAABIRA. REMEMBER HER? ONE OF THE NEW SLAYERS. SHE GREW UP UNDER THE TALIBAN. WASN'T EVEN ALLOWED TO GO TO SCHOOL.

SHE WAS *SO HAPPY* TO HAVE SOMEWHERE TO BELONG. WHERE SHE COULD FIGHT FOR THINGS THAT MATTERED. WITH SISTERS WHO VALUED AND CARED ABOUT HER.

I HELD HER HAND WHILE SHE DIED FROM A GUT SHOT IN TIBET. A BULLET FIRED BY THE PEOPLE YOU'RE WORKING FOR NOW.

I REMEMBER. I COULD NEVER *NOT* REMEMBER.

BUT I PUT IT ASIDE.

BECAUSE EVERYTHING ISN'T ABOUT *ME*.

SLAM

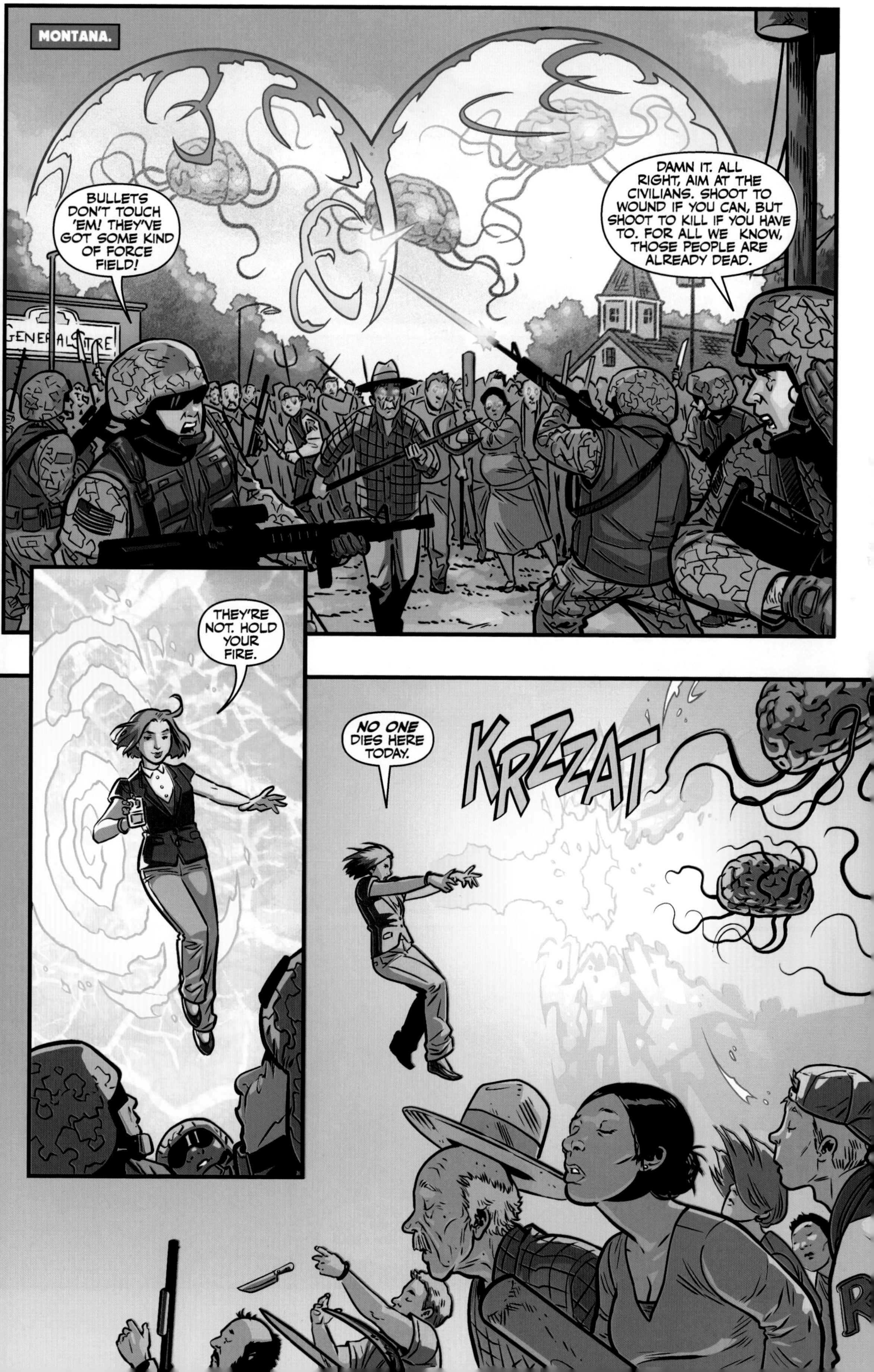
MONTANA.
GENERAL STORE
BULLETS DON'T TOUCH 'EM! THEY'VE GOT SOME KIND OF FORCE FIELD!
DAMN IT. ALL RIGHT, AIM AT THE CIVILIANS. SHOOT TO WOUND IF YOU CAN, BUT SHOOT TO KILL IF YOU HAVE TO. FOR ALL WE KNOW, THOSE PEOPLE ARE ALREADY DEAD.
THEY'RE NOT. HOLD YOUR FIRE.
NO ONE DIES HERE TODAY.
KRZZAT

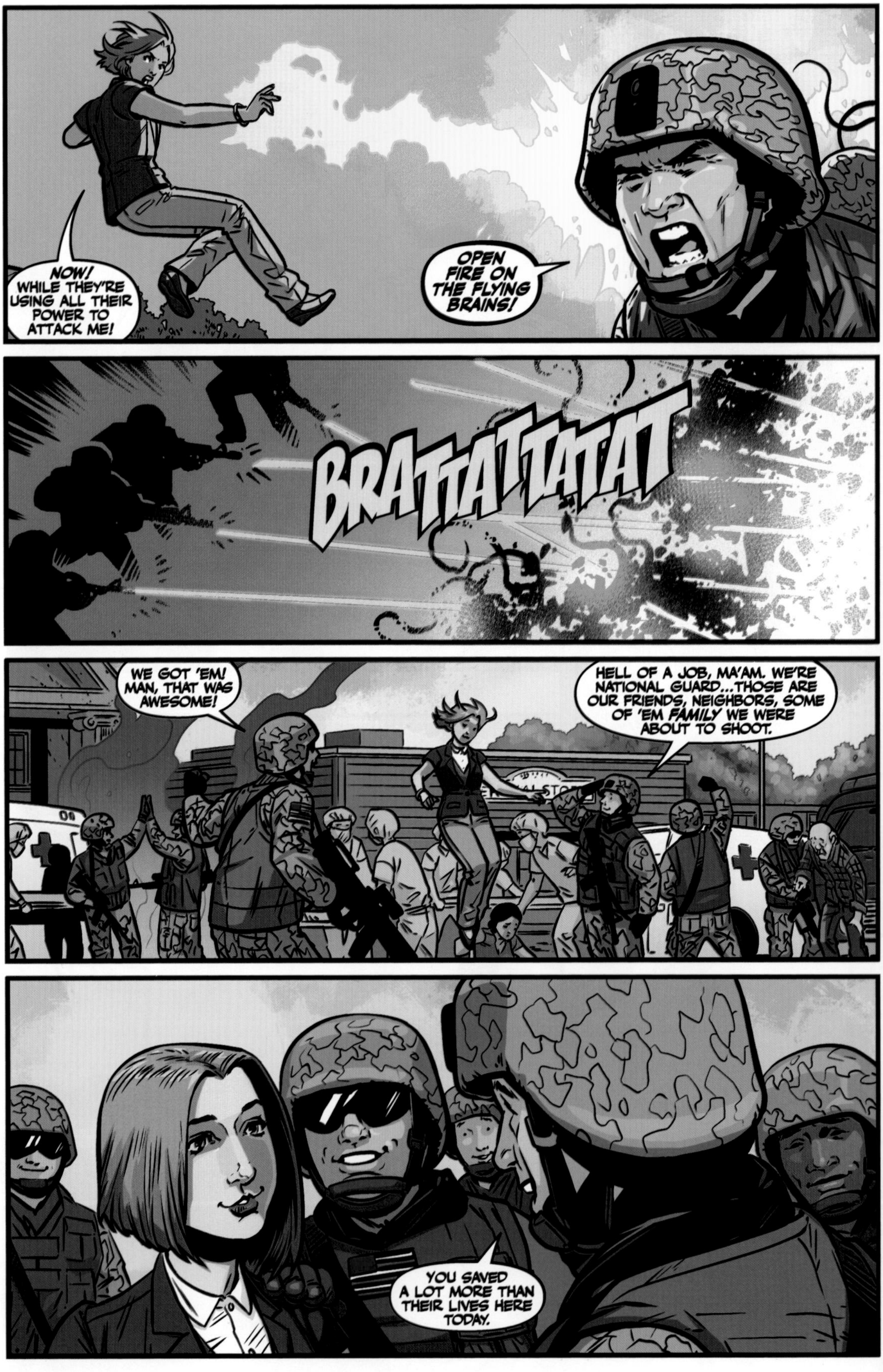
NOW! WHILE THEY'RE USING ALL THEIR POWER TO ATTACK ME!
OPEN FIRE ON THE FLYING BRAINS!
BRATTATTATAT
WE GOT 'EM! MAN, THAT WAS AWESOME!
HELL OF A JOB, MA'AM. WE'RE NATIONAL GUARD...THOSE ARE OUR FRIENDS, NEIGHBORS, SOME OF 'EM *FAMILY* WE WERE ABOUT TO SHOOT.
YOU SAVED A LOT MORE THAN THEIR LIVES HERE TODAY.

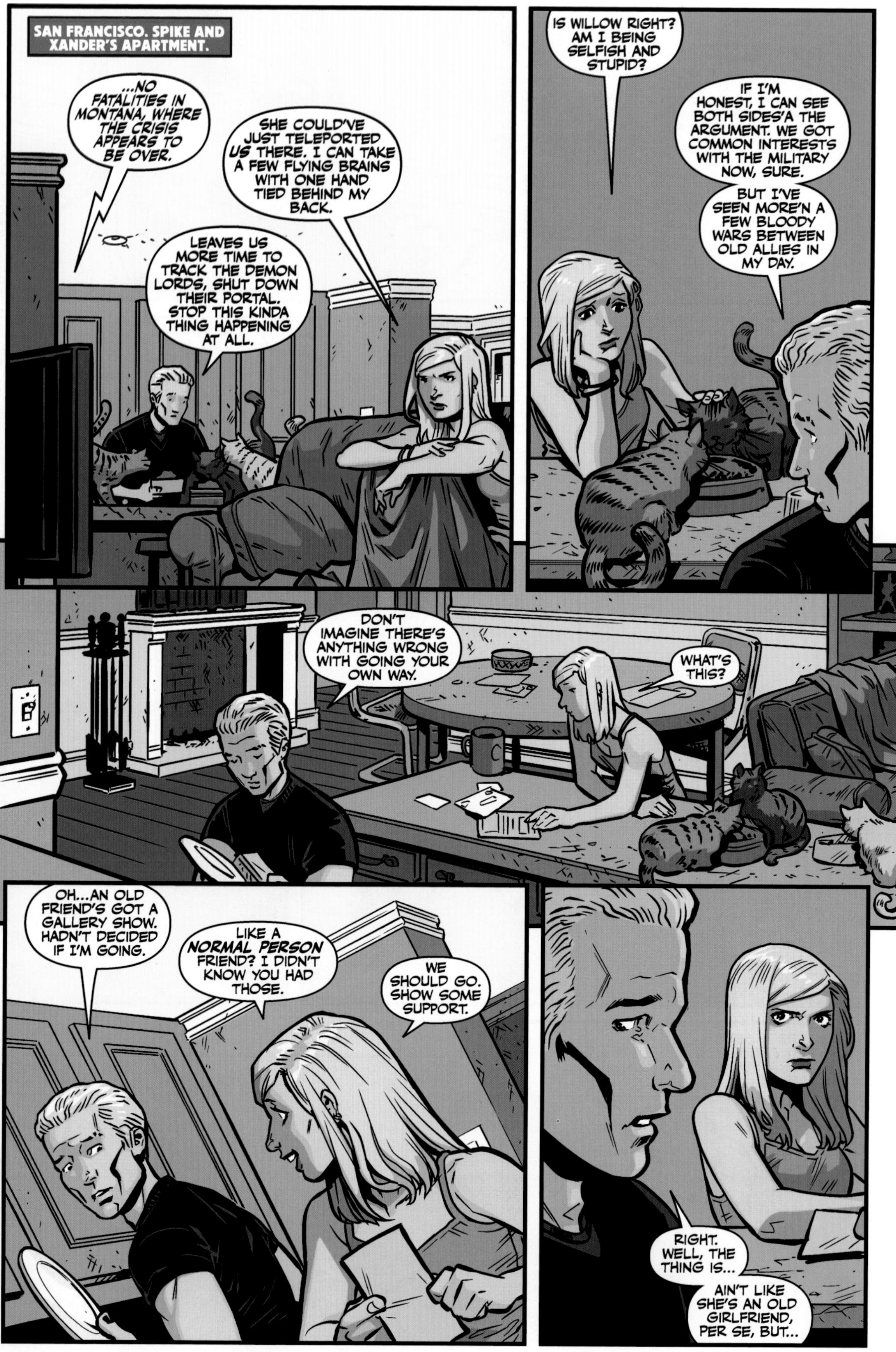

SAN FRANCISCO. SPIKE AND XANDER'S APARTMENT.
...NO FATALITIES IN MONTANA, WHERE THE CRISIS APPEARS TO BE OVER.
SHE COULD'VE JUST TELEPORTED US THERE. I CAN TAKE A FEW FLYING BRAINS WITH ONE HAND TIED BEHIND MY BACK.
LEAVES US MORE TIME TO TRACK THE DEMON LORDS, SHUT DOWN THEIR PORTAL. STOP THIS KINDA THING HAPPENING AT ALL.
IS WILLOW RIGHT? AM I BEING SELFISH AND STUPID?
IF I'M HONEST, I CAN SEE BOTH SIDES'A THE ARGUMENT. WE GOT COMMON INTERESTS WITH THE MILITARY NOW, SURE.
BUT I'VE SEEN MORE'N A FEW BLOODY WARS BETWEEN OLD ALLIES IN MY DAY.
DON'T IMAGINE THERE'S ANYTHING WRONG WITH GOING YOUR OWN WAY.
WHAT'S THIS?
OH...AN OLD FRIEND'S GOT A GALLERY SHOW. HADN'T DECIDED IF I'M GOING.
LIKE A NORMAL PERSON FRIEND? I DIDN'T KNOW YOU HAD THOSE.
WE SHOULD GO. SHOW SOME SUPPORT.
RIGHT. WELL, THE THING IS...
AIN'T LIKE SHE'S AN OLD GIRLFRIEND, PER SE, BUT...

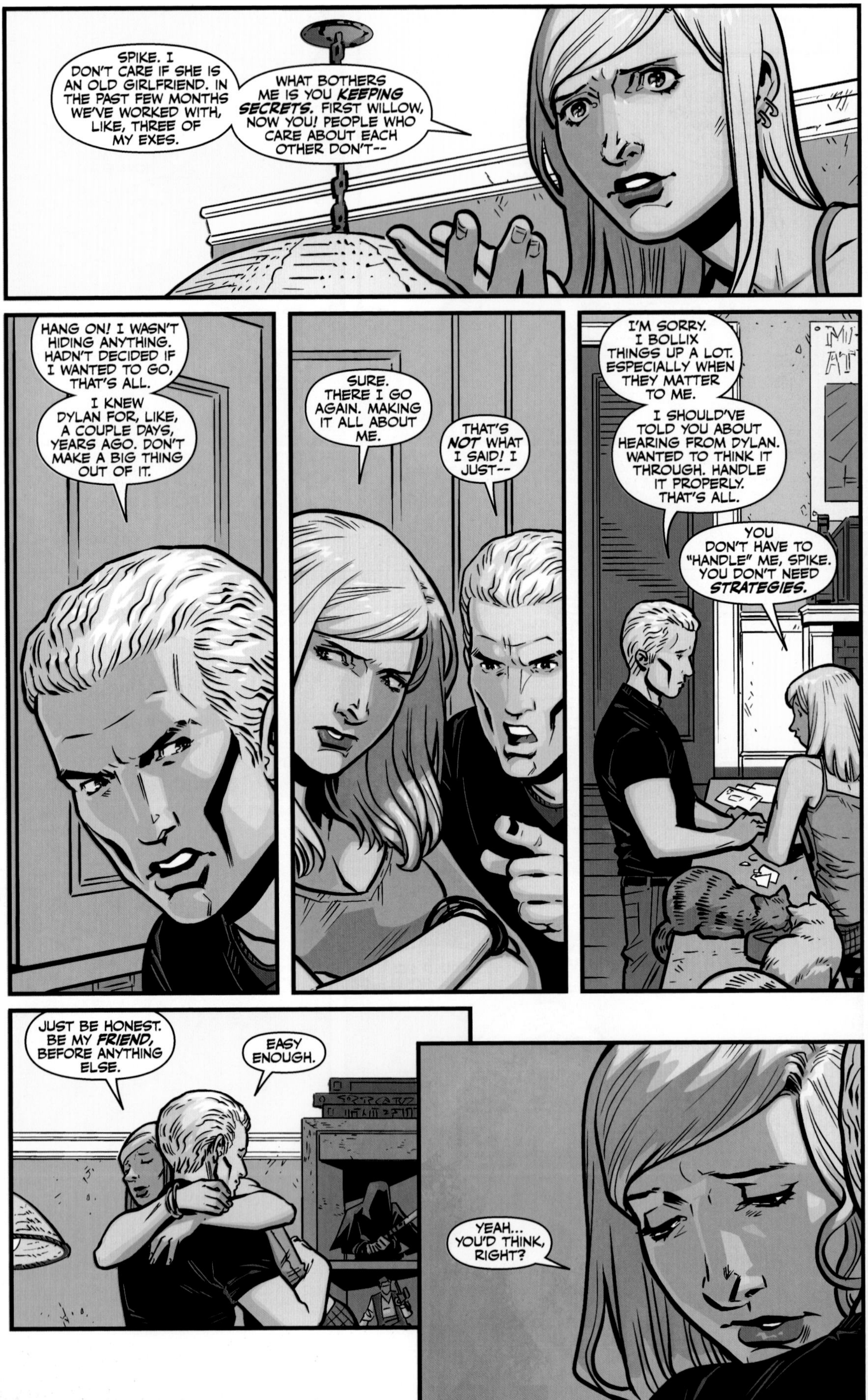
SPIKE. I DON'T CARE IF SHE IS AN OLD GIRLFRIEND. IN THE PAST FEW MONTHS WE'VE WORKED WITH, LIKE, THREE OF MY EXES.
WHAT BOTHERS ME IS YOU *KEEPING SECRETS.* FIRST WILLOW, NOW YOU! PEOPLE WHO CARE ABOUT EACH OTHER DON'T--
HANG ON! I WASN'T HIDING ANYTHING. HADN'T DECIDED IF I WANTED TO GO, THAT'S ALL.
I KNEW DYLAN FOR, LIKE, A COUPLE DAYS, YEARS AGO. DON'T MAKE A BIG THING OUT OF IT.
SURE. THERE I GO AGAIN. MAKING IT ALL ABOUT ME.
THAT'S *NOT* WHAT I SAID! I JUST--
I'M SORRY. I BOLLIX THINGS UP A LOT. ESPECIALLY WHEN THEY MATTER TO ME.
I SHOULD'VE TOLD YOU ABOUT HEARING FROM DYLAN. WANTED TO THINK IT THROUGH. HANDLE IT PROPERLY. THAT'S ALL.
YOU DON'T HAVE TO "HANDLE" ME, SPIKE. YOU DON'T NEED *STRATEGIES.*
JUST BE HONEST. BE MY *FRIEND,* BEFORE ANYTHING ELSE.
EASY ENOUGH.
YEAH... YOU'D THINK, RIGHT?

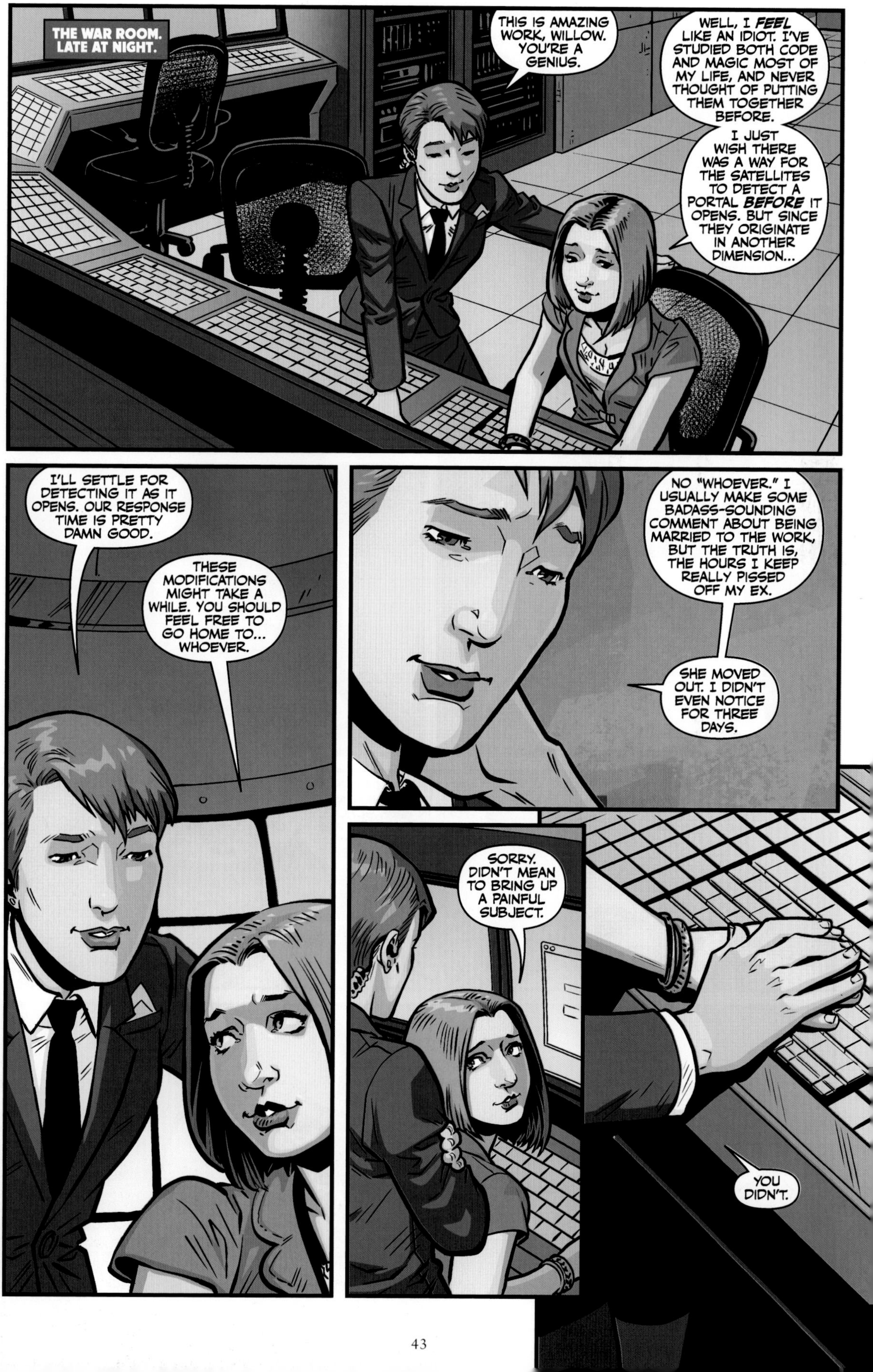
THE WAR ROOM. LATE AT NIGHT.
THIS IS AMAZING WORK, WILLOW. YOU'RE A GENIUS.
WELL, I FEEL LIKE AN IDIOT. I'VE STUDIED BOTH CODE AND MAGIC MOST OF MY LIFE, AND NEVER THOUGHT OF PUTTING THEM TOGETHER BEFORE.
I JUST WISH THERE WAS A WAY FOR THE SATELLITES TO DETECT A PORTAL BEFORE IT OPENS. BUT SINCE THEY ORIGINATE IN ANOTHER DIMENSION...
I'LL SETTLE FOR DETECTING IT AS IT OPENS. OUR RESPONSE TIME IS PRETTY DAMN GOOD.
THESE MODIFICATIONS MIGHT TAKE A WHILE. YOU SHOULD FEEL FREE TO GO HOME TO... WHOEVER.
NO "WHOEVER." I USUALLY MAKE SOME BADASS-SOUNDING COMMENT ABOUT BEING MARRIED TO THE WORK, BUT THE TRUTH IS, THE HOURS I KEEP REALLY PISSED OFF MY EX.
SHE MOVED OUT. I DIDN'T EVEN NOTICE FOR THREE DAYS.
SORRY. DIDN'T MEAN TO BRING UP A PAINFUL SUBJECT.
YOU DIDN'T.

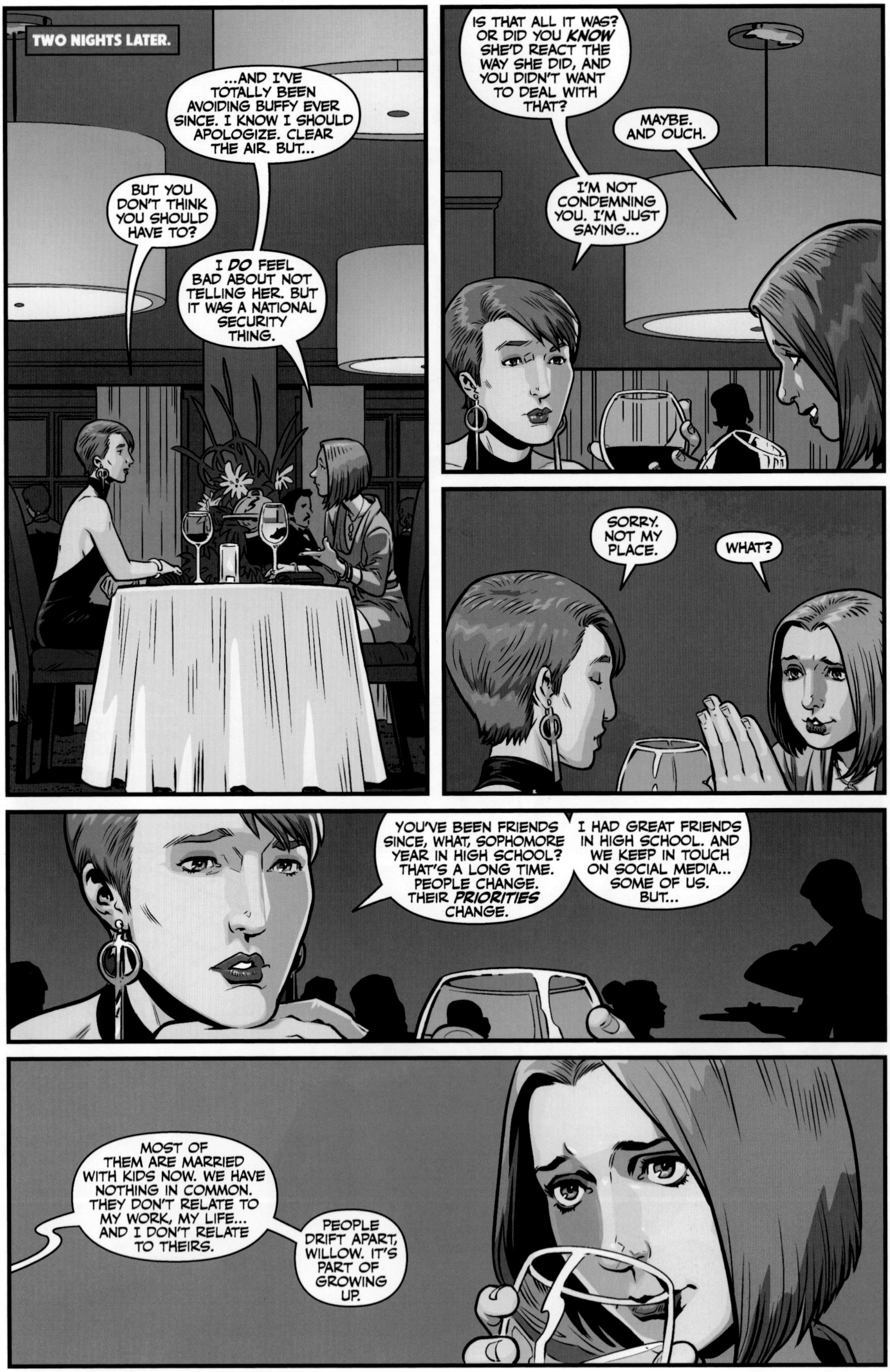
TWO NIGHTS LATER.
...AND I'VE TOTALLY BEEN AVOIDING BUFFY EVER SINCE. I KNOW I SHOULD APOLOGIZE. CLEAR THE AIR. BUT...
BUT YOU DON'T THINK YOU SHOULD HAVE TO?
I *DO* FEEL BAD ABOUT NOT TELLING HER. BUT IT WAS A NATIONAL SECURITY THING.
IS THAT ALL IT WAS? OR DID YOU *KNOW* SHE'D REACT THE WAY SHE DID, AND YOU DIDN'T WANT TO DEAL WITH THAT?
MAYBE. AND OUCH.
I'M NOT CONDEMNING YOU. I'M JUST SAYING...
SORRY. NOT MY PLACE.
WHAT?
YOU'VE BEEN FRIENDS SINCE, WHAT, SOPHOMORE YEAR IN HIGH SCHOOL? THAT'S A LONG TIME. PEOPLE CHANGE. THEIR *PRIORITIES* CHANGE.
I HAD GREAT FRIENDS IN HIGH SCHOOL. AND WE KEEP IN TOUCH ON SOCIAL MEDIA... SOME OF US. BUT...
MOST OF THEM ARE MARRIED WITH KIDS NOW. WE HAVE NOTHING IN COMMON. THEY DON'T RELATE TO MY WORK, MY LIFE... AND I DON'T RELATE TO THEIRS.
PEOPLE DRIFT APART, WILLOW. IT'S PART OF GROWING UP.

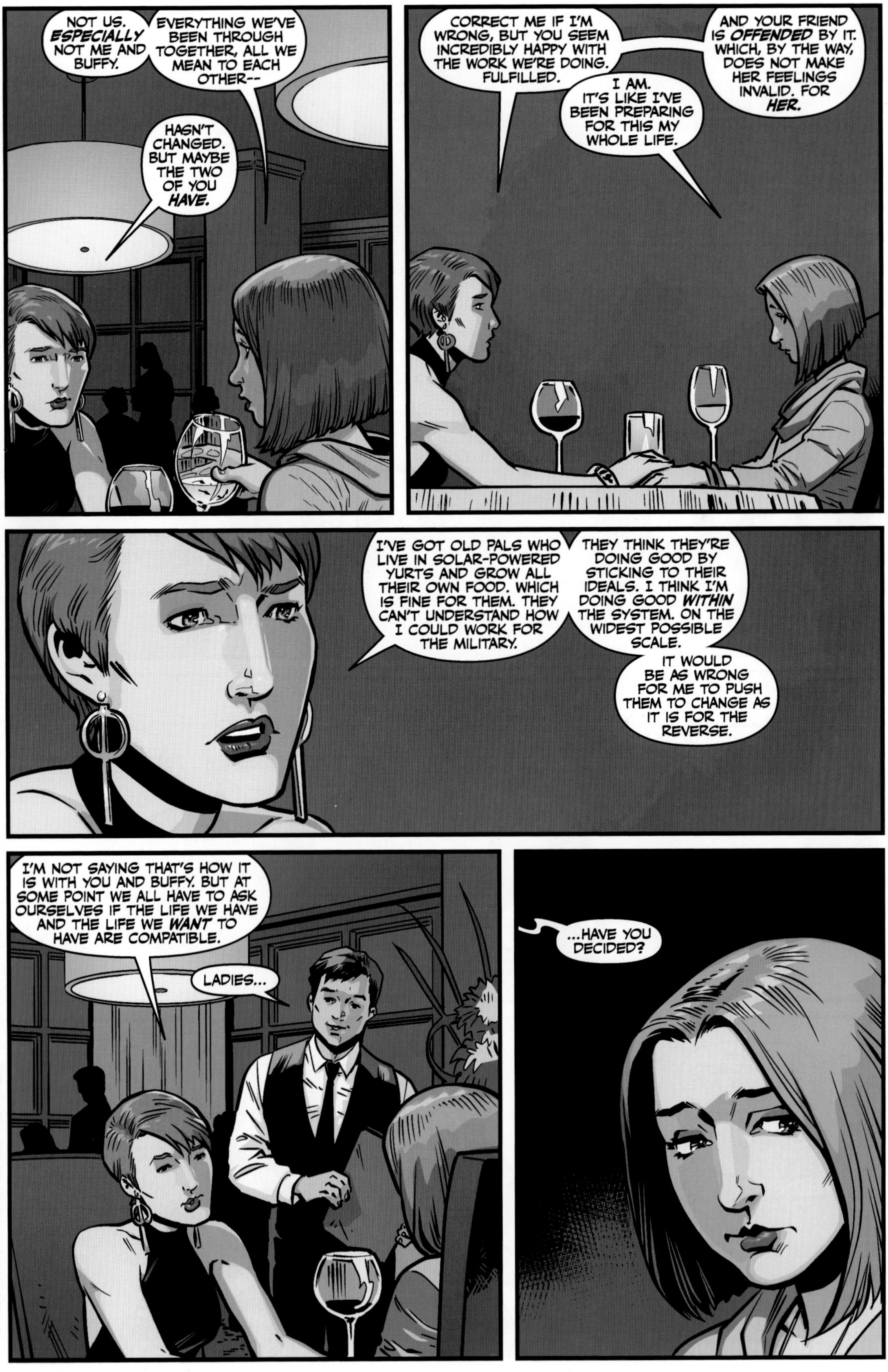
NOT US. ESPECIALLY NOT ME AND BUFFY.
EVERYTHING WE'VE BEEN THROUGH TOGETHER, ALL WE MEAN TO EACH OTHER--
HASN'T CHANGED. BUT MAYBE THE TWO OF YOU HAVE.
CORRECT ME IF I'M WRONG, BUT YOU SEEM INCREDIBLY HAPPY WITH THE WORK WE'RE DOING. FULFILLED.
I AM. IT'S LIKE I'VE BEEN PREPARING FOR THIS MY WHOLE LIFE.
AND YOUR FRIEND IS OFFENDED BY IT. WHICH, BY THE WAY, DOES NOT MAKE HER FEELINGS INVALID. FOR HER.
I'VE GOT OLD PALS WHO LIVE IN SOLAR-POWERED YURTS AND GROW ALL THEIR OWN FOOD. WHICH IS FINE FOR THEM. THEY CAN'T UNDERSTAND HOW I COULD WORK FOR THE MILITARY.
THEY THINK THEY'RE DOING GOOD BY STICKING TO THEIR IDEALS. I THINK I'M DOING GOOD WITHIN THE SYSTEM. ON THE WIDEST POSSIBLE SCALE.
IT WOULD BE AS WRONG FOR ME TO PUSH THEM TO CHANGE AS IT IS FOR THE REVERSE.
I'M NOT SAYING THAT'S HOW IT IS WITH YOU AND BUFFY. BUT AT SOME POINT WE ALL HAVE TO ASK OURSELVES IF THE LIFE WE HAVE AND THE LIFE WE WANT TO HAVE ARE COMPATIBLE.
LADIES...
...HAVE YOU DECIDED?

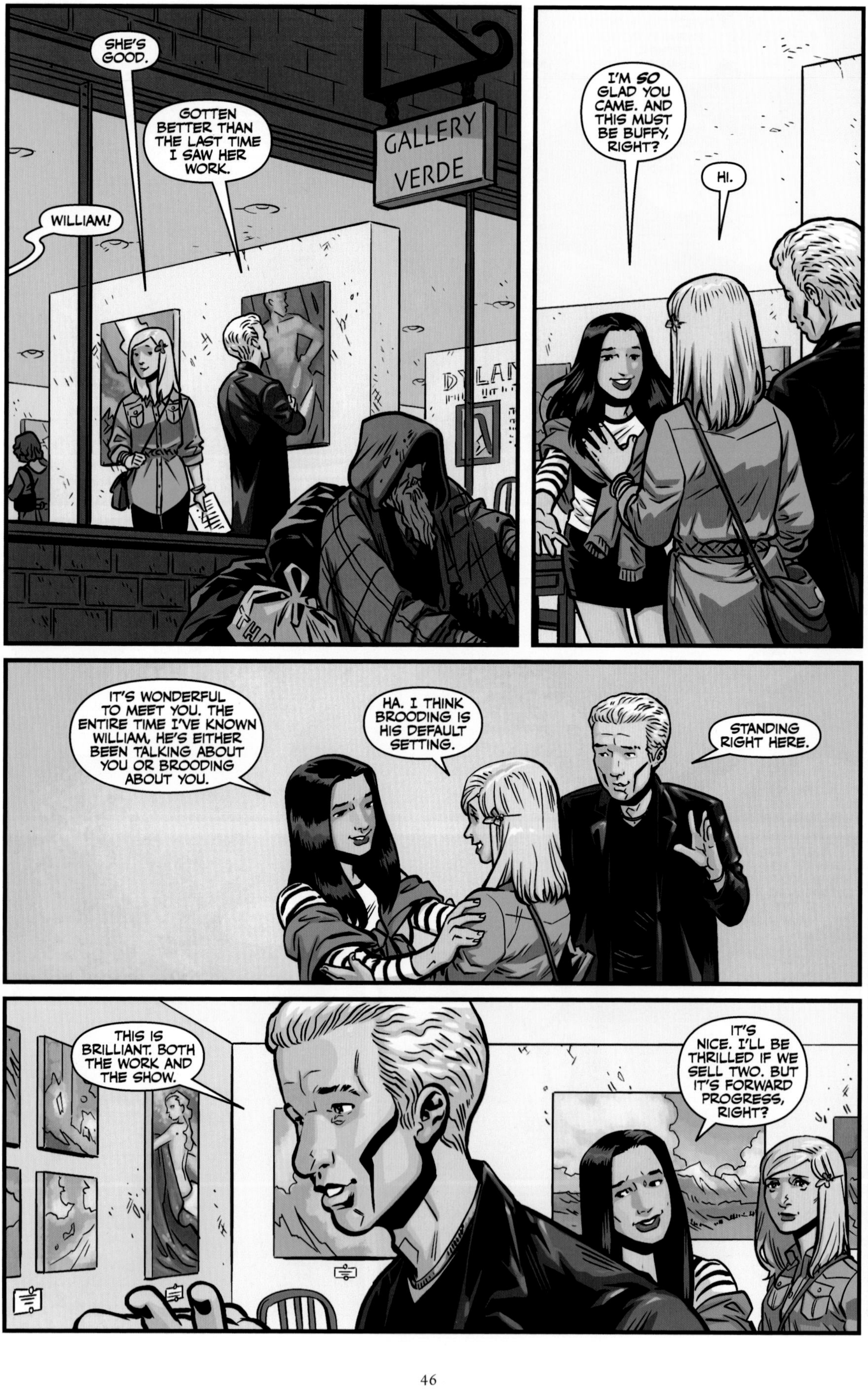
SHE'S GOOD.
GOTTEN BETTER THAN THE LAST TIME I SAW HER WORK.
GALLERY VERDE
WILLIAM!
I'M SO GLAD YOU CAME. AND THIS MUST BE BUFFY, RIGHT?
HI.
IT'S WONDERFUL TO MEET YOU. THE ENTIRE TIME I'VE KNOWN WILLIAM, HE'S EITHER BEEN TALKING ABOUT YOU OR BROODING ABOUT YOU.
HA. I THINK BROODING IS HIS DEFAULT SETTING.
STANDING RIGHT HERE.
THIS IS BRILLIANT. BOTH THE WORK AND THE SHOW.
IT'S NICE. I'LL BE THRILLED IF WE SELL TWO. BUT IT'S FORWARD PROGRESS, RIGHT?

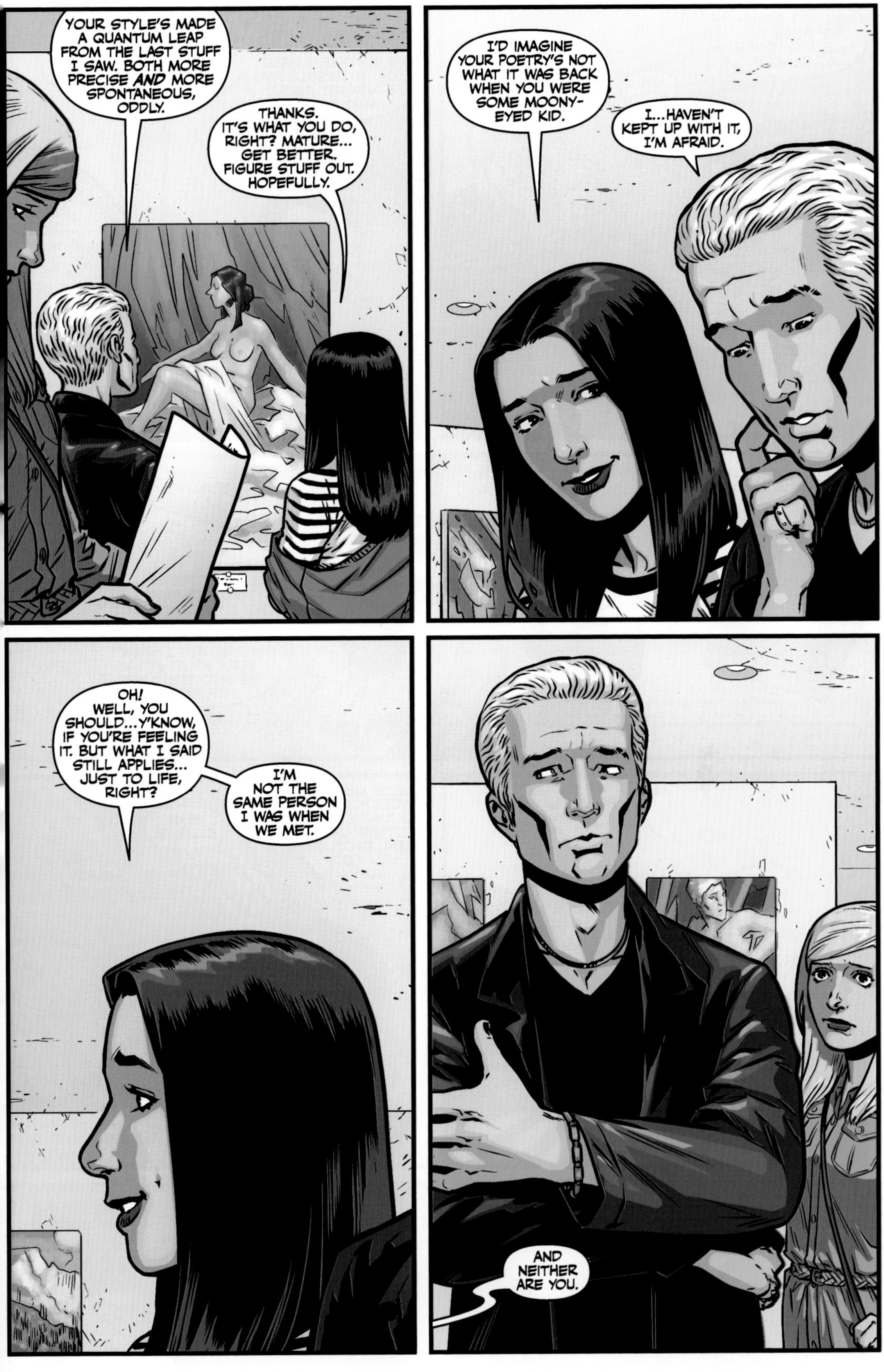
YOUR STYLE'S MADE A QUANTUM LEAP FROM THE LAST STUFF I SAW. BOTH MORE PRECISE AND MORE SPONTANEOUS, ODDLY.
THANKS. IT'S WHAT YOU DO, RIGHT? MATURE... GET BETTER. FIGURE STUFF OUT. HOPEFULLY.
I'D IMAGINE YOUR POETRY'S NOT WHAT IT WAS BACK WHEN YOU WERE SOME MOONY-EYED KID.
I...HAVEN'T KEPT UP WITH IT, I'M AFRAID.
OH! WELL, YOU SHOULD...Y'KNOW, IF YOU'RE FEELING IT. BUT WHAT I SAID STILL APPLIES... JUST TO LIFE, RIGHT?
I'M NOT THE SAME PERSON I WAS WHEN WE MET.
AND NEITHER ARE YOU.

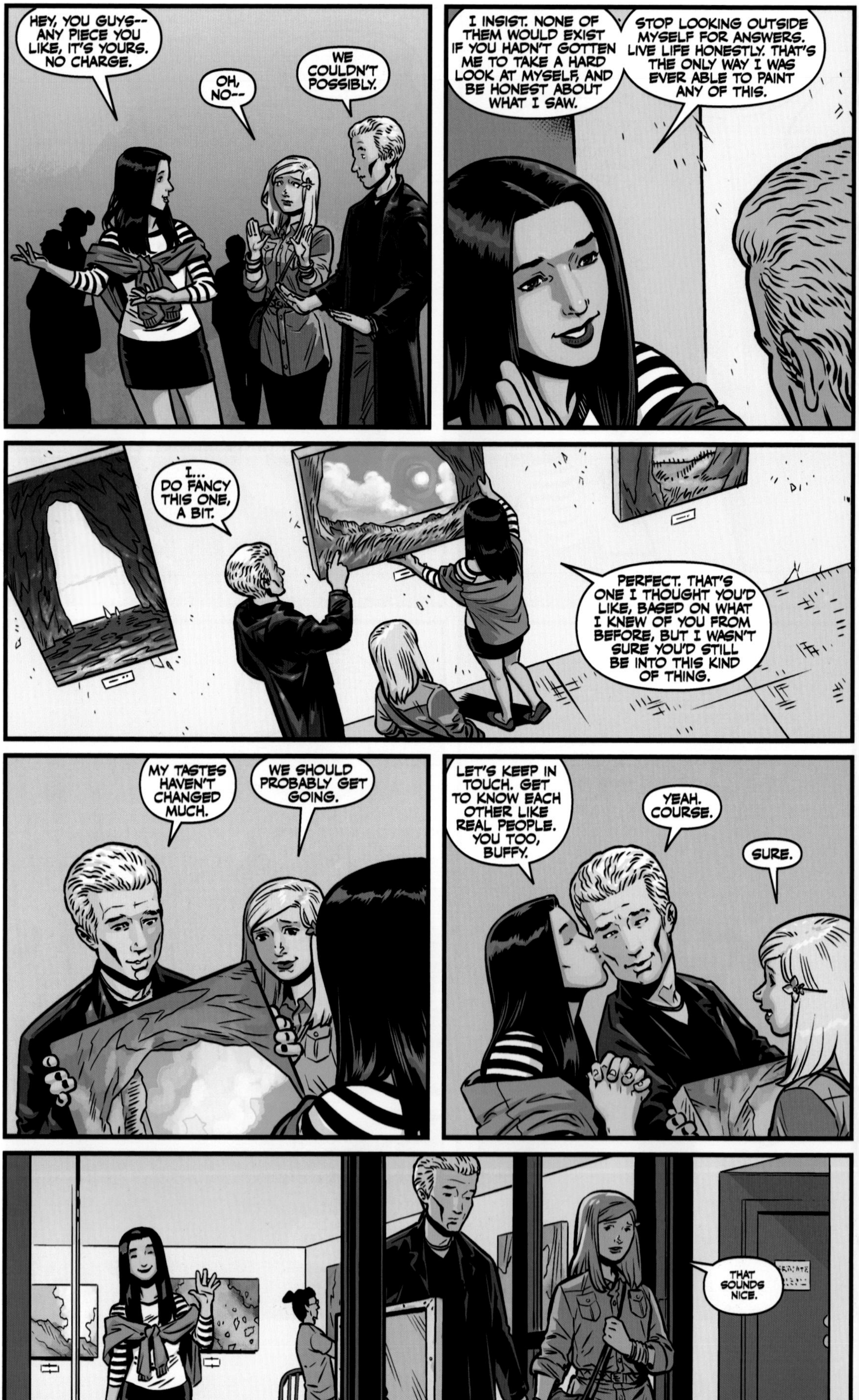
HEY, YOU GUYS-- ANY PIECE YOU LIKE, IT'S YOURS. NO CHARGE.
OH, NO--
WE COULDN'T POSSIBLY.
I INSIST. NONE OF THEM WOULD EXIST IF YOU HADN'T GOTTEN ME TO TAKE A HARD LOOK AT MYSELF, AND BE HONEST ABOUT WHAT I SAW.
STOP LOOKING OUTSIDE MYSELF FOR ANSWERS. LIVE LIFE HONESTLY. THAT'S THE ONLY WAY I WAS EVER ABLE TO PAINT ANY OF THIS.
I... DO FANCY THIS ONE, A BIT.
PERFECT. THAT'S ONE I THOUGHT YOU'D LIKE, BASED ON WHAT I KNEW OF YOU FROM BEFORE, BUT I WASN'T SURE YOU'D STILL BE INTO THIS KIND OF THING.
MY TASTES HAVEN'T CHANGED MUCH.
WE SHOULD PROBABLY GET GOING.
LET'S KEEP IN TOUCH. GET TO KNOW EACH OTHER LIKE REAL PEOPLE. YOU TOO, BUFFY.
YEAH. COURSE.
SURE.
THAT SOUNDS NICE.

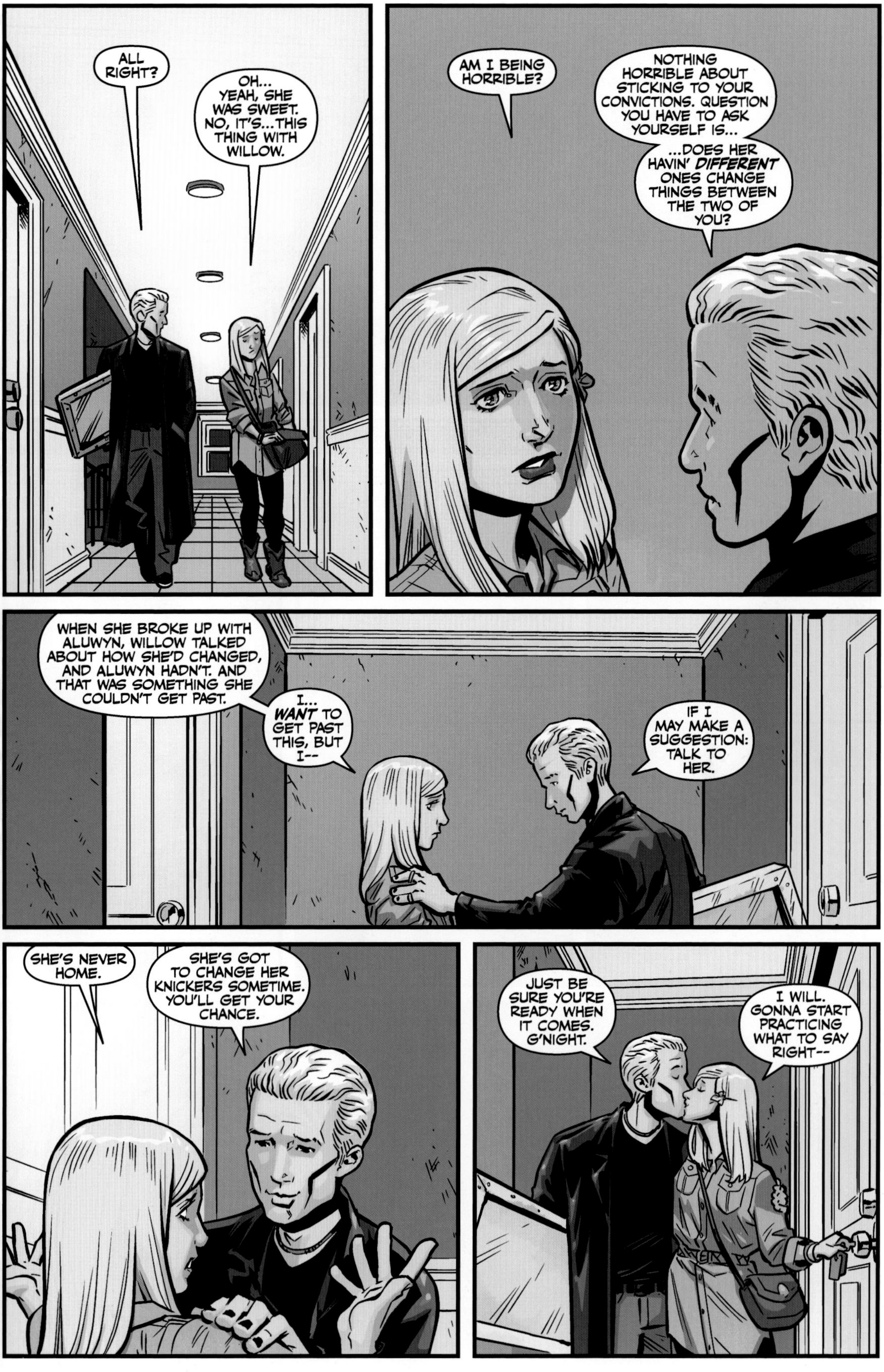
ALL RIGHT?
OH... YEAH, SHE WAS SWEET. NO, IT'S...THIS THING WITH WILLOW.
AM I BEING HORRIBLE?
NOTHING HORRIBLE ABOUT STICKING TO YOUR CONVICTIONS. QUESTION YOU HAVE TO ASK YOURSELF IS...
...DOES HER HAVIN' *DIFFERENT* ONES CHANGE THINGS BETWEEN THE TWO OF YOU?
WHEN SHE BROKE UP WITH ALUWYN, WILLOW TALKED ABOUT HOW SHE'D CHANGED, AND ALUWYN HADN'T. AND THAT WAS SOMETHING SHE COULDN'T GET PAST.
I... *WANT* TO GET PAST THIS, BUT I--
IF I MAY MAKE A SUGGESTION: TALK TO HER.
SHE'S NEVER HOME.
SHE'S GOT TO CHANGE HER KNICKERS SOMETIME. YOU'LL GET YOUR CHANCE.
JUST BE SURE YOU'RE READY WHEN IT COMES. G'NIGHT.
I WILL. GONNA START PRACTICING WHAT TO SAY RIGHT--

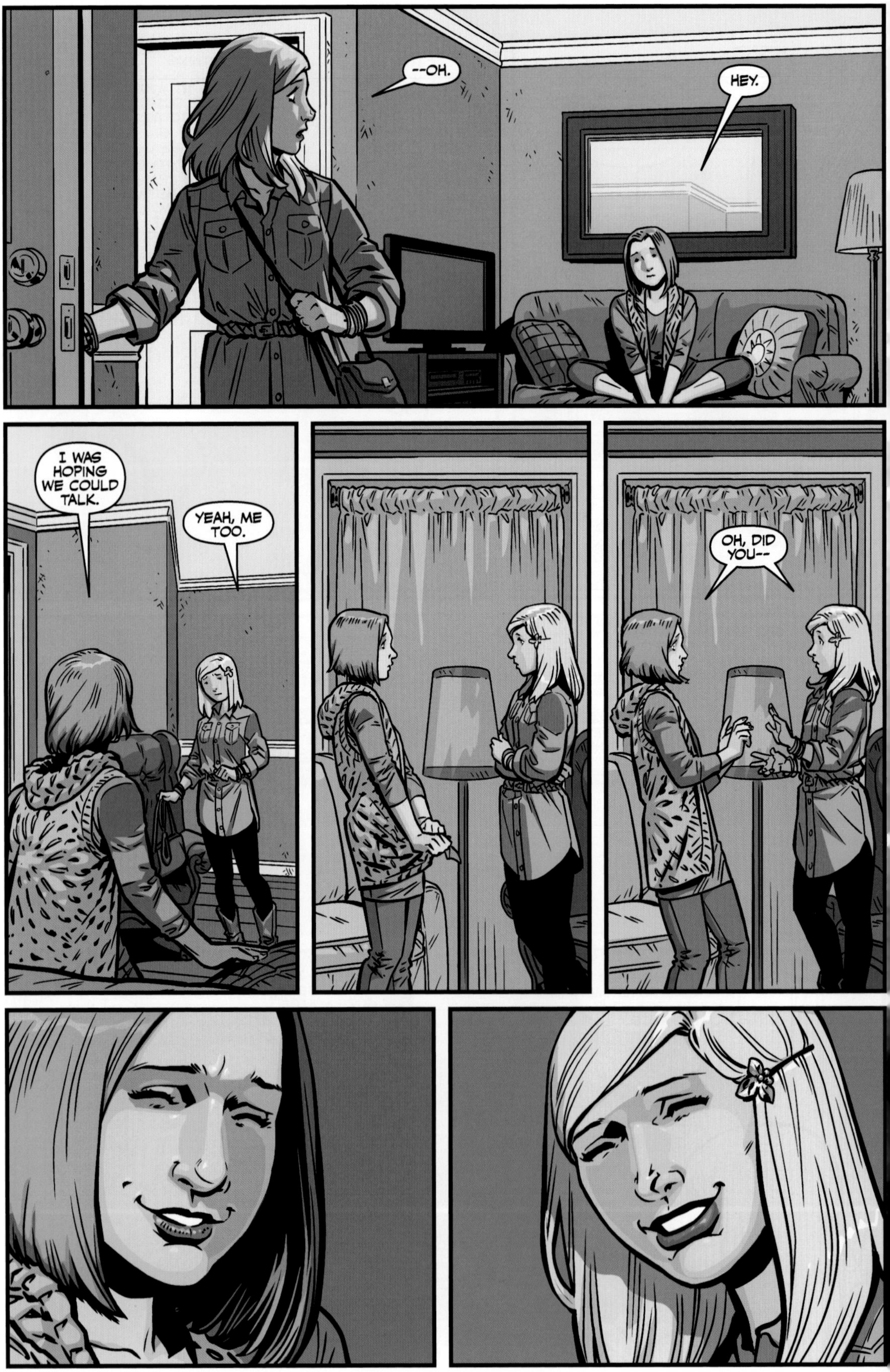
--OH.
HEY.
I WAS HOPING WE COULD TALK.
YEAH, ME TOO.
OH, DID YOU--

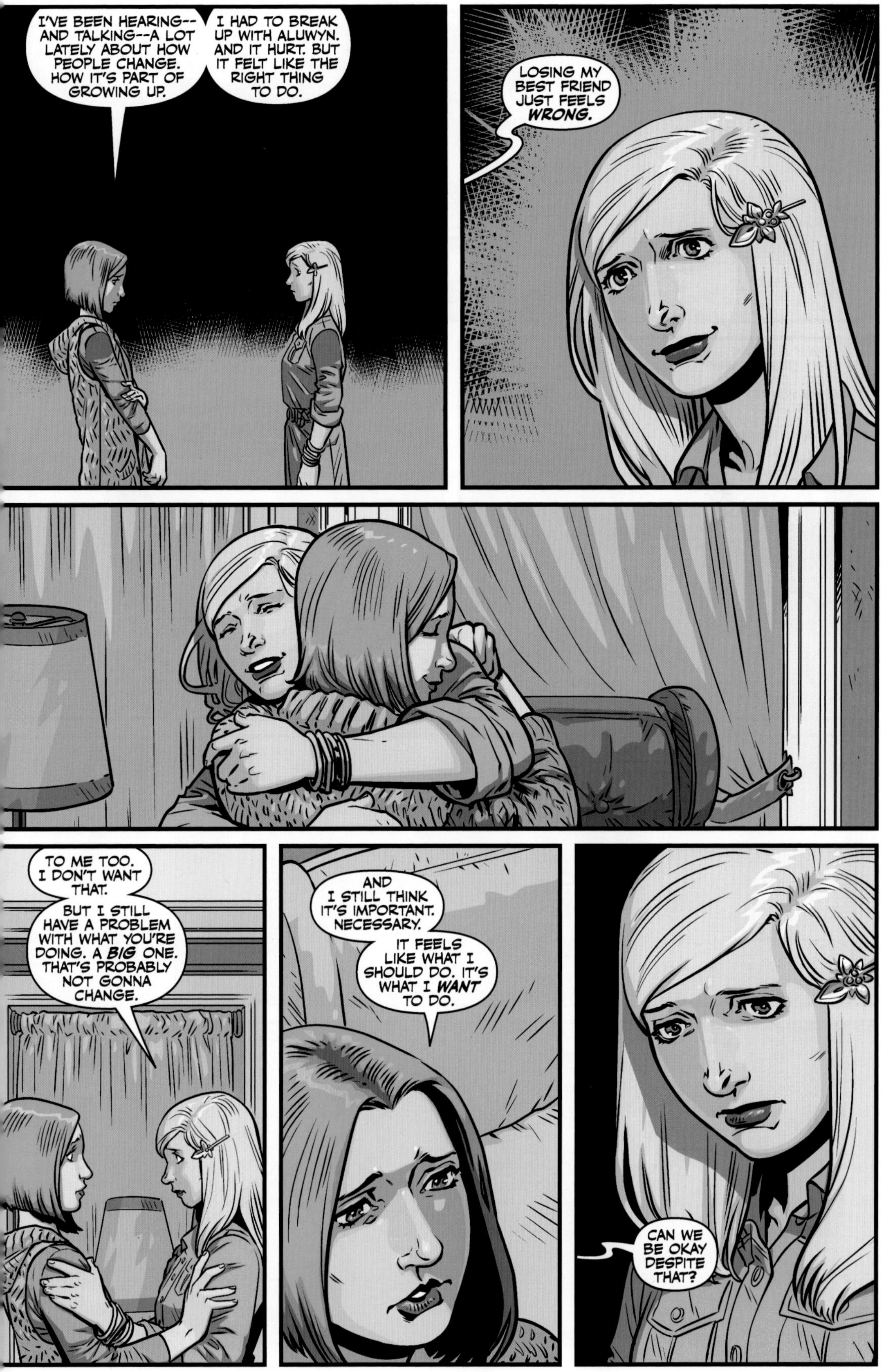
I'VE BEEN HEARING-- AND TALKING--A LOT LATELY ABOUT HOW PEOPLE CHANGE. HOW IT'S PART OF GROWING UP.
I HAD TO BREAK UP WITH ALUWYN. AND IT HURT. BUT IT FELT LIKE THE RIGHT THING TO DO.
LOSING MY BEST FRIEND JUST FEELS WRONG.
TO ME TOO. I DON'T WANT THAT.
BUT I STILL HAVE A PROBLEM WITH WHAT YOU'RE DOING. A BIG ONE. THAT'S PROBABLY NOT GONNA CHANGE.
AND I STILL THINK IT'S IMPORTANT. NECESSARY.
IT FEELS LIKE WHAT I SHOULD DO. IT'S WHAT I WANT TO DO.
CAN WE BE OKAY DESPITE THAT?

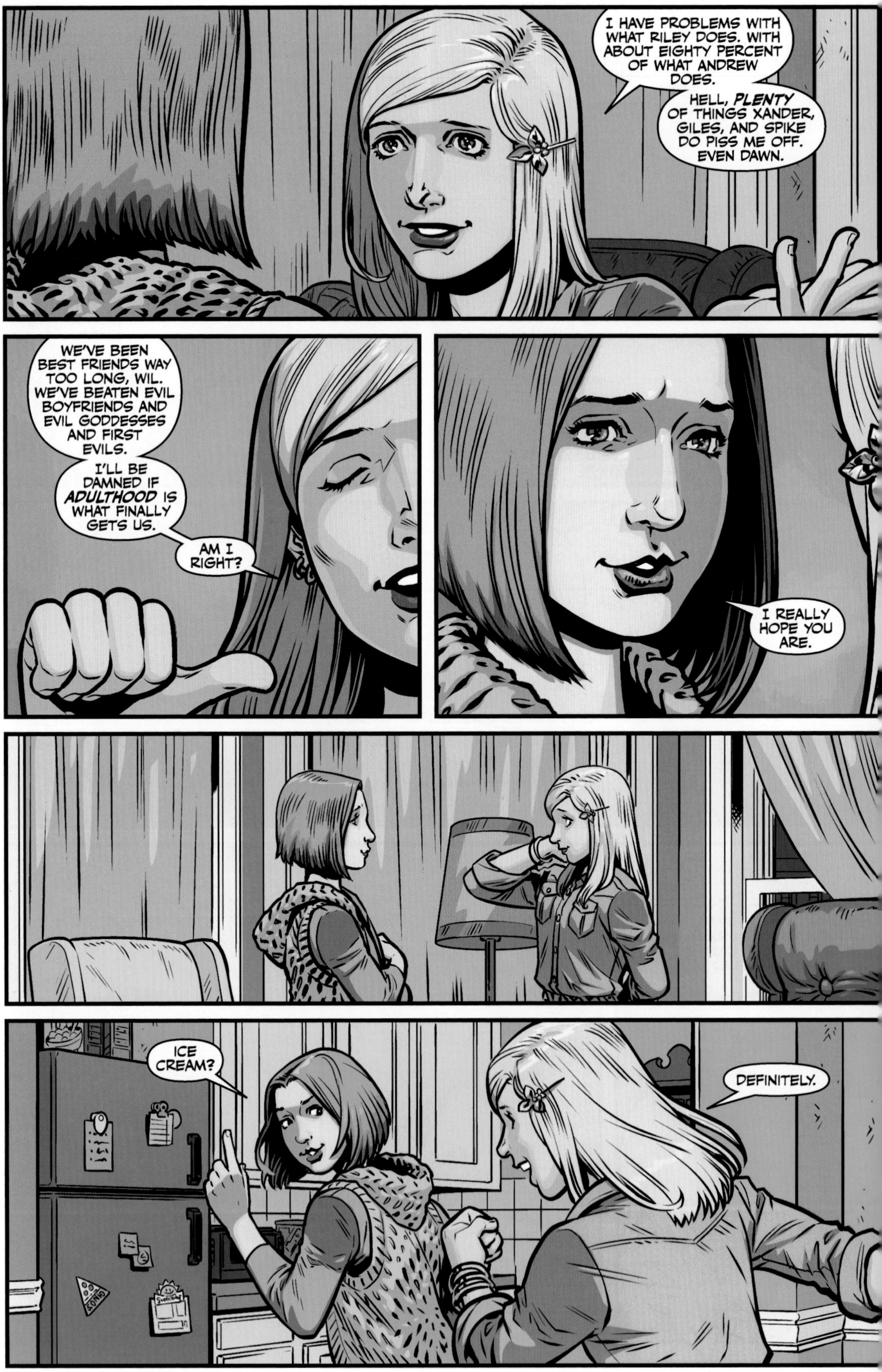
I HAVE PROBLEMS WITH WHAT RILEY DOES. WITH ABOUT EIGHTY PERCENT OF WHAT ANDREW DOES.
HELL, PLENTY OF THINGS XANDER, GILES, AND SPIKE DO PISS ME OFF. EVEN DAWN.
WE'VE BEEN BEST FRIENDS WAY TOO LONG, WIL. WE'VE BEATEN EVIL BOYFRIENDS AND EVIL GODDESSES AND FIRST EVILS.
I'LL BE DAMNED IF ADULTHOOD IS WHAT FINALLY GETS US.
AM I RIGHT?
I REALLY HOPE YOU ARE.
ICE CREAM?
DEFINITELY.

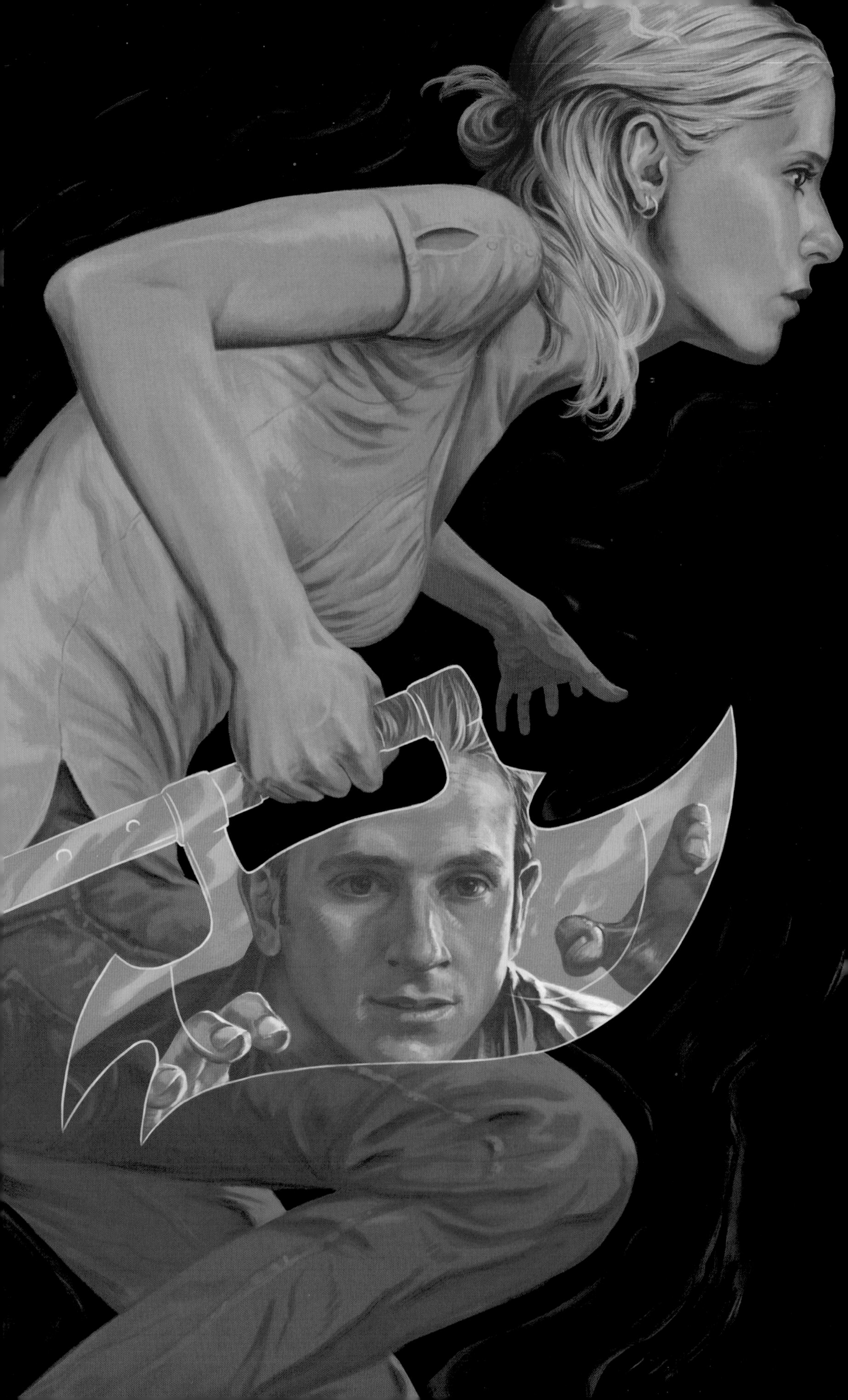

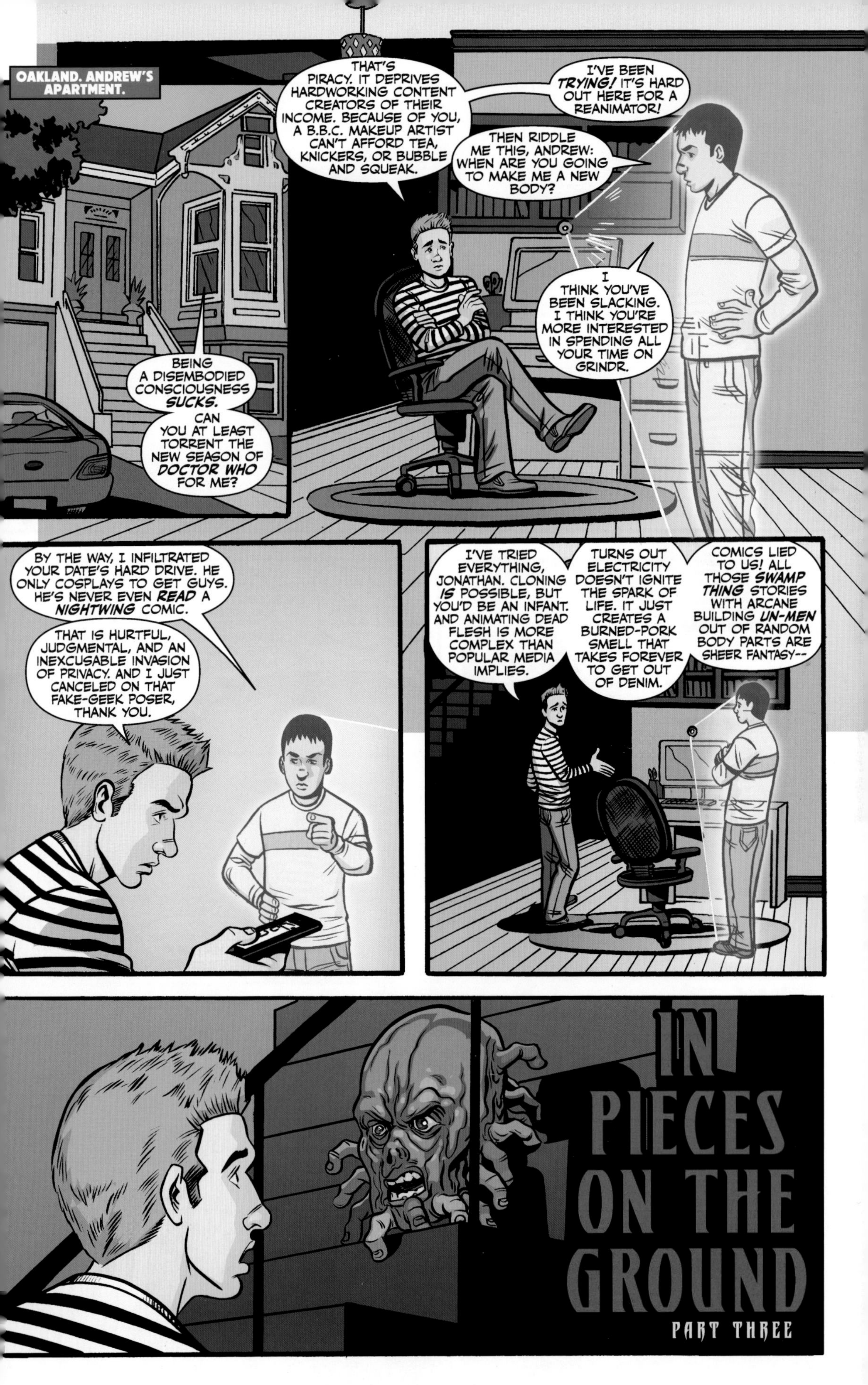
OAKLAND. ANDREW'S APARTMENT.
BEING A DISEMBODIED CONSCIOUSNESS SUCKS.
CAN YOU AT LEAST TORRENT THE NEW SEASON OF DOCTOR WHO FOR ME?
THAT'S PIRACY. IT DEPRIVES HARDWORKING CONTENT CREATORS OF THEIR INCOME. BECAUSE OF YOU, A B.B.C. MAKEUP ARTIST CAN'T AFFORD TEA, KNICKERS, OR BUBBLE AND SQUEAK.
THEN RIDDLE ME THIS, ANDREW: WHEN ARE YOU GOING TO MAKE ME A NEW BODY?
I'VE BEEN TRYING! IT'S HARD OUT HERE FOR A REANIMATOR!
I THINK YOU'VE BEEN SLACKING. I THINK YOU'RE MORE INTERESTED IN SPENDING ALL YOUR TIME ON GRINDR.
BY THE WAY, I INFILTRATED YOUR DATE'S HARD DRIVE. HE ONLY COSPLAYS TO GET GUYS. HE'S NEVER EVEN READ A NIGHTWING COMIC.
THAT IS HURTFUL, JUDGMENTAL, AND AN INEXCUSABLE INVASION OF PRIVACY. AND I JUST CANCELED ON THAT FAKE-GEEK POSER, THANK YOU.
I'VE TRIED EVERYTHING, JONATHAN. CLONING IS POSSIBLE, BUT YOU'D BE AN INFANT. AND ANIMATING DEAD FLESH IS MORE COMPLEX THAN POPULAR MEDIA IMPLIES.
TURNS OUT ELECTRICITY DOESN'T IGNITE THE SPARK OF LIFE. IT JUST CREATES A BURNED-PORK SMELL THAT TAKES FOREVER TO GET OUT OF DENIM.
COMICS LIED TO US! ALL THOSE SWAMP THING STORIES WITH ARCANE BUILDING UN-MEN OUT OF RANDOM BODY PARTS ARE SHEER FANTASY--
IN PIECES ON THE GROUND
PART THREE

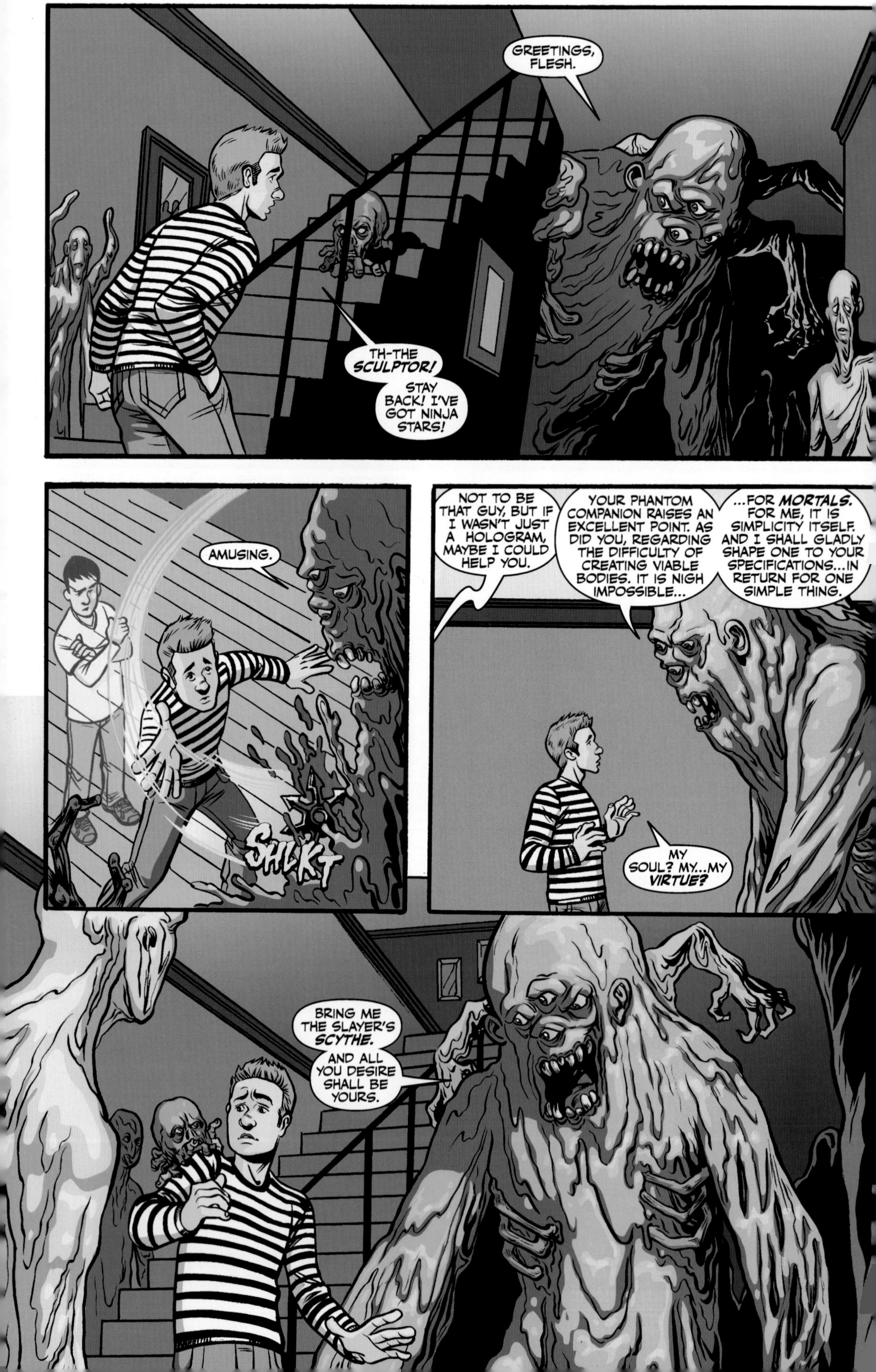
GREETINGS, FLESH.
TH-THE SCULPTOR!
STAY BACK! I'VE GOT NINJA STARS!
AMUSING.
SHLKT
NOT TO BE THAT GUY, BUT IF I WASN'T JUST A HOLOGRAM, MAYBE I COULD HELP YOU.
YOUR PHANTOM COMPANION RAISES AN EXCELLENT POINT. AS DID YOU, REGARDING THE DIFFICULTY OF CREATING VIABLE BODIES. IT IS NIGH IMPOSSIBLE...
...FOR MORTALS. FOR ME, IT IS SIMPLICITY ITSELF. AND I SHALL GLADLY SHAPE ONE TO YOUR SPECIFICATIONS...IN RETURN FOR ONE SIMPLE THING.
MY SOUL? MY...MY VIRTUE?
BRING ME THE SLAYER'S SCYTHE.
AND ALL YOU DESIRE SHALL BE YOURS.

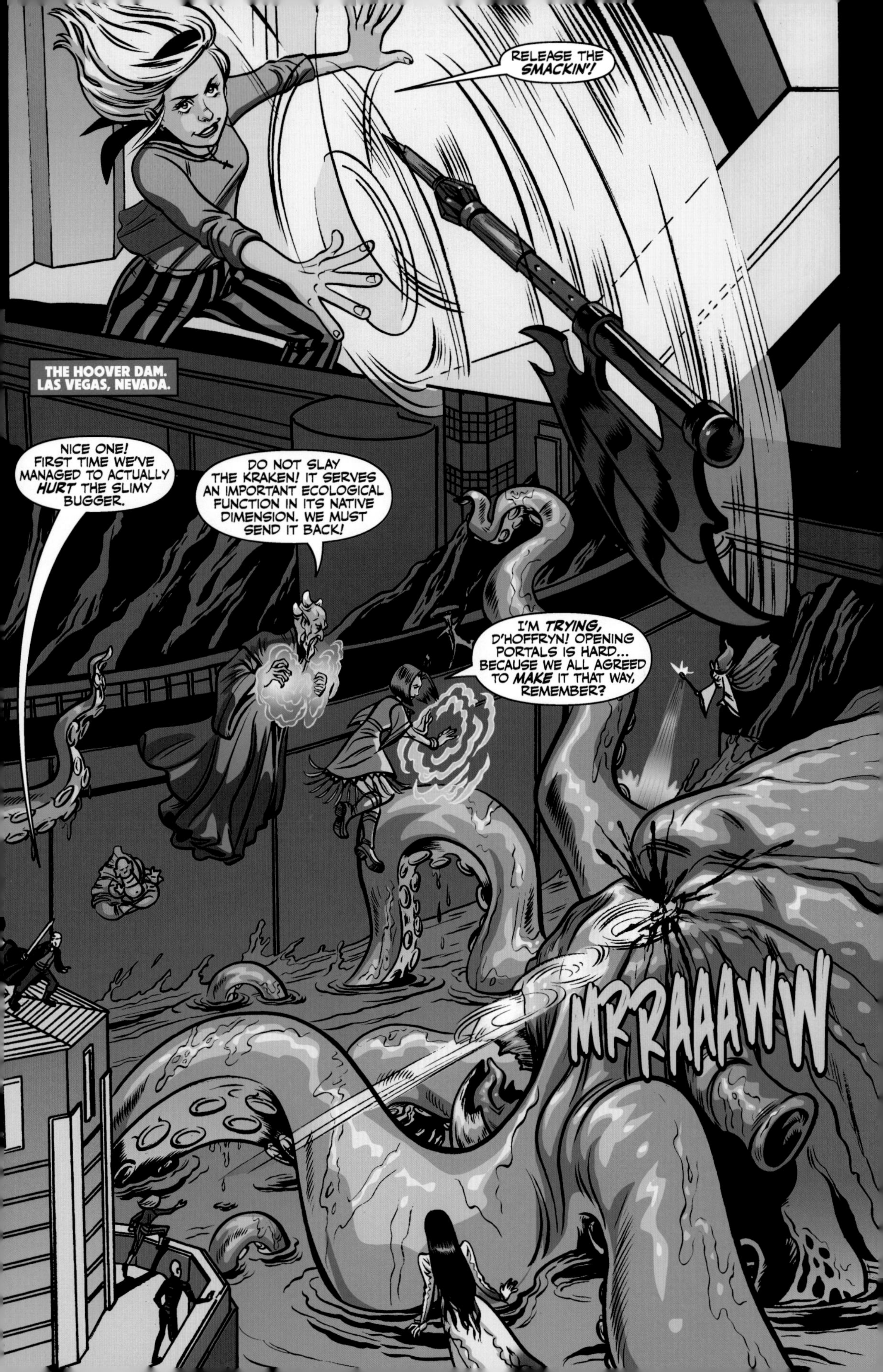
RELEASE THE *SMACKIN'!*
THE HOOVER DAM. LAS VEGAS, NEVADA.
NICE ONE! FIRST TIME WE'VE MANAGED TO ACTUALLY *HURT* THE SLIMY BUGGER.
DO NOT SLAY THE KRAKEN! IT SERVES AN IMPORTANT ECOLOGICAL FUNCTION IN ITS NATIVE DIMENSION. WE MUST SEND IT BACK!
I'M *TRYING,* D'HOFFRYN! OPENING PORTALS IS HARD... BECAUSE WE ALL AGREED TO *MAKE* IT THAT WAY, REMEMBER?
MRRAAAWW

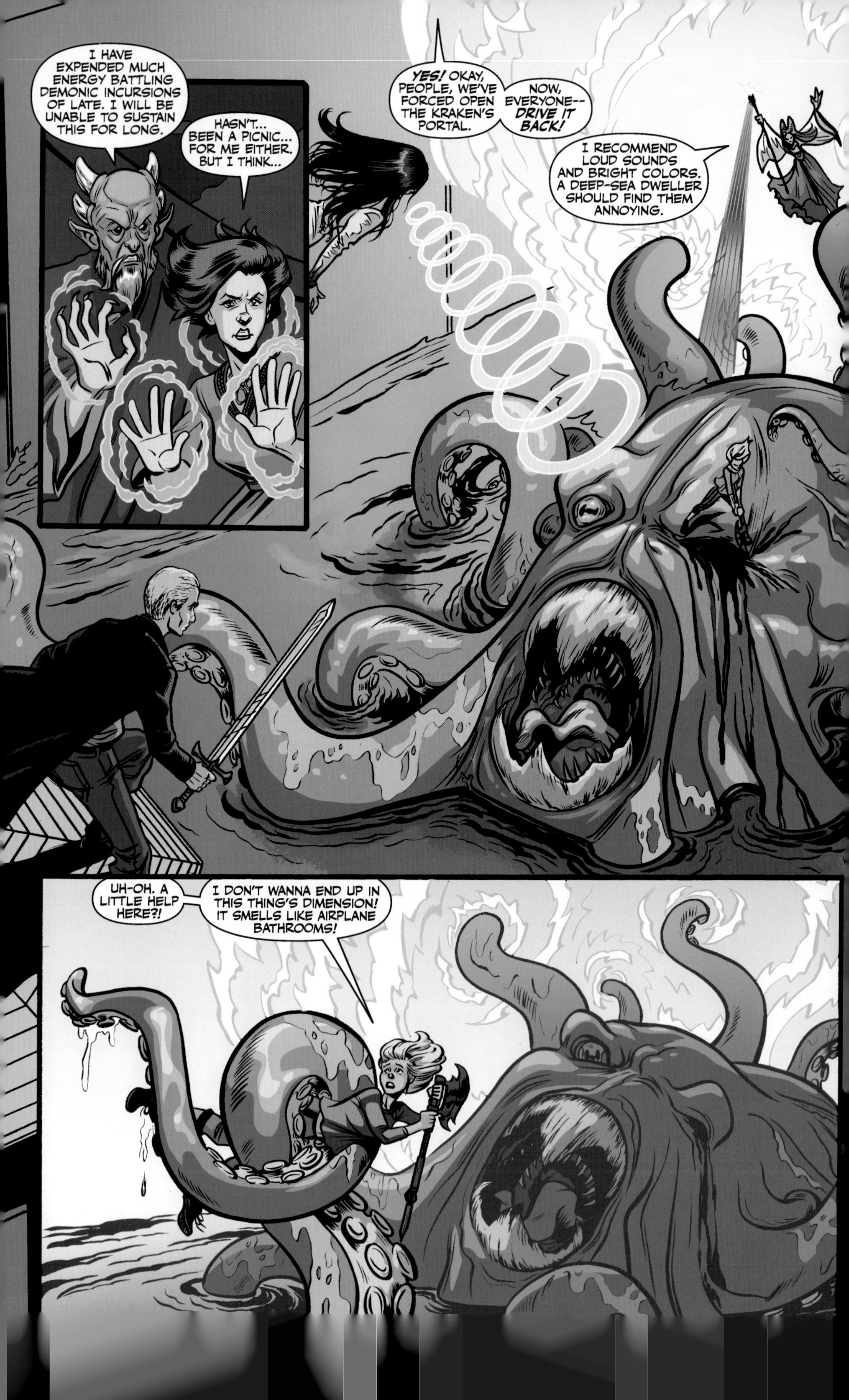
I HAVE EXPENDED MUCH ENERGY BATTLING DEMONIC INCURSIONS OF LATE. I WILL BE UNABLE TO SUSTAIN THIS FOR LONG.
HASN'T... BEEN A PICNIC... FOR ME EITHER. BUT I THINK...
YES! OKAY, PEOPLE, WE'VE FORCED OPEN THE KRAKEN'S PORTAL.
NOW, EVERYONE-- DRIVE IT BACK!
I RECOMMEND LOUD SOUNDS AND BRIGHT COLORS. A DEEP-SEA DWELLER SHOULD FIND THEM ANNOYING.
UH-OH. A LITTLE HELP HERE?!
I DON'T WANNA END UP IN THIS THING'S DIMENSION! IT SMELLS LIKE AIRPLANE BATHROOMS!

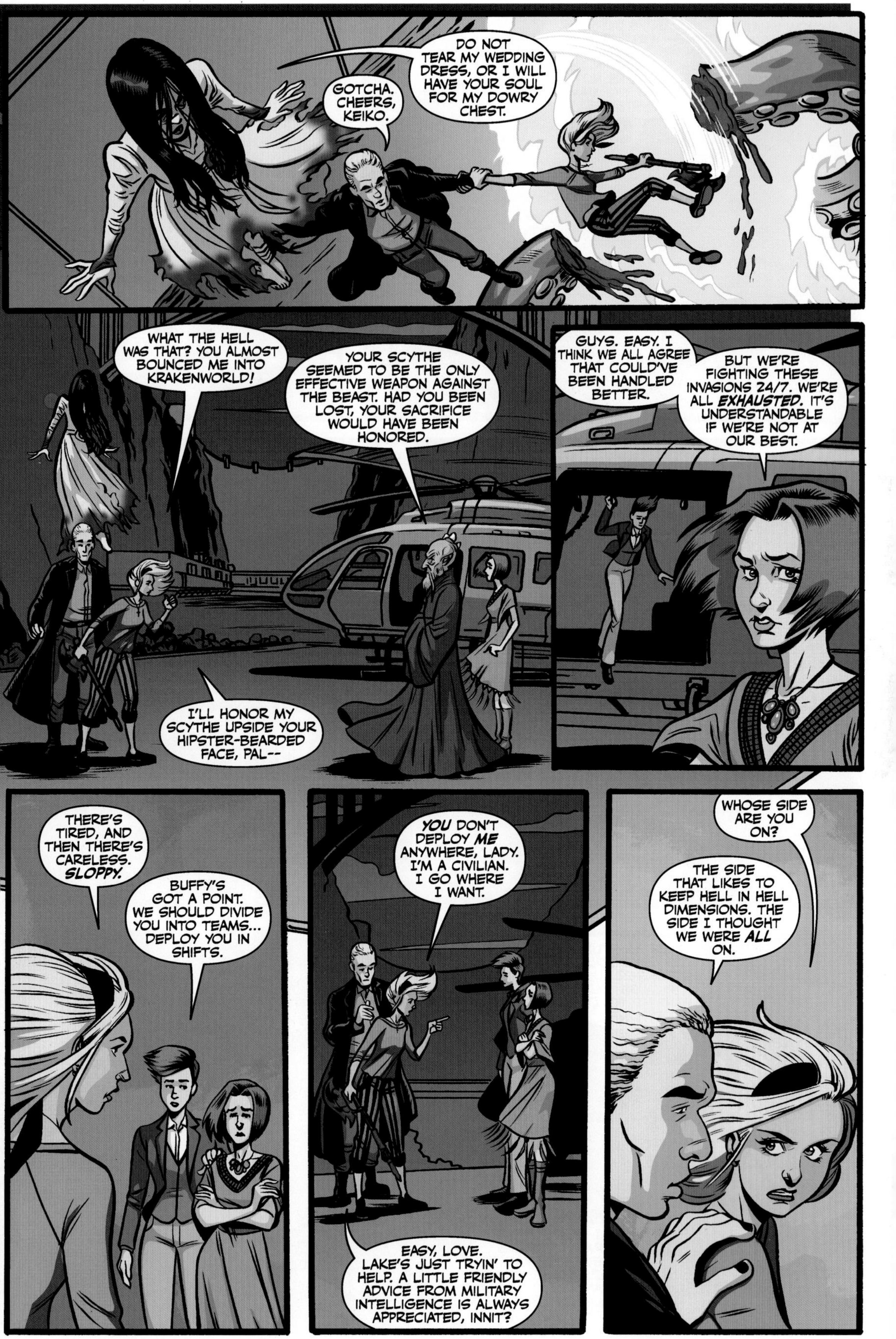
DO NOT TEAR MY WEDDING DRESS, OR I WILL HAVE YOUR SOUL FOR MY DOWRY CHEST.
GOTCHA. CHEERS, KEIKO.
WHAT THE HELL WAS THAT? YOU ALMOST BOUNCED ME INTO KRAKENWORLD!
YOUR SCYTHE SEEMED TO BE THE ONLY EFFECTIVE WEAPON AGAINST THE BEAST. HAD YOU BEEN LOST, YOUR SACRIFICE WOULD HAVE BEEN HONORED.
I'LL HONOR MY SCYTHE UPSIDE YOUR HIPSTER-BEARDED FACE, PAL--
GUYS. EASY. I THINK WE ALL AGREE THAT COULD'VE BEEN HANDLED BETTER.
BUT WE'RE FIGHTING THESE INVASIONS 24/7. WE'RE ALL *EXHAUSTED*. IT'S UNDERSTANDABLE IF WE'RE NOT AT OUR BEST.
THERE'S TIRED, AND THEN THERE'S CARELESS. *SLOPPY.*
BUFFY'S GOT A POINT. WE SHOULD DIVIDE YOU INTO TEAMS... DEPLOY YOU IN SHIFTS.
YOU DON'T DEPLOY *ME* ANYWHERE, LADY. I'M A CIVILIAN. I GO WHERE I WANT.
EASY, LOVE. LAKE'S JUST TRYIN' TO HELP. A LITTLE FRIENDLY ADVICE FROM MILITARY INTELLIGENCE IS ALWAYS APPRECIATED, INNIT?
WHOSE SIDE ARE YOU ON?
THE SIDE THAT LIKES TO KEEP HELL IN HELL DIMENSIONS. THE SIDE I THOUGHT WE WERE *ALL* ON.

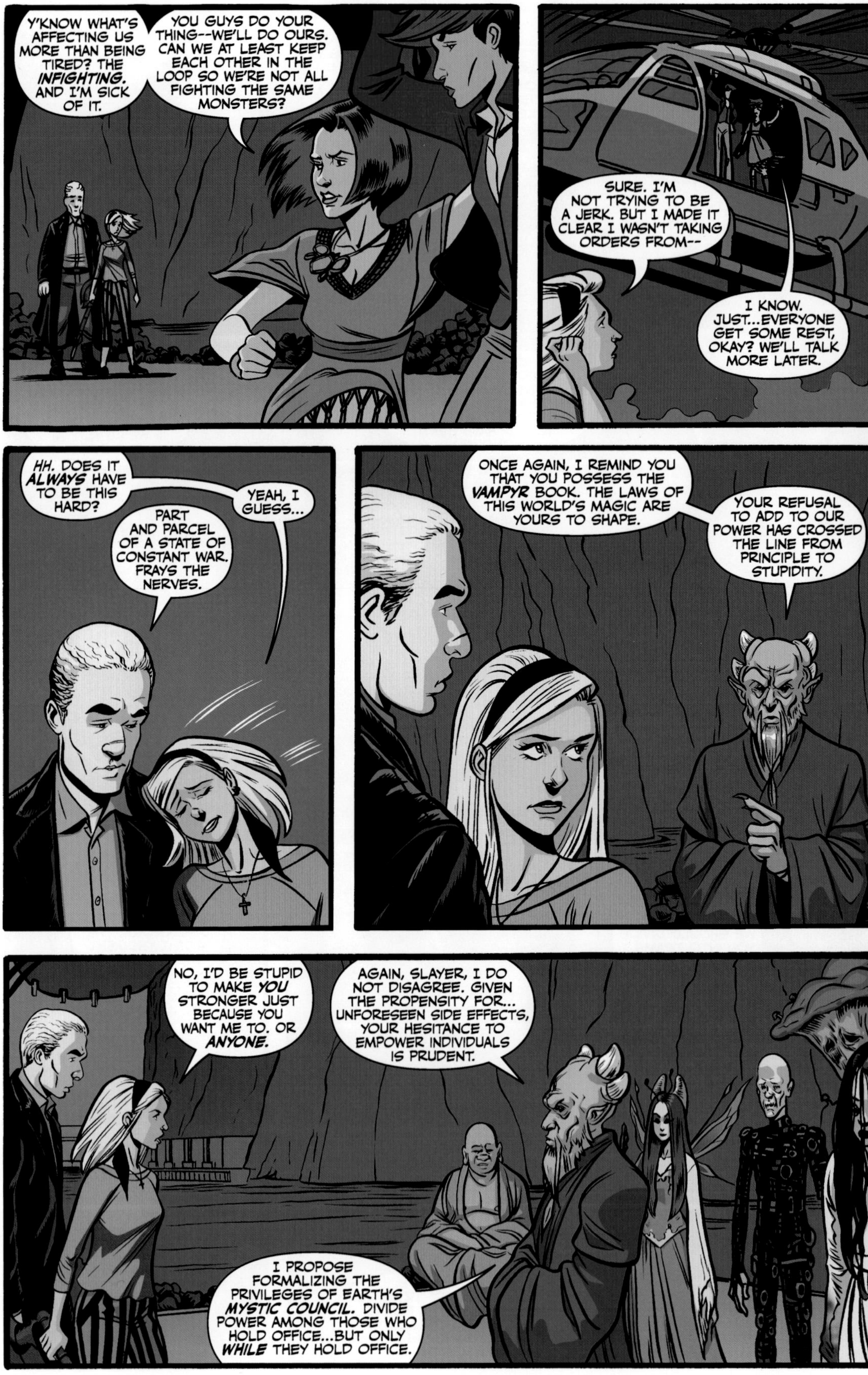
Y'KNOW WHAT'S AFFECTING US MORE THAN BEING TIRED? THE *INFIGHTING.* AND I'M SICK OF IT.
YOU GUYS DO YOUR THING--WE'LL DO OURS. CAN WE AT LEAST KEEP EACH OTHER IN THE LOOP SO WE'RE NOT ALL FIGHTING THE SAME MONSTERS?
SURE. I'M NOT TRYING TO BE A JERK. BUT I MADE IT CLEAR I WASN'T TAKING ORDERS FROM--
I KNOW. JUST...EVERYONE GET SOME REST, OKAY? WE'LL TALK MORE LATER.
HH. DOES IT *ALWAYS* HAVE TO BE THIS HARD?
YEAH, I GUESS...
PART AND PARCEL OF A STATE OF CONSTANT WAR. FRAYS THE NERVES.
ONCE AGAIN, I REMIND YOU THAT YOU POSSESS THE *VAMPYR* BOOK. THE LAWS OF THIS WORLD'S MAGIC ARE YOURS TO SHAPE.
YOUR REFUSAL TO ADD TO OUR POWER HAS CROSSED THE LINE FROM PRINCIPLE TO STUPIDITY.
NO, I'D BE STUPID TO MAKE *YOU* STRONGER JUST BECAUSE YOU WANT ME TO. OR *ANYONE.*
AGAIN, SLAYER, I DO NOT DISAGREE. GIVEN THE PROPENSITY FOR... UNFORESEEN SIDE EFFECTS, YOUR HESITANCE TO EMPOWER INDIVIDUALS IS PRUDENT.
I PROPOSE FORMALIZING THE PRIVILEGES OF EARTH'S *MYSTIC COUNCIL.* DIVIDE POWER AMONG THOSE WHO HOLD OFFICE...BUT ONLY *WHILE* THEY HOLD OFFICE.

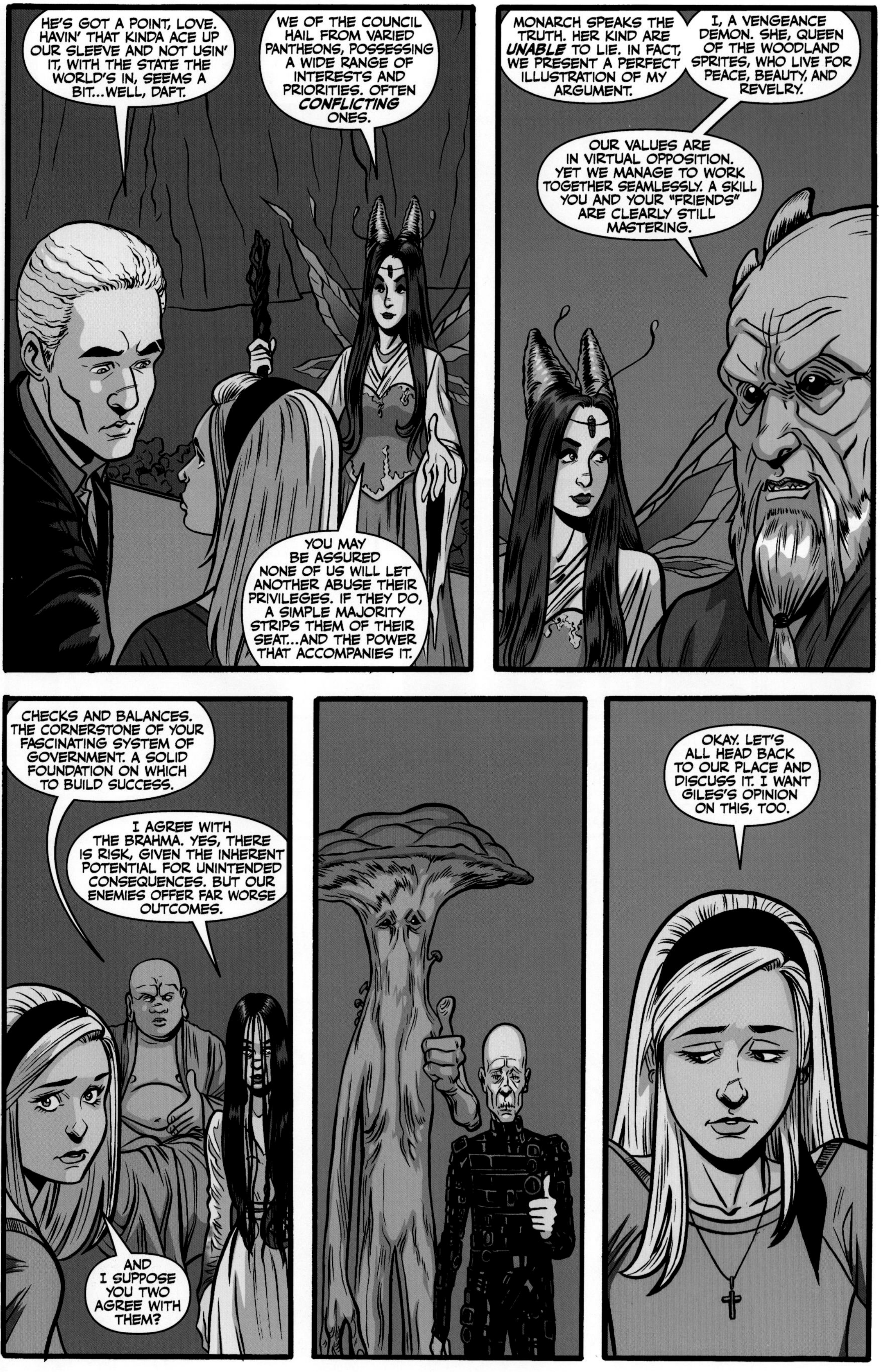
HE'S GOT A POINT, LOVE. HAVIN' THAT KINDA ACE UP OUR SLEEVE AND NOT USIN' IT, WITH THE STATE THE WORLD'S IN, SEEMS A BIT...WELL, DAFT.
WE OF THE COUNCIL HAIL FROM VARIED PANTHEONS, POSSESSING A WIDE RANGE OF INTERESTS AND PRIORITIES. OFTEN *CONFLICTING* ONES.
YOU MAY BE ASSURED NONE OF US WILL LET ANOTHER ABUSE THEIR PRIVILEGES. IF THEY DO, A SIMPLE MAJORITY STRIPS THEM OF THEIR SEAT...AND THE POWER THAT ACCOMPANIES IT.
MONARCH SPEAKS THE TRUTH. HER KIND ARE *UNABLE* TO LIE. IN FACT, WE PRESENT A PERFECT ILLUSTRATION OF MY ARGUMENT.
I, A VENGEANCE DEMON. SHE, QUEEN OF THE WOODLAND SPRITES, WHO LIVE FOR PEACE, BEAUTY, AND REVELRY.
OUR VALUES ARE IN VIRTUAL OPPOSITION. YET WE MANAGE TO WORK TOGETHER SEAMLESSLY. A SKILL YOU AND YOUR "FRIENDS" ARE CLEARLY STILL MASTERING.
CHECKS AND BALANCES. THE CORNERSTONE OF YOUR FASCINATING SYSTEM OF GOVERNMENT. A SOLID FOUNDATION ON WHICH TO BUILD SUCCESS.
I AGREE WITH THE BRAHMA. YES, THERE IS RISK, GIVEN THE INHERENT POTENTIAL FOR UNINTENDED CONSEQUENCES. BUT OUR ENEMIES OFFER FAR WORSE OUTCOMES.
AND I SUPPOSE YOU TWO AGREE WITH THEM?
OKAY. LET'S ALL HEAD BACK TO OUR PLACE AND DISCUSS IT. I WANT GILES'S OPINION ON THIS, TOO.

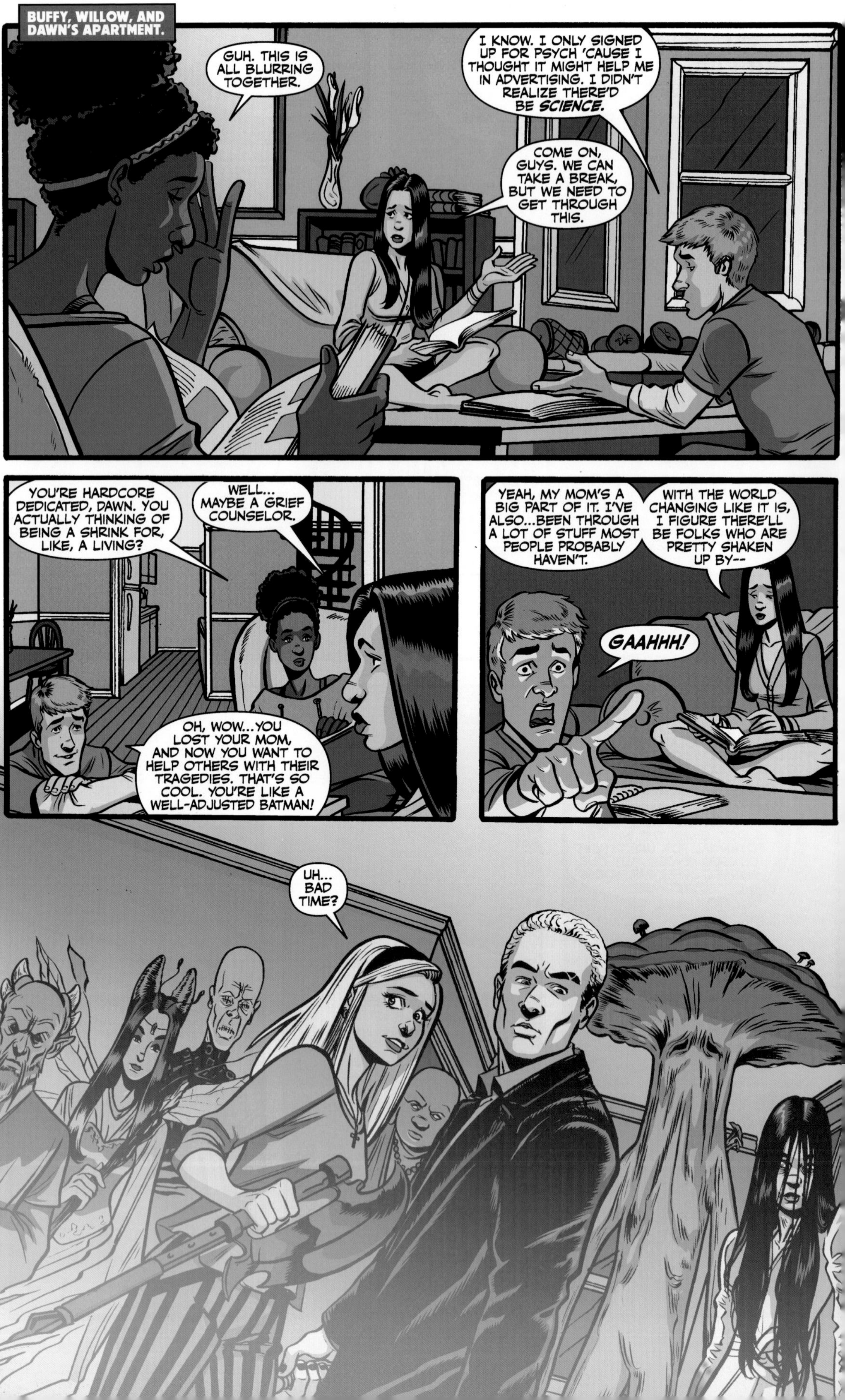
BUFFY, WILLOW, AND DAWN'S APARTMENT.
GUH. THIS IS ALL BLURRING TOGETHER.
I KNOW. I ONLY SIGNED UP FOR PSYCH 'CAUSE I THOUGHT IT MIGHT HELP ME IN ADVERTISING. I DIDN'T REALIZE THERE'D BE *SCIENCE*.
COME ON, GUYS. WE CAN TAKE A BREAK, BUT WE NEED TO GET THROUGH THIS.
YOU'RE HARDCORE DEDICATED, DAWN. YOU ACTUALLY THINKING OF BEING A SHRINK FOR, LIKE, A LIVING?
WELL... MAYBE A GRIEF COUNSELOR.
OH, WOW...YOU LOST YOUR MOM, AND NOW YOU WANT TO HELP OTHERS WITH THEIR TRAGEDIES. THAT'S SO COOL. YOU'RE LIKE A WELL-ADJUSTED BATMAN!
YEAH, MY MOM'S A BIG PART OF IT. I'VE ALSO...BEEN THROUGH A LOT OF STUFF MOST PEOPLE PROBABLY HAVEN'T.
WITH THE WORLD CHANGING LIKE IT IS, I FIGURE THERE'LL BE FOLKS WHO ARE PRETTY SHAKEN UP BY--
GAAHHH!
UH... BAD TIME?

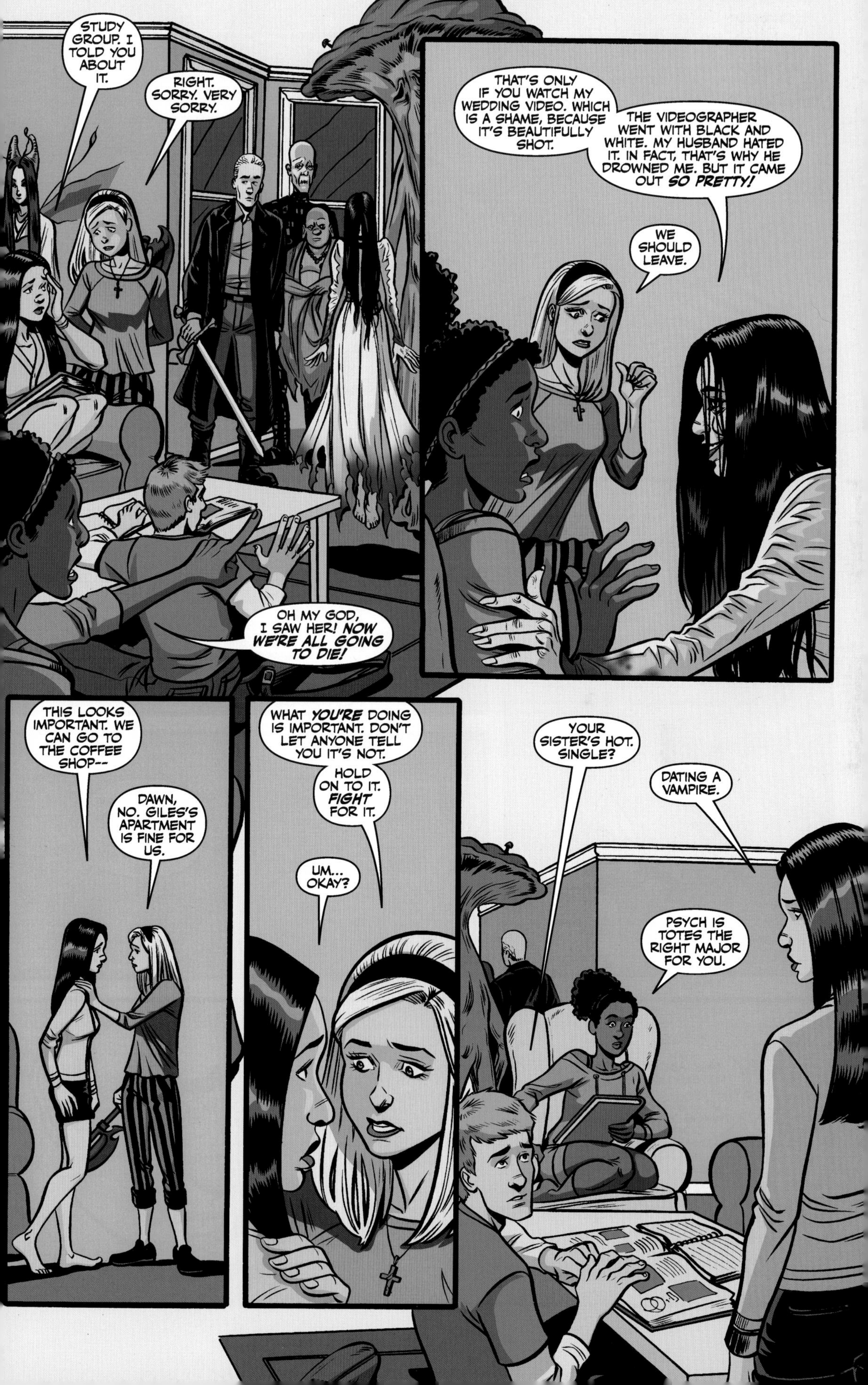
STUDY GROUP. I TOLD YOU ABOUT IT.
RIGHT. SORRY. VERY SORRY.
OH MY GOD, I SAW HER! NOW WE'RE ALL GOING TO DIE!
THAT'S ONLY IF YOU WATCH MY WEDDING VIDEO. WHICH IS A SHAME, BECAUSE IT'S BEAUTIFULLY SHOT.
THE VIDEOGRAPHER WENT WITH BLACK AND WHITE. MY HUSBAND HATED IT. IN FACT, THAT'S WHY HE DROWNED ME. BUT IT CAME OUT SO PRETTY!
WE SHOULD LEAVE.
THIS LOOKS IMPORTANT. WE CAN GO TO THE COFFEE SHOP--
DAWN, NO. GILES'S APARTMENT IS FINE FOR US.
WHAT YOU'RE DOING IS IMPORTANT. DON'T LET ANYONE TELL YOU IT'S NOT.
HOLD ON TO IT. FIGHT FOR IT.
UM... OKAY?
YOUR SISTER'S HOT. SINGLE?
DATING A VAMPIRE.
PSYCH IS TOTES THE RIGHT MAJOR FOR YOU.

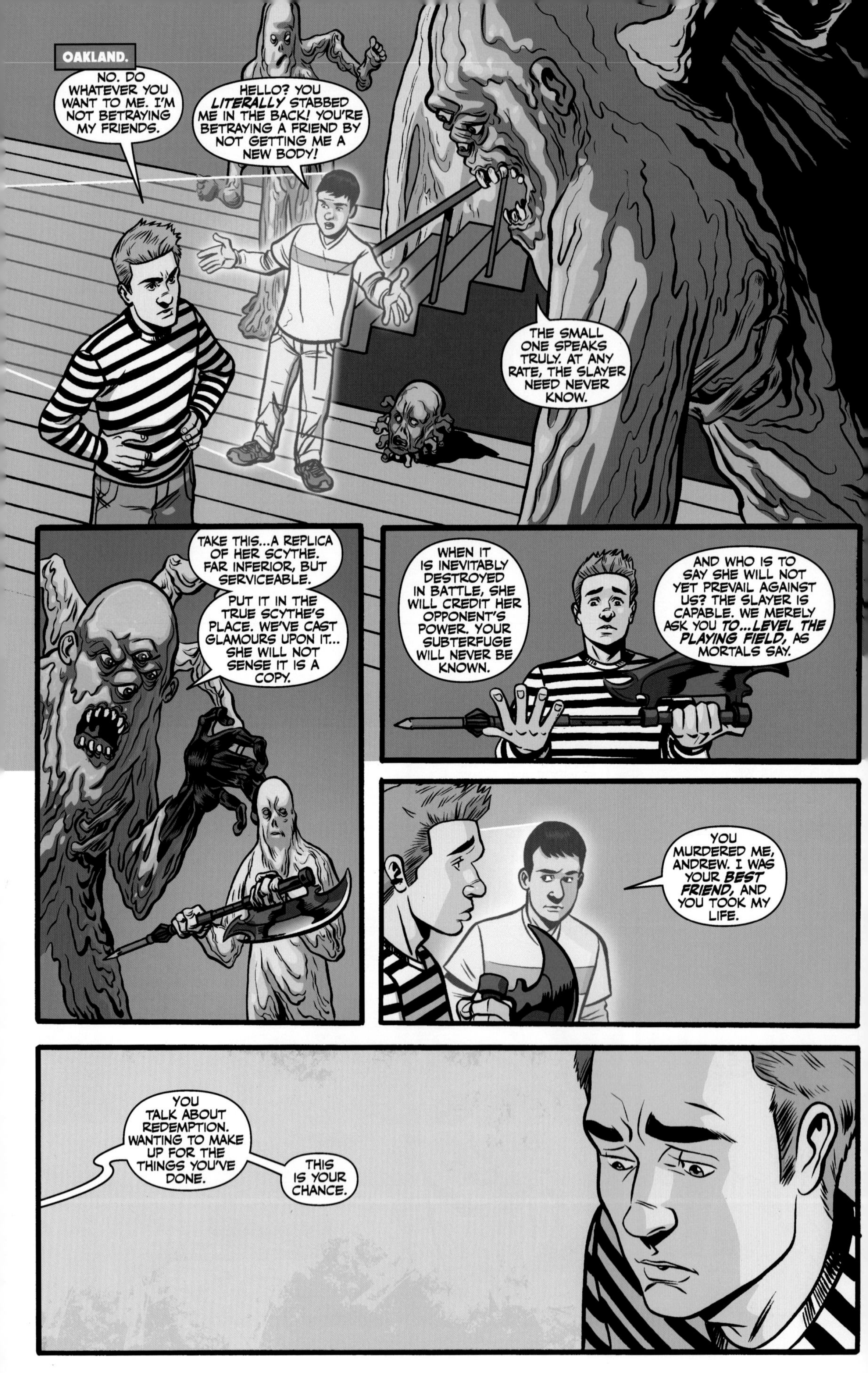
OAKLAND.
NO. DO WHATEVER YOU WANT TO ME. I'M NOT BETRAYING MY FRIENDS.
HELLO? YOU *LITERALLY* STABBED ME IN THE BACK! YOU'RE BETRAYING A FRIEND BY NOT GETTING ME A NEW BODY!
THE SMALL ONE SPEAKS TRULY. AT ANY RATE, THE SLAYER NEED NEVER KNOW.
TAKE THIS...A REPLICA OF HER SCYTHE. FAR INFERIOR, BUT SERVICEABLE.
PUT IT IN THE TRUE SCYTHE'S PLACE. WE'VE CAST GLAMOURS UPON IT... SHE WILL NOT SENSE IT IS A COPY.
WHEN IT IS INEVITABLY DESTROYED IN BATTLE, SHE WILL CREDIT HER OPPONENT'S POWER. YOUR SUBTERFUGE WILL NEVER BE KNOWN.
AND WHO IS TO SAY SHE WILL NOT YET PREVAIL AGAINST US? THE SLAYER IS CAPABLE. WE MERELY ASK YOU *TO...LEVEL THE PLAYING FIELD,* AS MORTALS SAY.
YOU MURDERED ME, ANDREW. I WAS YOUR *BEST FRIEND,* AND YOU TOOK MY LIFE.
YOU TALK ABOUT REDEMPTION. WANTING TO MAKE UP FOR THE THINGS YOU'VE DONE.
THIS IS YOUR CHANCE.

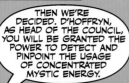

THEN WE'RE DECIDED. D'HOFFRYN, AS HEAD OF THE COUNCIL, YOU WILL BE GRANTED THE POWER TO DETECT AND PINPOINT THE USAGE OF CONCENTRATED MYSTIC ENERGY.

MONARCH, YOU SHALL HAVE THE ABILITY TO DRAIN THE MAGIC POWER OF ANY BEING NOT NATIVE TO THIS DIMENSION.

TO COUNTER PURELY *PHYSICAL* ASSAULTS, KEIKO WILL HENCEFORTH BE ABLE TO ABSORB AND REDIRECT THE KINETIC ENERGY OF AN ATTACK.

YAY!

THE *QUIET MAN* SHALL POSSESS THE POWER TO RETURN ANY BEING TO ITS NATIVE DIMENSION.

AND TO THE BRAHMA GOES THE ABILITY TO SENSE ANY OPPONENT'S GREATEST WEAKNESS...

...WHILE MATANGO IS GRANTED INVULNERABILITY TO MAGICAL ATTACKS, THOUGH NOT PHYSICAL ONES.

PLEASE REMOVE YOUR SPORES FROM MY SINK.

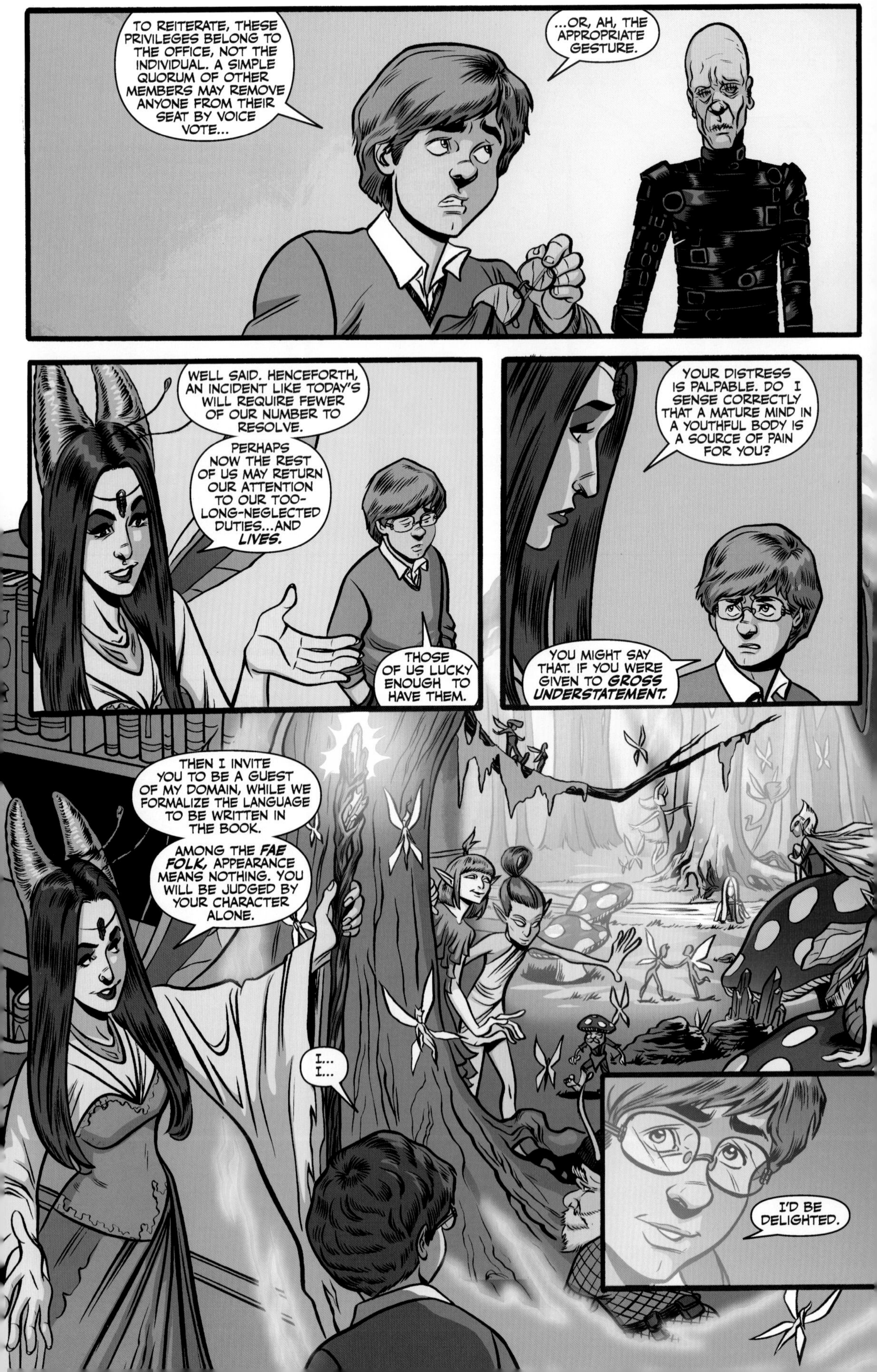
TO REITERATE, THESE PRIVILEGES BELONG TO THE OFFICE, NOT THE INDIVIDUAL. A SIMPLE QUORUM OF OTHER MEMBERS MAY REMOVE ANYONE FROM THEIR SEAT BY VOICE VOTE...
...OR, AH, THE APPROPRIATE GESTURE.
WELL SAID. HENCEFORTH, AN INCIDENT LIKE TODAY'S WILL REQUIRE FEWER OF OUR NUMBER TO RESOLVE.
PERHAPS NOW THE REST OF US MAY RETURN OUR ATTENTION TO OUR TOO-LONG-NEGLECTED DUTIES...AND LIVES.
THOSE OF US LUCKY ENOUGH TO HAVE THEM.
YOUR DISTRESS IS PALPABLE. DO I SENSE CORRECTLY THAT A MATURE MIND IN A YOUTHFUL BODY IS A SOURCE OF PAIN FOR YOU?
YOU MIGHT SAY THAT. IF YOU WERE GIVEN TO GROSS UNDERSTATEMENT.
THEN I INVITE YOU TO BE A GUEST OF MY DOMAIN, WHILE WE FORMALIZE THE LANGUAGE TO BE WRITTEN IN THE BOOK.
AMONG THE FAE FOLK, APPEARANCE MEANS NOTHING. YOU WILL BE JUDGED BY YOUR CHARACTER ALONE.
I... I...
I'D BE DELIGHTED.

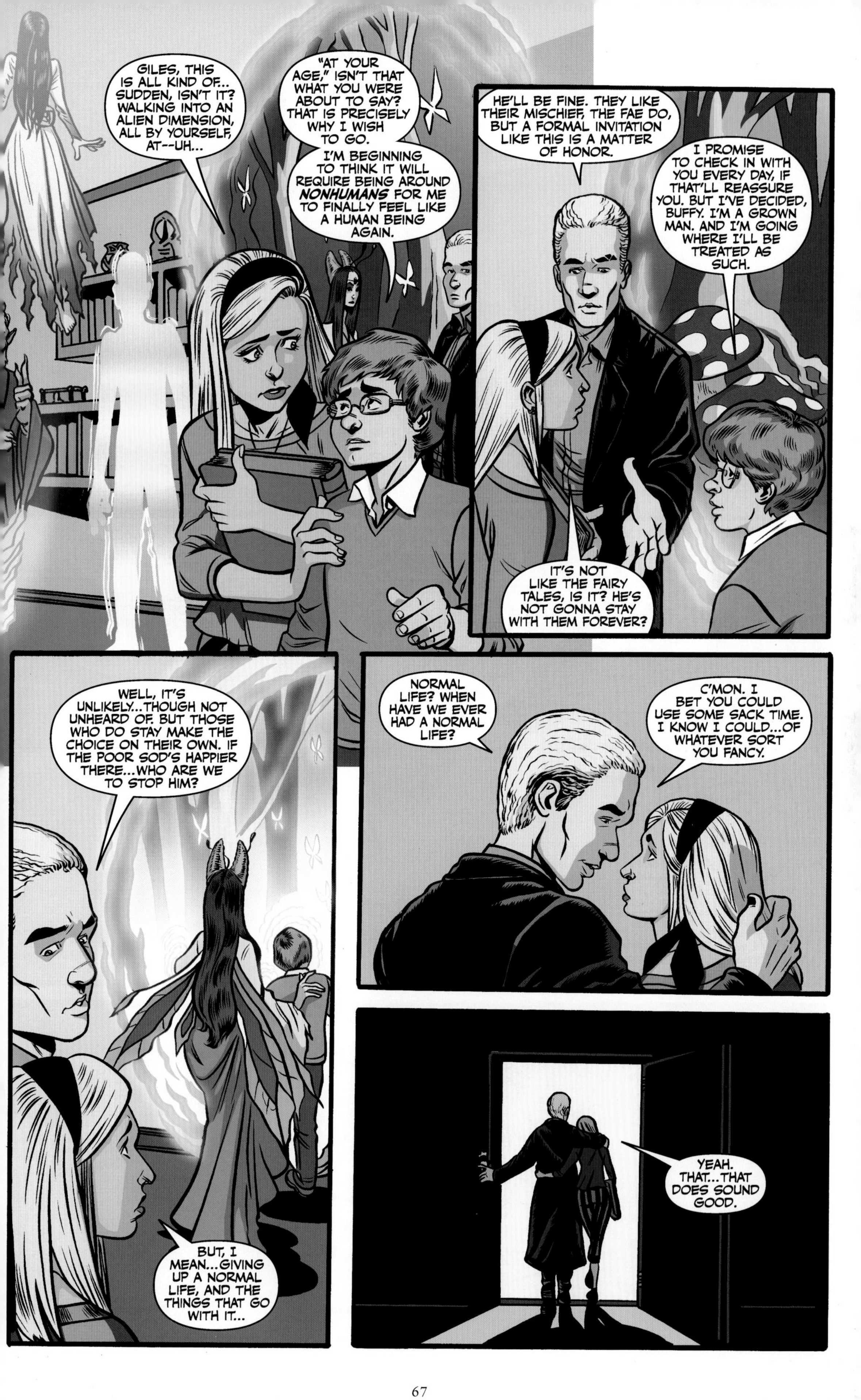
GILES, THIS IS ALL KIND OF... SUDDEN, ISN'T IT? WALKING INTO AN ALIEN DIMENSION, ALL BY YOURSELF, AT--UH...
"AT YOUR AGE," ISN'T THAT WHAT YOU WERE ABOUT TO SAY? THAT IS PRECISELY WHY I WISH TO GO.
I'M BEGINNING TO THINK IT WILL REQUIRE BEING AROUND NONHUMANS FOR ME TO FINALLY FEEL LIKE A HUMAN BEING AGAIN.
HE'LL BE FINE. THEY LIKE THEIR MISCHIEF, THE FAE DO, BUT A FORMAL INVITATION LIKE THIS IS A MATTER OF HONOR.
I PROMISE TO CHECK IN WITH YOU EVERY DAY, IF THAT'LL REASSURE YOU. BUT I'VE DECIDED, BUFFY. I'M A GROWN MAN. AND I'M GOING WHERE I'LL BE TREATED AS SUCH.
IT'S NOT LIKE THE FAIRY TALES, IS IT? HE'S NOT GONNA STAY WITH THEM FOREVER?
WELL, IT'S UNLIKELY...THOUGH NOT UNHEARD OF. BUT THOSE WHO DO STAY MAKE THE CHOICE ON THEIR OWN. IF THE POOR SOD'S HAPPIER THERE...WHO ARE WE TO STOP HIM?
BUT, I MEAN...GIVING UP A NORMAL LIFE, AND THE THINGS THAT GO WITH IT...
NORMAL LIFE? WHEN HAVE WE EVER HAD A NORMAL LIFE?
C'MON. I BET YOU COULD USE SOME SACK TIME. I KNOW I COULD...OF WHATEVER SORT YOU FANCY.
YEAH. THAT...THAT DOES SOUND GOOD.

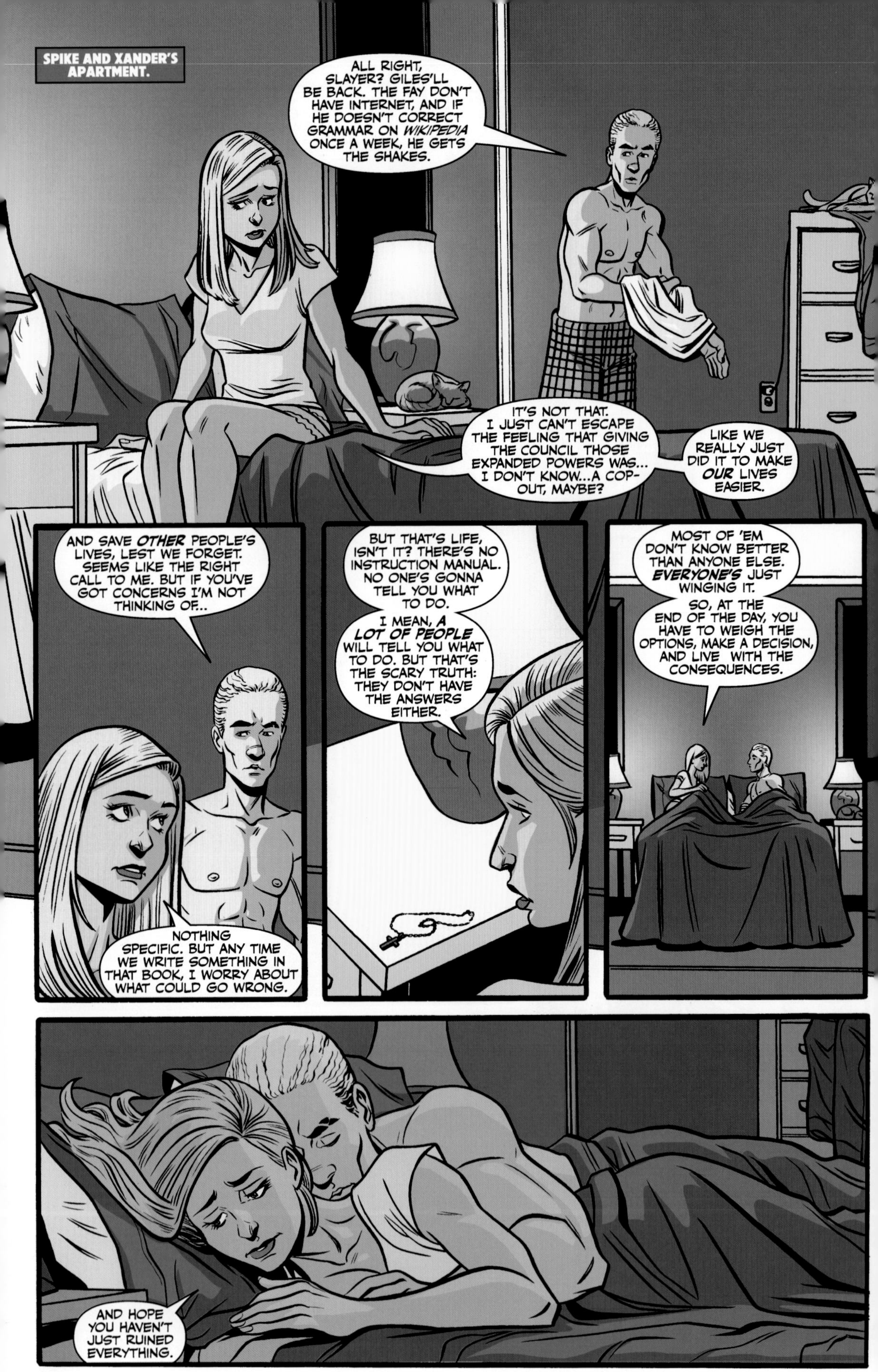

SPIKE AND XANDER'S APARTMENT.
ALL RIGHT, SLAYER? GILES'LL BE BACK. THE FAY DON'T HAVE INTERNET, AND IF HE DOESN'T CORRECT GRAMMAR ON WIKIPEDIA ONCE A WEEK, HE GETS THE SHAKES.
IT'S NOT THAT. I JUST CAN'T ESCAPE THE FEELING THAT GIVING THE COUNCIL THOSE EXPANDED POWERS WAS... I DON'T KNOW...A COP-OUT, MAYBE?
LIKE WE REALLY JUST DID IT TO MAKE OUR LIVES EASIER.
AND SAVE OTHER PEOPLE'S LIVES, LEST WE FORGET. SEEMS LIKE THE RIGHT CALL TO ME. BUT IF YOU'VE GOT CONCERNS I'M NOT THINKING OF...
NOTHING SPECIFIC. BUT ANY TIME WE WRITE SOMETHING IN THAT BOOK, I WORRY ABOUT WHAT COULD GO WRONG.
BUT THAT'S LIFE, ISN'T IT? THERE'S NO INSTRUCTION MANUAL. NO ONE'S GONNA TELL YOU WHAT TO DO.
I MEAN, A LOT OF PEOPLE WILL TELL YOU WHAT TO DO. BUT THAT'S THE SCARY TRUTH: THEY DON'T HAVE THE ANSWERS EITHER.
MOST OF 'EM DON'T KNOW BETTER THAN ANYONE ELSE. EVERYONE'S JUST WINGING IT.
SO, AT THE END OF THE DAY, YOU HAVE TO WEIGH THE OPTIONS, MAKE A DECISION, AND LIVE WITH THE CONSEQUENCES.
AND HOPE YOU HAVEN'T JUST RUINED EVERYTHING.

MORNING, SUNSHINE. OR RATHER, MIDAFTERNOON. SAY, I'VE AN IDEA. WHY DON'T WE TAKE THE DAY OFF?

ONCE THE NEW RULES ARE IN THE BOOK, D'HOFFRYN SHOULD BE ABLE TO TRACK DOWN OUR DEMON LORDS SHARPISH. AND TILL THEN, WE'VE EARNED A BREAK.

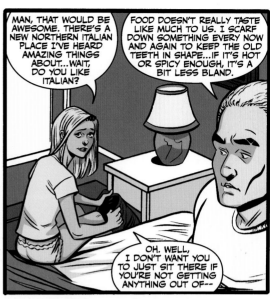

MAN, THAT WOULD BE AWESOME. THERE'S A NEW NORTHERN ITALIAN PLACE I'VE HEARD AMAZING THINGS ABOUT...WAIT, DO YOU LIKE ITALIAN?

FOOD DOESN'T REALLY TASTE LIKE MUCH TO US. I SCARF DOWN SOMETHING EVERY NOW AND AGAIN TO KEEP THE OLD TEETH IN SHAPE...IF IT'S HOT OR SPICY ENOUGH, IT'S A BIT LESS BLAND.

OH. WELL, I DON'T WANT YOU TO JUST SIT THERE IF YOU'RE NOT GETTING ANYTHING OUT OF--

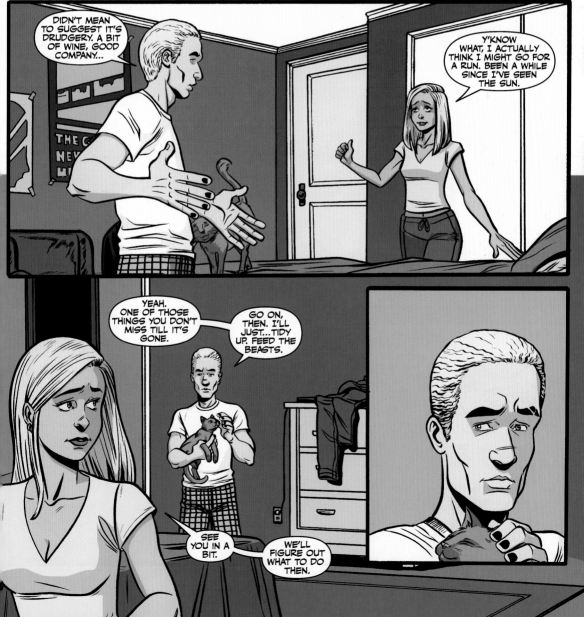

DIDN'T MEAN TO SUGGEST IT'S DRUDGERY. A BIT OF WINE, GOOD COMPANY...

Y'KNOW WHAT, I ACTUALLY THINK I MIGHT GO FOR A RUN. BEEN A WHILE SINCE I'VE SEEN THE SUN.

YEAH. ONE OF THOSE THINGS YOU DON'T MISS TILL IT'S GONE.

GO ON, THEN. I'LL JUST...TIDY UP. FEED THE BEASTS.

SEE YOU IN A BIT.

WE'LL FIGURE OUT WHAT TO DO THEN.

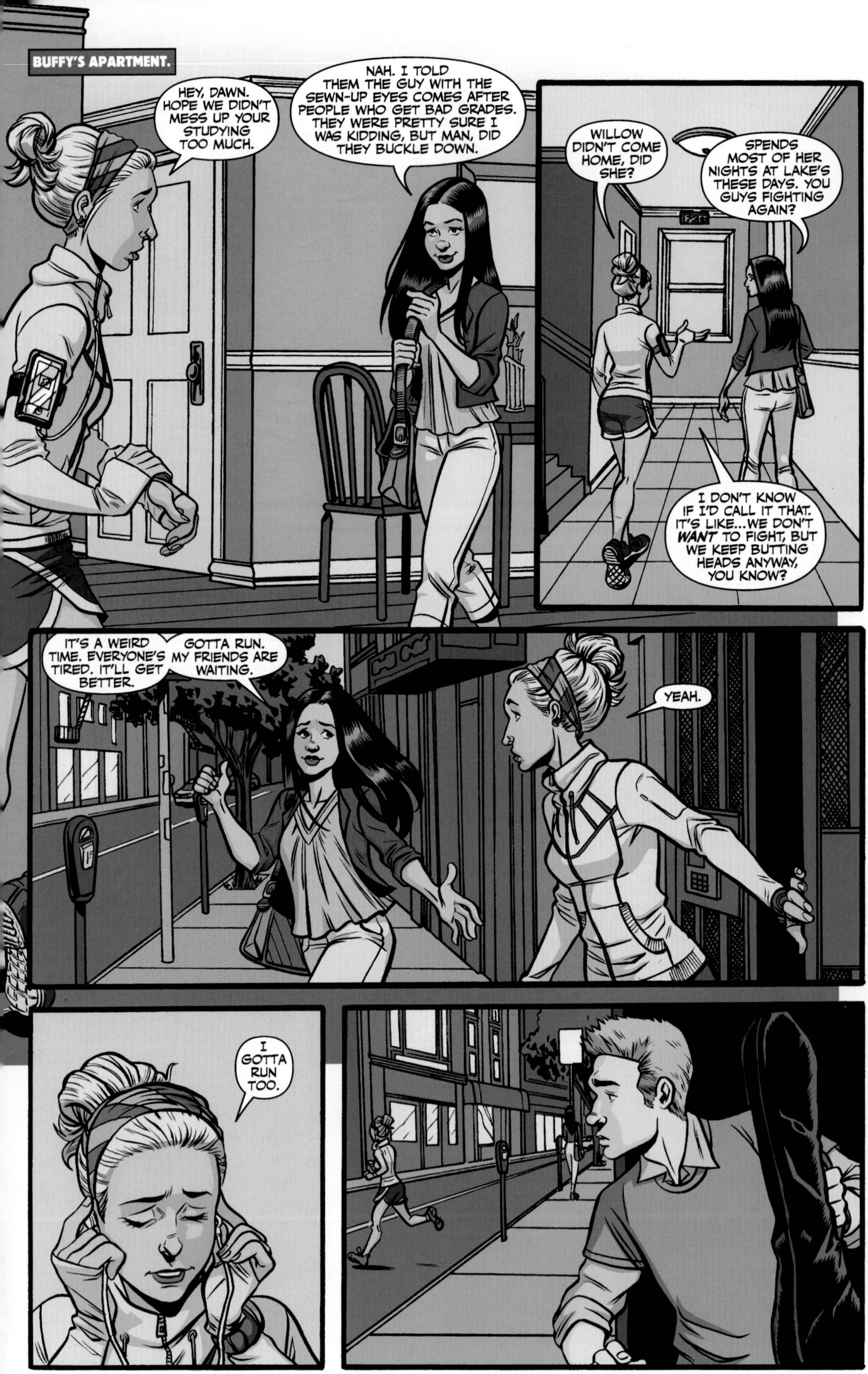

BUFFY'S APARTMENT.
HEY, DAWN. HOPE WE DIDN'T MESS UP YOUR STUDYING TOO MUCH.
NAH. I TOLD THEM THE GUY WITH THE SEWN-UP EYES COMES AFTER PEOPLE WHO GET BAD GRADES. THEY WERE PRETTY SURE I WAS KIDDING, BUT MAN, DID THEY BUCKLE DOWN.
WILLOW DIDN'T COME HOME, DID SHE?
SPENDS MOST OF HER NIGHTS AT LAKE'S THESE DAYS. YOU GUYS FIGHTING AGAIN?
EXIT
I DON'T KNOW IF I'D CALL IT THAT. IT'S LIKE...WE DON'T WANT TO FIGHT, BUT WE KEEP BUTTING HEADS ANYWAY, YOU KNOW?
IT'S A WEIRD TIME. EVERYONE'S TIRED. IT'LL GET BETTER.
GOTTA RUN. MY FRIENDS ARE WAITING.
YEAH.
I GOTTA RUN TOO.

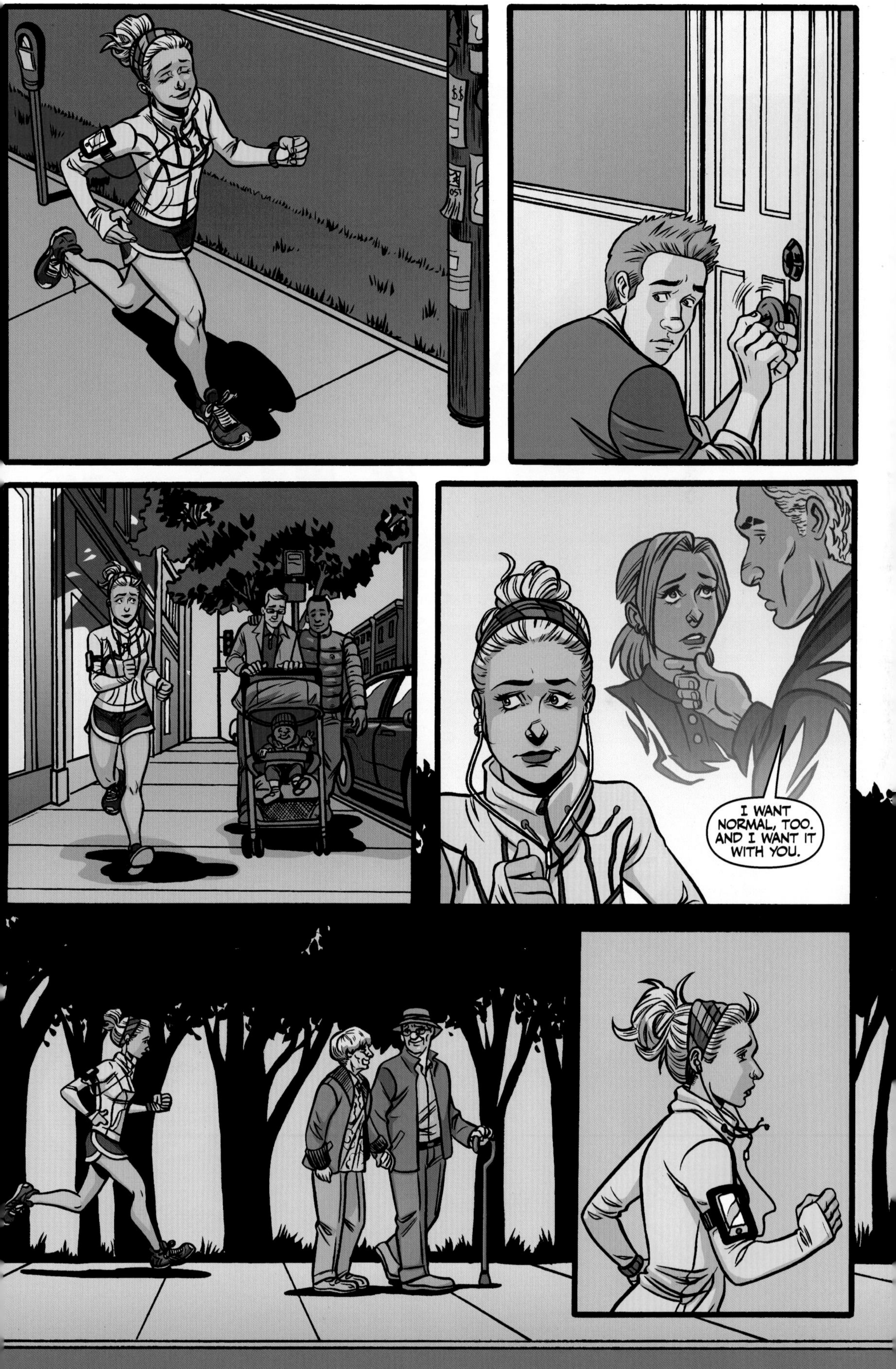
I WANT NORMAL, TOO. AND I WANT IT WITH YOU.

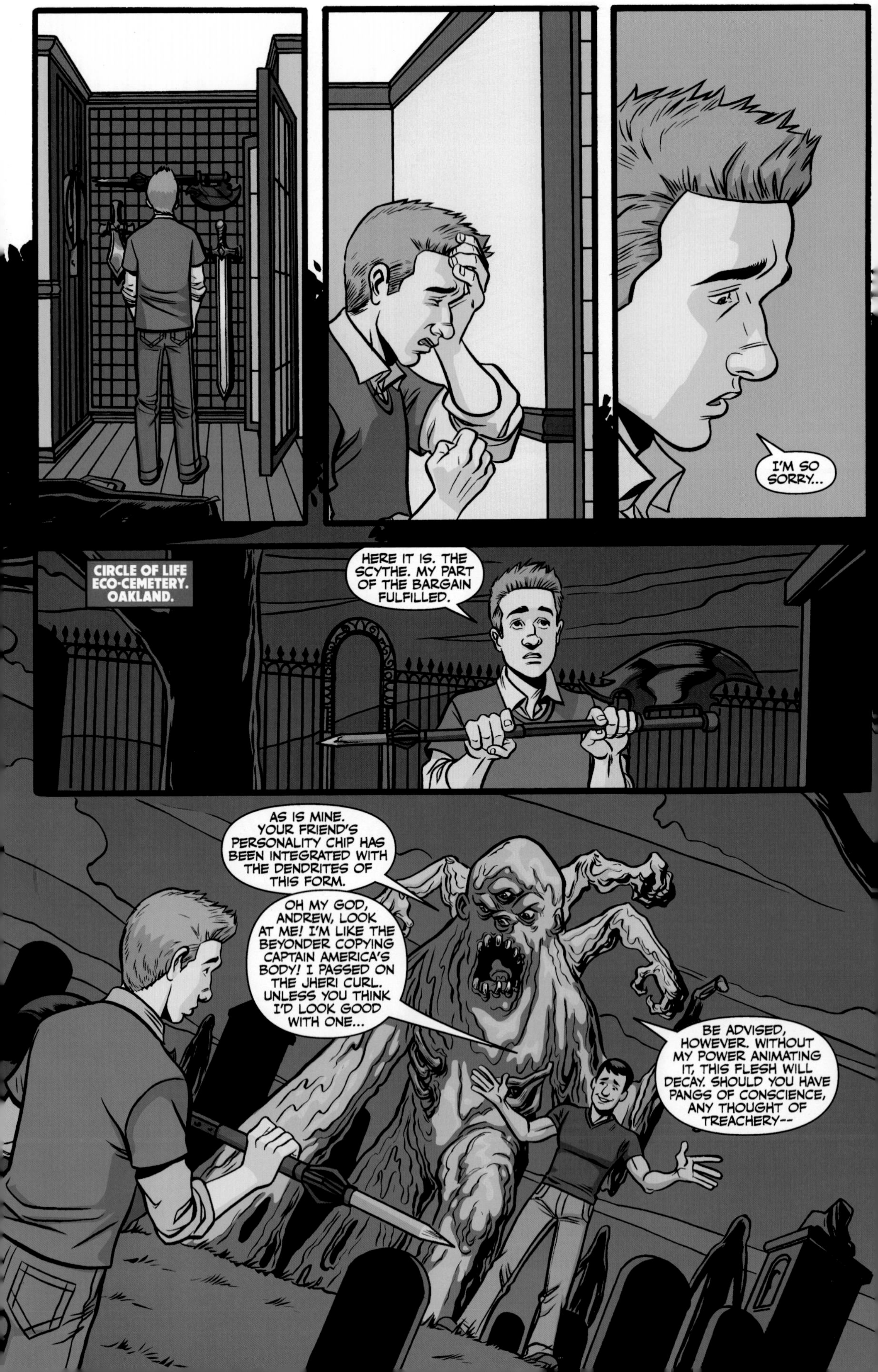
I'M SO SORRY...
CIRCLE OF LIFE ECO-CEMETERY. OAKLAND.
HERE IT IS. THE SCYTHE. MY PART OF THE BARGAIN FULFILLED.
AS IS MINE. YOUR FRIEND'S PERSONALITY CHIP HAS BEEN INTEGRATED WITH THE DENDRITES OF THIS FORM.
OH MY GOD, ANDREW, LOOK AT ME! I'M LIKE THE BEYONDER COPYING CAPTAIN AMERICA'S BODY! I PASSED ON THE JHERI CURL. UNLESS YOU THINK I'D LOOK GOOD WITH ONE...
BE ADVISED, HOWEVER. WITHOUT MY POWER ANIMATING IT, THIS FLESH WILL DECAY. SHOULD YOU HAVE PANGS OF CONSCIENCE, ANY THOUGHT OF TREACHERY--

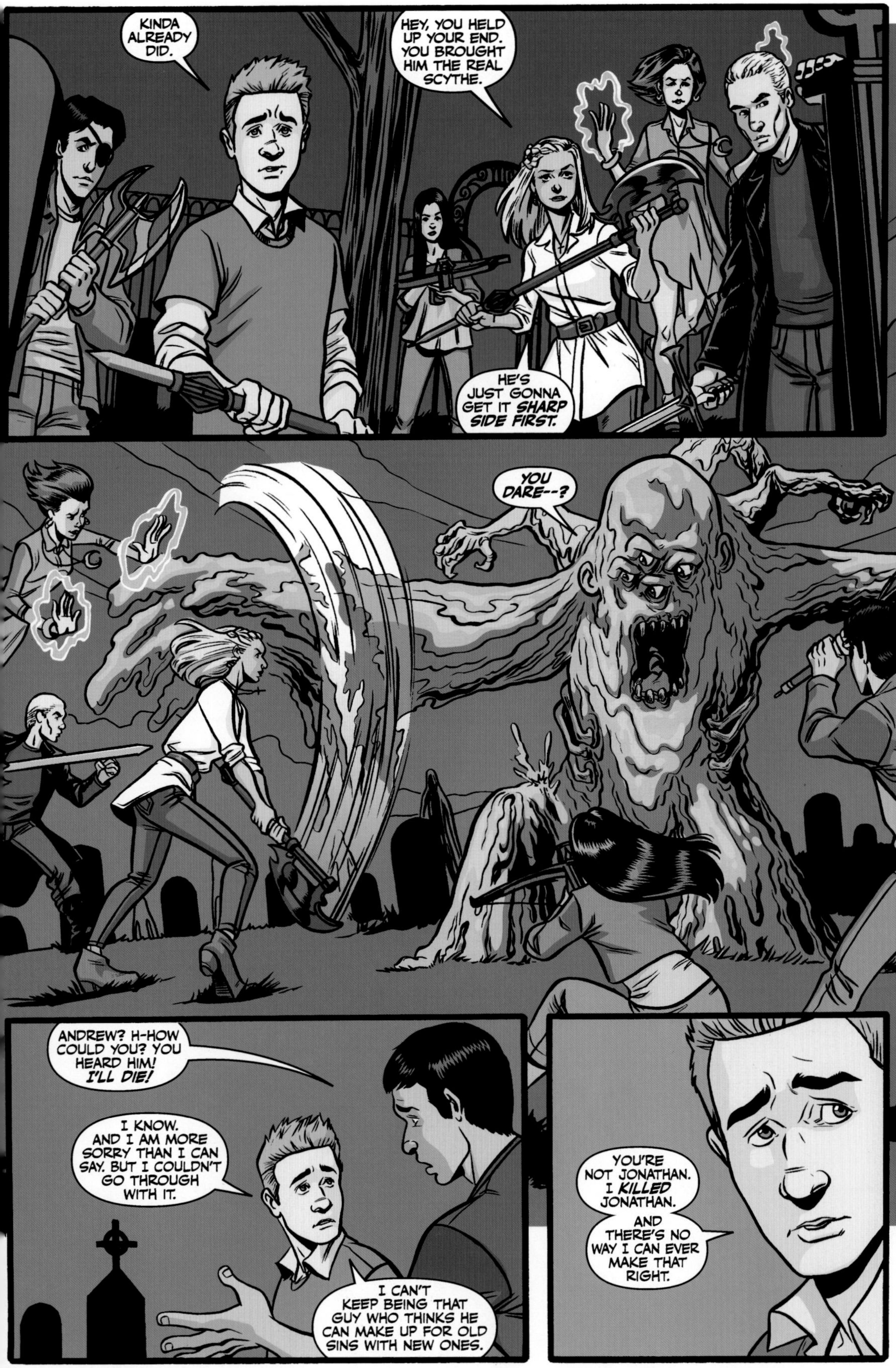
KINDA ALREADY DID.
HEY, YOU HELD UP YOUR END. YOU BROUGHT HIM THE REAL SCYTHE.
HE'S JUST GONNA GET IT SHARP SIDE FIRST.
YOU DARE--?
ANDREW? H-HOW COULD YOU? YOU HEARD HIM! I'LL DIE!
I KNOW. AND I AM MORE SORRY THAN I CAN SAY. BUT I COULDN'T GO THROUGH WITH IT.
I CAN'T KEEP BEING THAT GUY WHO THINKS HE CAN MAKE UP FOR OLD SINS WITH NEW ONES.
YOU'RE NOT JONATHAN. I KILLED JONATHAN.
AND THERE'S NO WAY I CAN EVER MAKE THAT RIGHT.

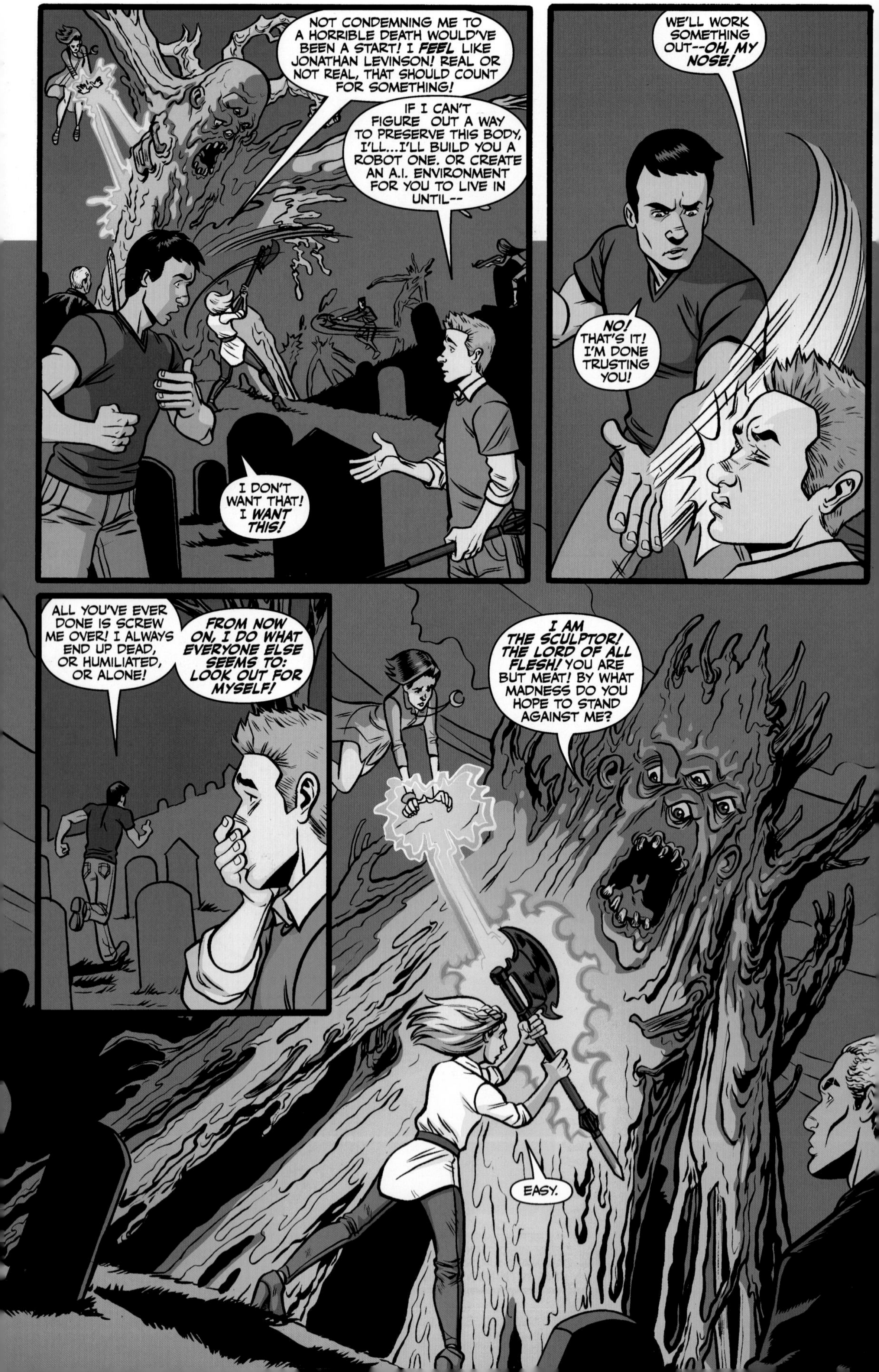
NOT CONDEMNING ME TO A HORRIBLE DEATH WOULD'VE BEEN A START! I FEEL LIKE JONATHAN LEVINSON! REAL OR NOT REAL, THAT SHOULD COUNT FOR SOMETHING!
IF I CAN'T FIGURE OUT A WAY TO PRESERVE THIS BODY, I'LL...I'LL BUILD YOU A ROBOT ONE. OR CREATE AN A.I. ENVIRONMENT FOR YOU TO LIVE IN UNTIL--
I DON'T WANT THAT! I WANT THIS!
WE'LL WORK SOMETHING OUT--OH, MY NOSE!
NO! THAT'S IT! I'M DONE TRUSTING YOU!
ALL YOU'VE EVER DONE IS SCREW ME OVER! I ALWAYS END UP DEAD, OR HUMILIATED, OR ALONE!
FROM NOW ON, I DO WHAT EVERYONE ELSE SEEMS TO: LOOK OUT FOR MYSELF!
I AM THE SCULPTOR! THE LORD OF ALL FLESH! YOU ARE BUT MEAT! BY WHAT MADNESS DO YOU HOPE TO STAND AGAINST ME?
EASY.

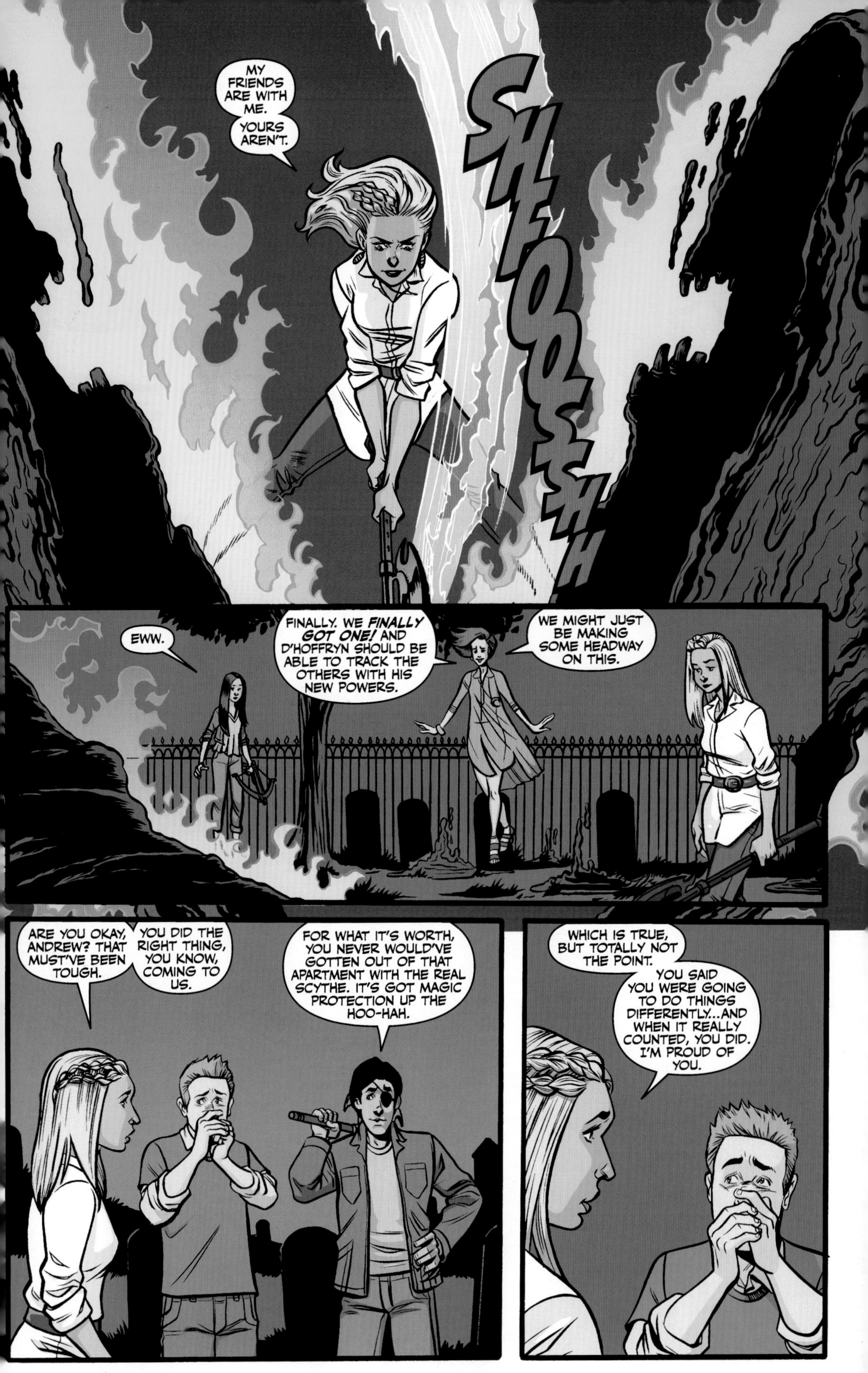
MY FRIENDS ARE WITH ME.
YOURS AREN'T.
SHHOOOSHH
EWW.
FINALLY. WE *FINALLY GOT ONE!* AND D'HOFFRYN SHOULD BE ABLE TO TRACK THE OTHERS WITH HIS NEW POWERS.
WE MIGHT JUST BE MAKING SOME HEADWAY ON THIS.
ARE YOU OKAY, ANDREW? THAT MUST'VE BEEN TOUGH.
YOU DID THE RIGHT THING, YOU KNOW, COMING TO US.
FOR WHAT IT'S WORTH, YOU NEVER WOULD'VE GOTTEN OUT OF THAT APARTMENT WITH THE REAL SCYTHE. IT'S GOT MAGIC PROTECTION UP THE HOO-HAH.
WHICH IS TRUE, BUT TOTALLY NOT THE POINT.
YOU SAID YOU WERE GOING TO DO THINGS DIFFERENTLY...AND WHEN IT REALLY COUNTED, YOU DID. I'M PROUD OF YOU.

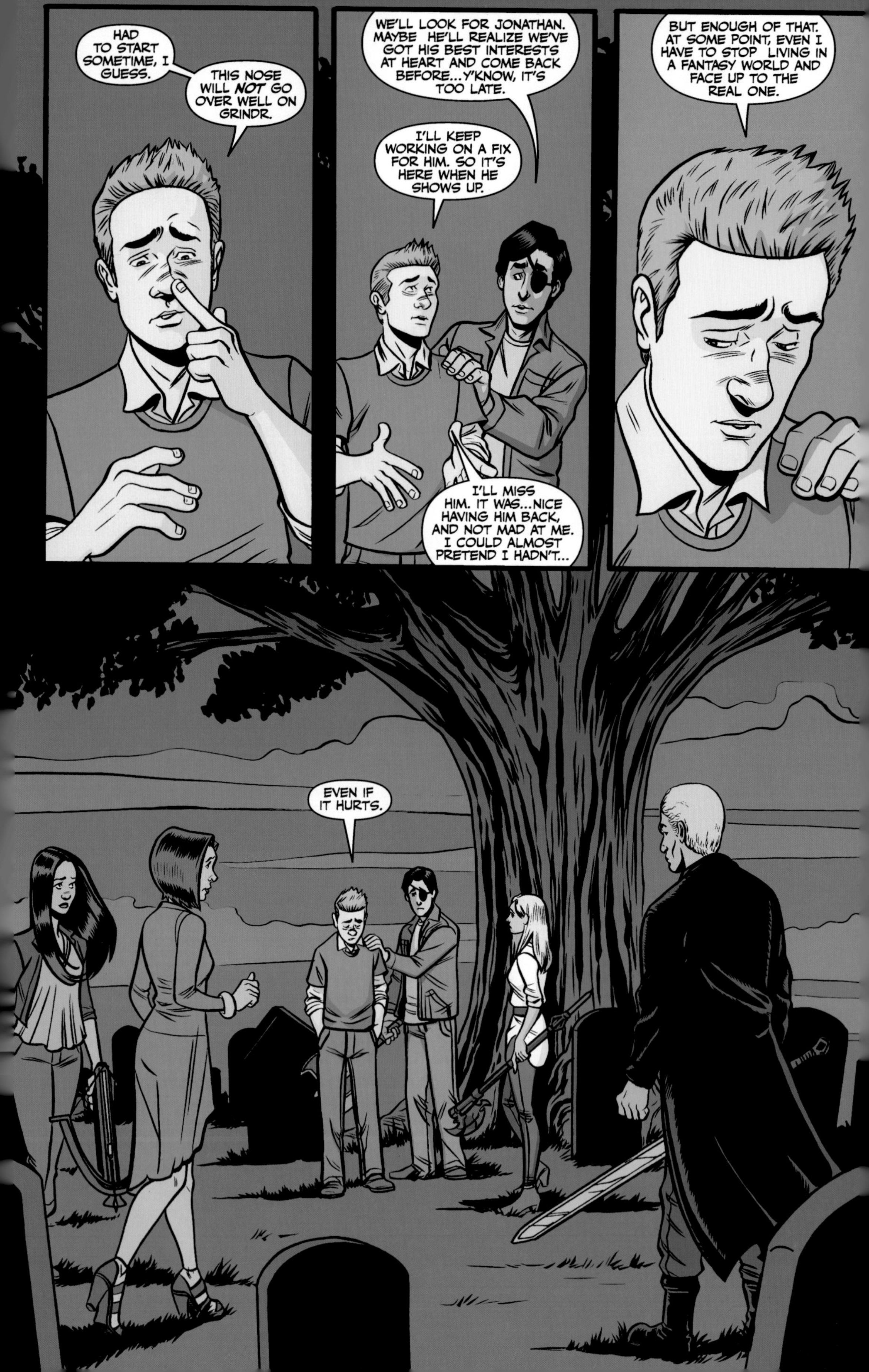

HAD TO START SOMETIME, I GUESS.
THIS NOSE WILL *NOT* GO OVER WELL ON GRINDR.
WE'LL LOOK FOR JONATHAN. MAYBE HE'LL REALIZE WE'VE GOT HIS BEST INTERESTS AT HEART AND COME BACK BEFORE...Y'KNOW, IT'S TOO LATE.
I'LL KEEP WORKING ON A FIX FOR HIM. SO IT'S HERE WHEN HE SHOWS UP.
I'LL MISS HIM. IT WAS...NICE HAVING HIM BACK, AND NOT MAD AT ME. I COULD ALMOST PRETEND I HADN'T...
BUT ENOUGH OF THAT. AT SOME POINT, EVEN I HAVE TO STOP LIVING IN A FANTASY WORLD AND FACE UP TO THE REAL ONE.
EVEN IF IT HURTS.

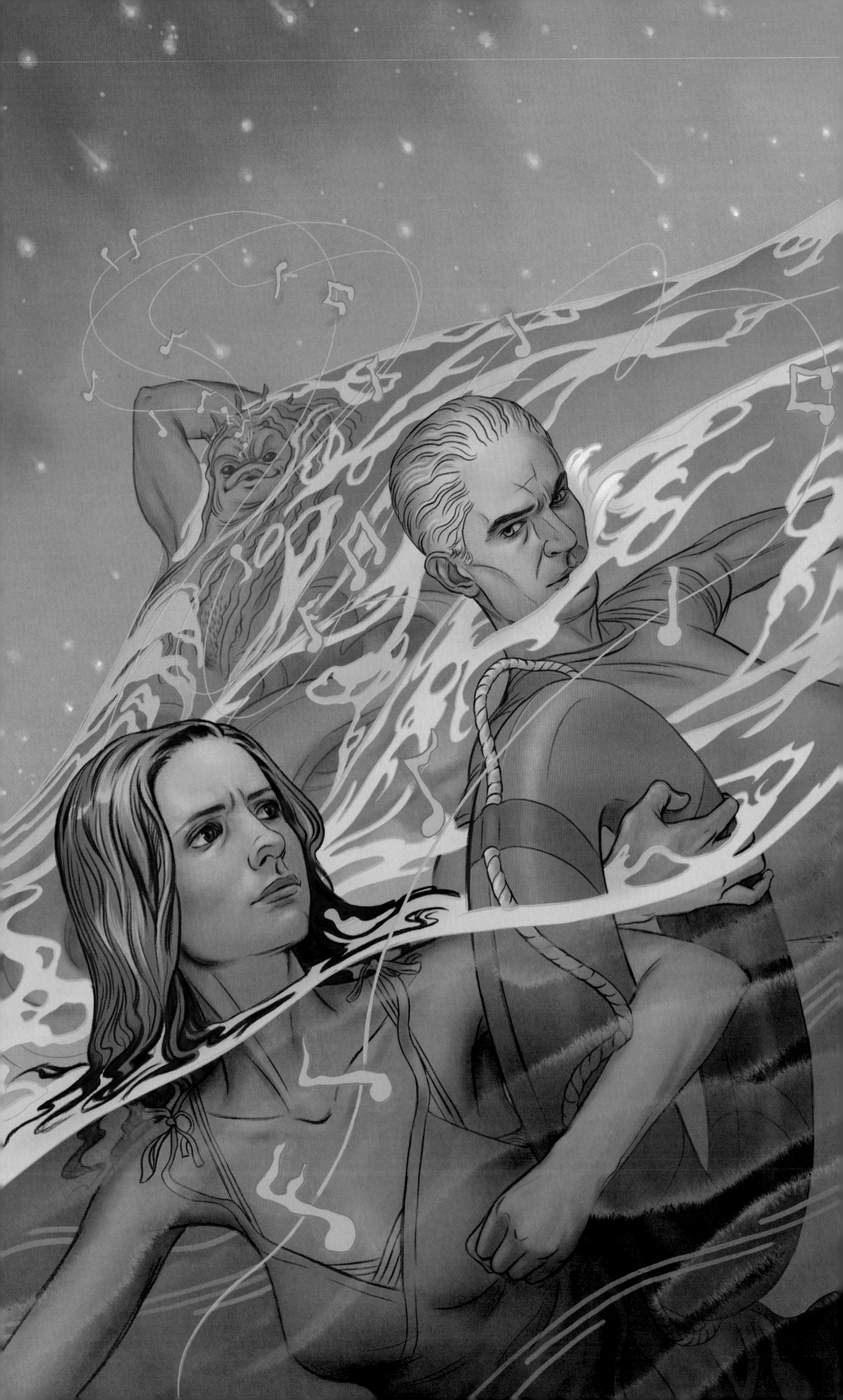

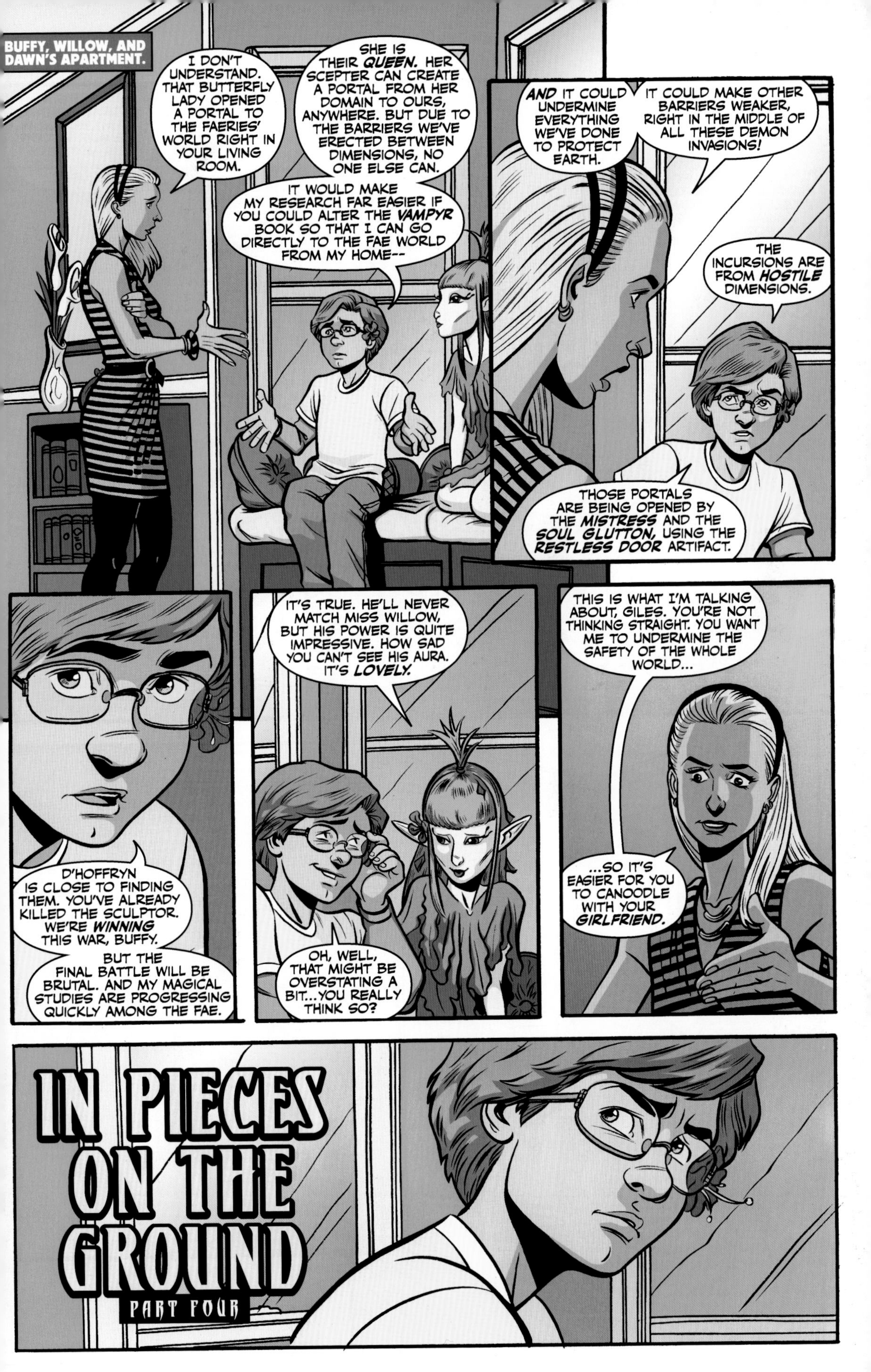
BUFFY, WILLOW, AND DAWN'S APARTMENT.
I DON'T UNDERSTAND. THAT BUTTERFLY LADY OPENED A PORTAL TO THE FAERIES' WORLD RIGHT IN YOUR LIVING ROOM.
SHE IS THEIR QUEEN. HER SCEPTER CAN CREATE A PORTAL FROM HER DOMAIN TO OURS, ANYWHERE. BUT DUE TO THE BARRIERS WE'VE ERECTED BETWEEN DIMENSIONS, NO ONE ELSE CAN.
IT WOULD MAKE MY RESEARCH FAR EASIER IF YOU COULD ALTER THE VAMPYR BOOK SO THAT I CAN GO DIRECTLY TO THE FAE WORLD FROM MY HOME--
AND IT COULD UNDERMINE EVERYTHING WE'VE DONE TO PROTECT EARTH.
IT COULD MAKE OTHER BARRIERS WEAKER, RIGHT IN THE MIDDLE OF ALL THESE DEMON INVASIONS!
THE INCURSIONS ARE FROM HOSTILE DIMENSIONS.
THOSE PORTALS ARE BEING OPENED BY THE MISTRESS AND THE SOUL GLUTTON, USING THE RESTLESS DOOR ARTIFACT.
D'HOFFRYN IS CLOSE TO FINDING THEM. YOU'VE ALREADY KILLED THE SCULPTOR. WE'RE WINNING THIS WAR, BUFFY.
BUT THE FINAL BATTLE WILL BE BRUTAL. AND MY MAGICAL STUDIES ARE PROGRESSING QUICKLY AMONG THE FAE.
IT'S TRUE. HE'LL NEVER MATCH MISS WILLOW, BUT HIS POWER IS QUITE IMPRESSIVE. HOW SAD YOU CAN'T SEE HIS AURA. IT'S LOVELY.
OH, WELL, THAT MIGHT BE OVERSTATING A BIT...YOU REALLY THINK SO?
THIS IS WHAT I'M TALKING ABOUT, GILES. YOU'RE NOT THINKING STRAIGHT. YOU WANT ME TO UNDERMINE THE SAFETY OF THE WHOLE WORLD...
...SO IT'S EASIER FOR YOU TO CANOODLE WITH YOUR GIRLFRIEND.
IN PIECES ON THE GROUND
PART FOUR

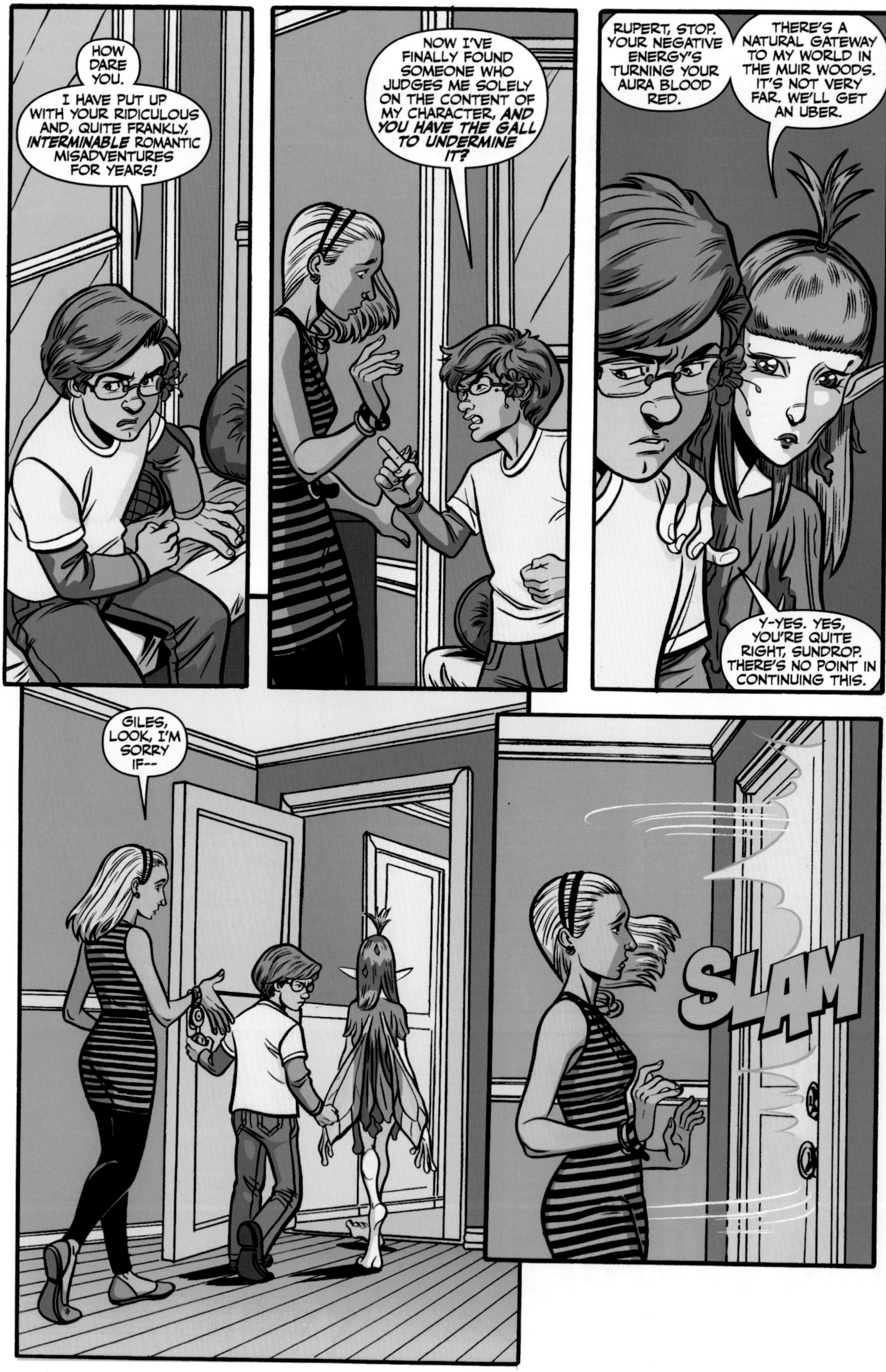
HOW DARE YOU.
I HAVE PUT UP WITH YOUR RIDICULOUS AND, QUITE FRANKLY, *INTERMINABLE* ROMANTIC MISADVENTURES FOR YEARS!
NOW I'VE FINALLY FOUND SOMEONE WHO JUDGES ME SOLELY ON THE CONTENT OF MY CHARACTER, *AND YOU HAVE THE GALL TO UNDERMINE IT?*
RUPERT, STOP. YOUR NEGATIVE ENERGY'S TURNING YOUR AURA BLOOD RED.
THERE'S A NATURAL GATEWAY TO MY WORLD IN THE MUIR WOODS. IT'S NOT VERY FAR. WE'LL GET AN UBER.
Y-YES. YES, YOU'RE QUITE RIGHT, SUNDROP. THERE'S NO POINT IN CONTINUING THIS.
GILES, LOOK, I'M SORRY IF--
SLAM

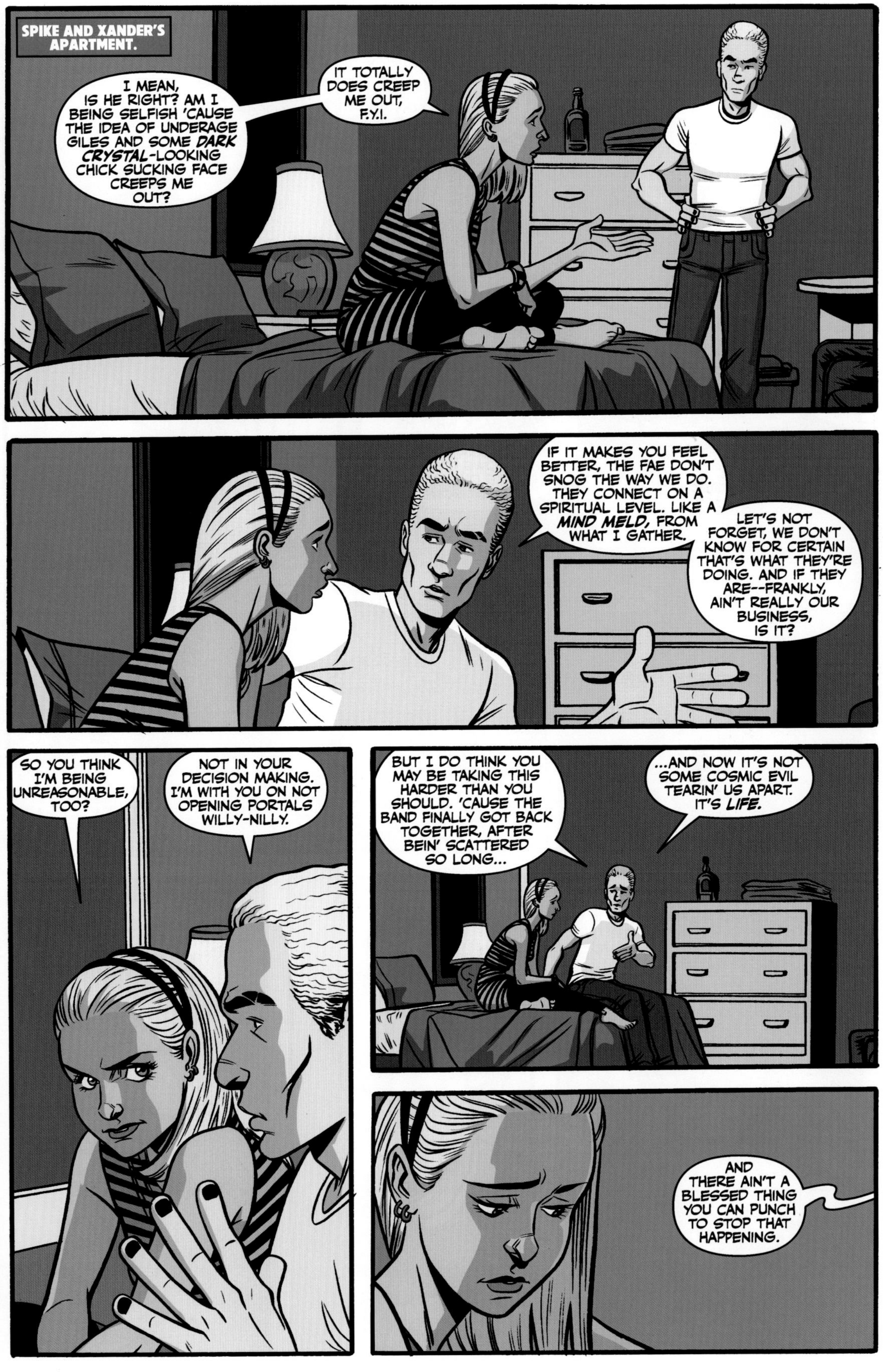
SPIKE AND XANDER'S APARTMENT.
I MEAN, IS HE RIGHT? AM I BEING SELFISH 'CAUSE THE IDEA OF UNDERAGE GILES AND SOME *DARK CRYSTAL*-LOOKING CHICK SUCKING FACE CREEPS ME OUT?
IT TOTALLY DOES CREEP ME OUT, F.Y.I.
IF IT MAKES YOU FEEL BETTER, THE FAE DON'T SNOG THE WAY WE DO. THEY CONNECT ON A SPIRITUAL LEVEL. LIKE A *MIND MELD,* FROM WHAT I GATHER.
LET'S NOT FORGET, WE DON'T KNOW FOR CERTAIN THAT'S WHAT THEY'RE DOING. AND IF THEY ARE--FRANKLY, AIN'T REALLY OUR BUSINESS, IS IT?
SO YOU THINK I'M BEING UNREASONABLE, TOO?
NOT IN YOUR DECISION MAKING. I'M WITH YOU ON NOT OPENING PORTALS WILLY-NILLY.
BUT I DO THINK YOU MAY BE TAKING THIS HARDER THAN YOU SHOULD. 'CAUSE THE BAND FINALLY GOT BACK TOGETHER, AFTER BEIN' SCATTERED SO LONG...
...AND NOW IT'S NOT SOME COSMIC EVIL TEARIN' US APART. IT'S *LIFE.*
AND THERE AIN'T A BLESSED THING YOU CAN PUNCH TO STOP THAT HAPPENING.

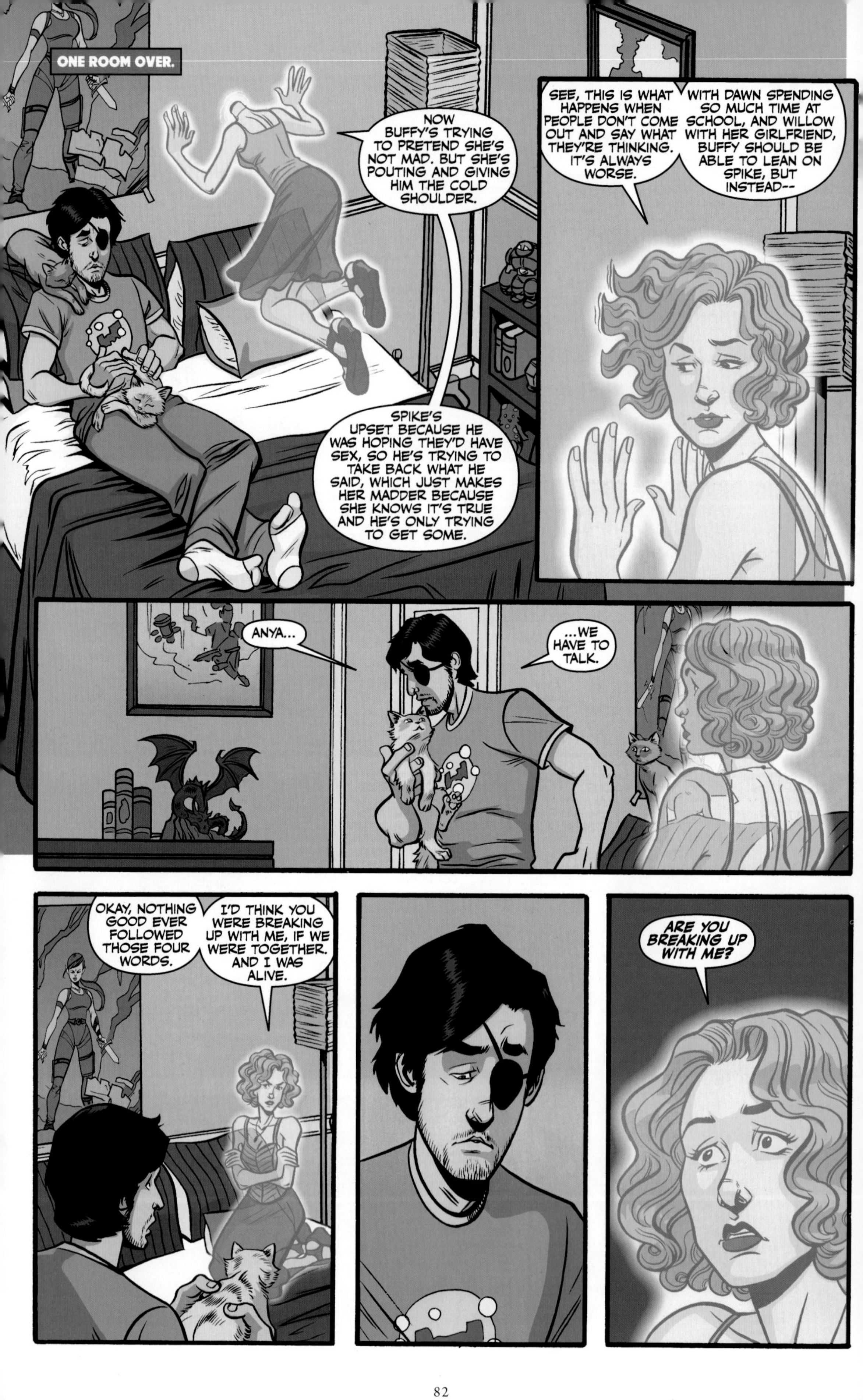
ONE ROOM OVER.
NOW BUFFY'S TRYING TO PRETEND SHE'S NOT MAD. BUT SHE'S POUTING AND GIVING HIM THE COLD SHOULDER.
SPIKE'S UPSET BECAUSE HE WAS HOPING THEY'D HAVE SEX, SO HE'S TRYING TO TAKE BACK WHAT HE SAID, WHICH JUST MAKES HER MADDER BECAUSE SHE KNOWS IT'S TRUE AND HE'S ONLY TRYING TO GET SOME.
SEE, THIS IS WHAT HAPPENS WHEN PEOPLE DON'T COME OUT AND SAY WHAT THEY'RE THINKING. IT'S ALWAYS WORSE.
WITH DAWN SPENDING SO MUCH TIME AT SCHOOL, AND WILLOW WITH HER GIRLFRIEND, BUFFY SHOULD BE ABLE TO LEAN ON SPIKE, BUT INSTEAD--
ANYA...
...WE HAVE TO TALK.
OKAY, NOTHING GOOD EVER FOLLOWED THOSE FOUR WORDS.
I'D THINK YOU WERE BREAKING UP WITH ME, IF WE WERE TOGETHER. AND I WAS ALIVE.
ARE YOU BREAKING UP WITH ME?

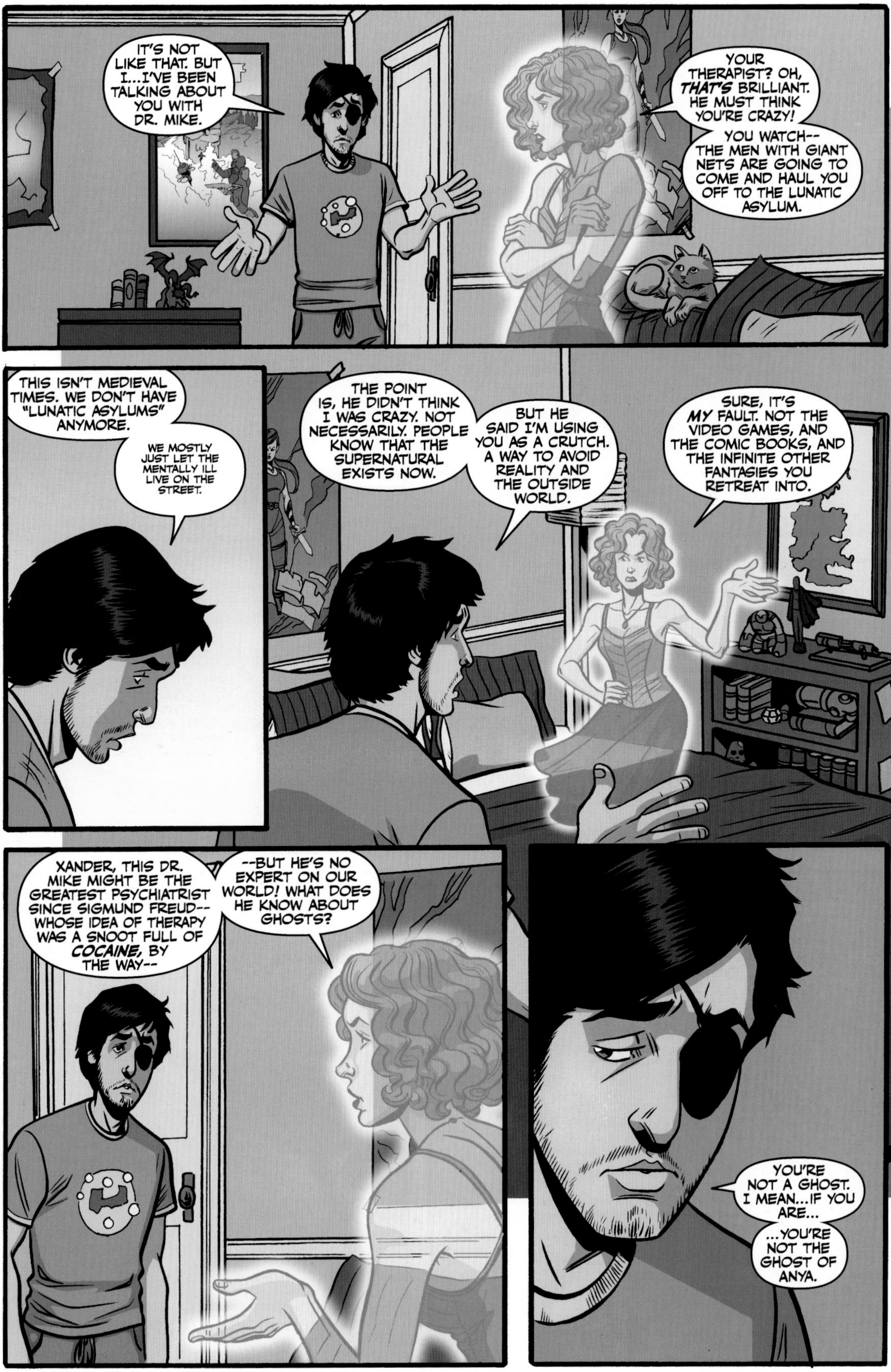
IT'S NOT LIKE THAT. BUT I...I'VE BEEN TALKING ABOUT YOU WITH DR. MIKE.
YOUR THERAPIST? OH, *THAT'S* BRILLIANT. HE MUST THINK YOU'RE CRAZY!
YOU WATCH-- THE MEN WITH GIANT NETS ARE GOING TO COME AND HAUL YOU OFF TO THE LUNATIC ASYLUM.
THIS ISN'T MEDIEVAL TIMES. WE DON'T HAVE "LUNATIC ASYLUMS" ANYMORE.
WE MOSTLY JUST LET THE MENTALLY ILL LIVE ON THE STREET.
THE POINT IS, HE DIDN'T THINK I WAS CRAZY. NOT NECESSARILY. PEOPLE KNOW THAT THE SUPERNATURAL EXISTS NOW.
BUT HE SAID I'M USING YOU AS A CRUTCH. A WAY TO AVOID REALITY AND THE OUTSIDE WORLD.
SURE, IT'S *MY* FAULT. NOT THE VIDEO GAMES, AND THE COMIC BOOKS, AND THE INFINITE OTHER FANTASIES YOU RETREAT INTO.
XANDER, THIS DR. MIKE MIGHT BE THE GREATEST PSYCHIATRIST SINCE SIGMUND FREUD-- WHOSE IDEA OF THERAPY WAS A SNOOT FULL OF *COCAINE,* BY THE WAY--
--BUT HE'S NO EXPERT ON OUR WORLD! WHAT DOES HE KNOW ABOUT GHOSTS?
YOU'RE NOT A GHOST. I MEAN...IF YOU ARE...
...YOU'RE NOT THE GHOST OF ANYA.

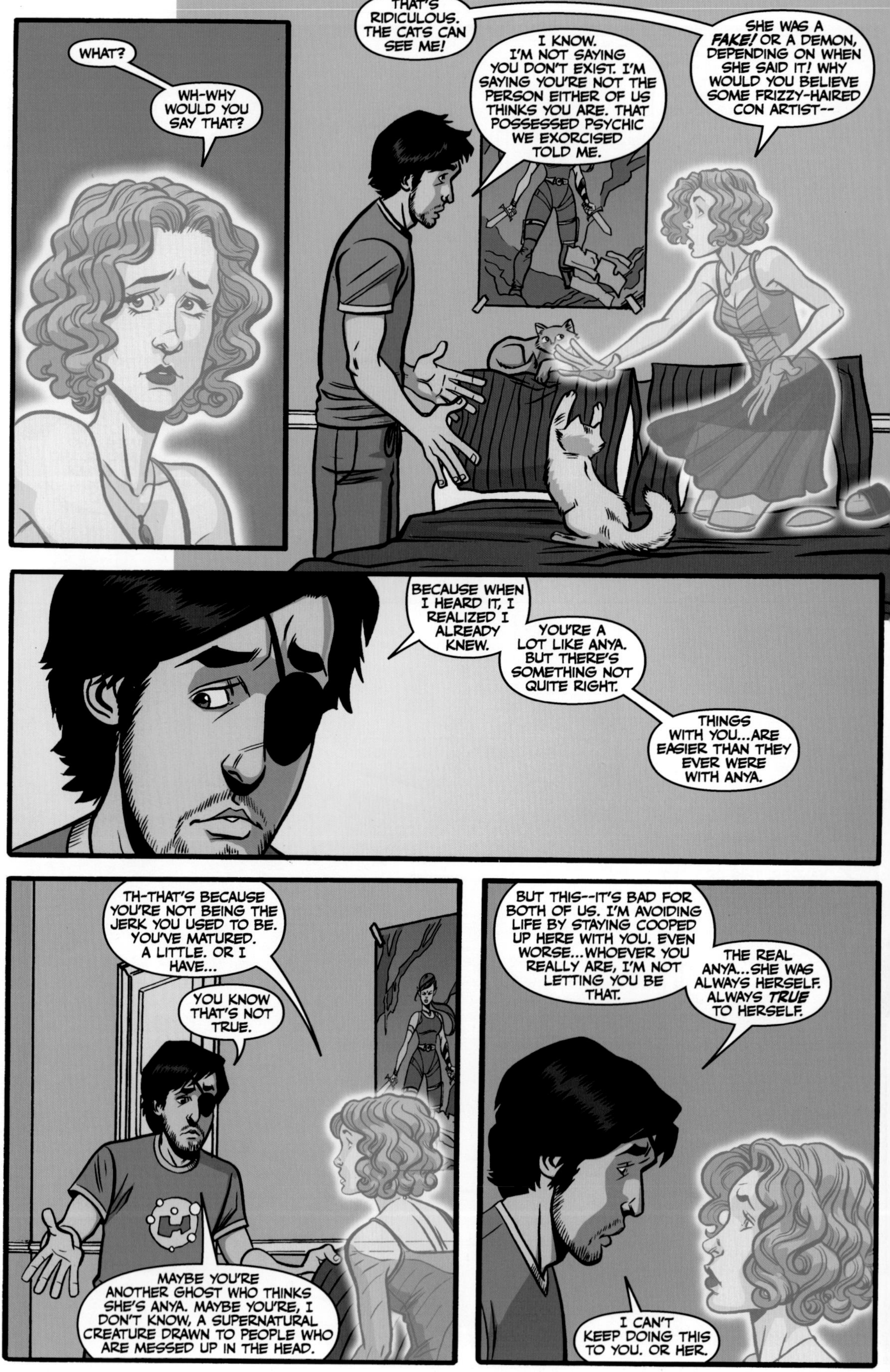

WHAT?
WH-WHY WOULD YOU SAY THAT?
THAT'S RIDICULOUS. THE CATS CAN SEE ME!
I KNOW. I'M NOT SAYING YOU DON'T EXIST. I'M SAYING YOU'RE NOT THE PERSON EITHER OF US THINKS YOU ARE. THAT POSSESSED PSYCHIC WE EXORCISED TOLD ME.
SHE WAS A *FAKE!* OR A DEMON, DEPENDING ON WHEN SHE SAID IT! WHY WOULD YOU BELIEVE SOME FRIZZY-HAIRED CON ARTIST--
BECAUSE WHEN I HEARD IT, I REALIZED I ALREADY KNEW.
YOU'RE A LOT LIKE ANYA. BUT THERE'S SOMETHING NOT QUITE RIGHT.
THINGS WITH YOU...ARE EASIER THAN THEY EVER WERE WITH ANYA.
TH-THAT'S BECAUSE YOU'RE NOT BEING THE JERK YOU USED TO BE. YOU'VE MATURED. A LITTLE. OR I HAVE...
YOU KNOW THAT'S NOT TRUE.
MAYBE YOU'RE ANOTHER GHOST WHO THINKS SHE'S ANYA. MAYBE YOU'RE, I DON'T KNOW, A SUPERNATURAL CREATURE DRAWN TO PEOPLE WHO ARE MESSED UP IN THE HEAD.
BUT THIS--IT'S BAD FOR BOTH OF US. I'M AVOIDING LIFE BY STAYING COOPED UP HERE WITH YOU. EVEN WORSE...WHOEVER YOU REALLY ARE, I'M NOT LETTING YOU BE THAT.
THE REAL ANYA...SHE WAS ALWAYS HERSELF. ALWAYS *TRUE* TO HERSELF.
I CAN'T KEEP DOING THIS TO YOU. OR HER.

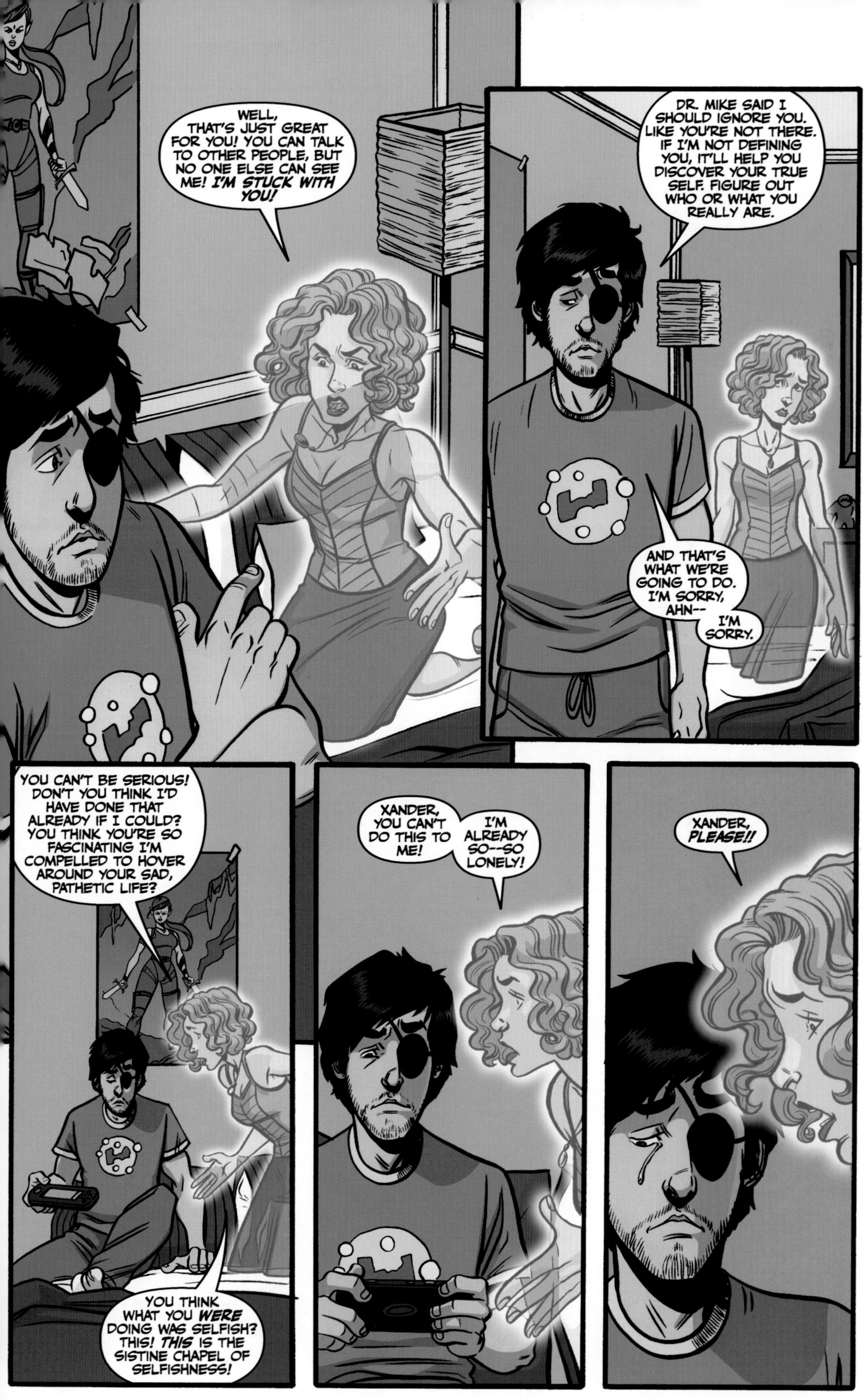
WELL, THAT'S JUST GREAT FOR YOU! YOU CAN TALK TO OTHER PEOPLE, BUT NO ONE ELSE CAN SEE ME! I'M STUCK WITH YOU!
DR. MIKE SAID I SHOULD IGNORE YOU. LIKE YOU'RE NOT THERE. IF I'M NOT DEFINING YOU, IT'LL HELP YOU DISCOVER YOUR TRUE SELF. FIGURE OUT WHO OR WHAT YOU REALLY ARE.
AND THAT'S WHAT WE'RE GOING TO DO. I'M SORRY, AHN--
I'M SORRY.
YOU CAN'T BE SERIOUS! DON'T YOU THINK I'D HAVE DONE THAT ALREADY IF I COULD? YOU THINK YOU'RE SO FASCINATING I'M COMPELLED TO HOVER AROUND YOUR SAD, PATHETIC LIFE?
YOU THINK WHAT YOU WERE DOING WAS SELFISH? THIS! THIS IS THE SISTINE CHAPEL OF SELFISHNESS!
XANDER, YOU CAN'T DO THIS TO ME!
I'M ALREADY SO--SO LONELY!
XANDER, PLEASE!!

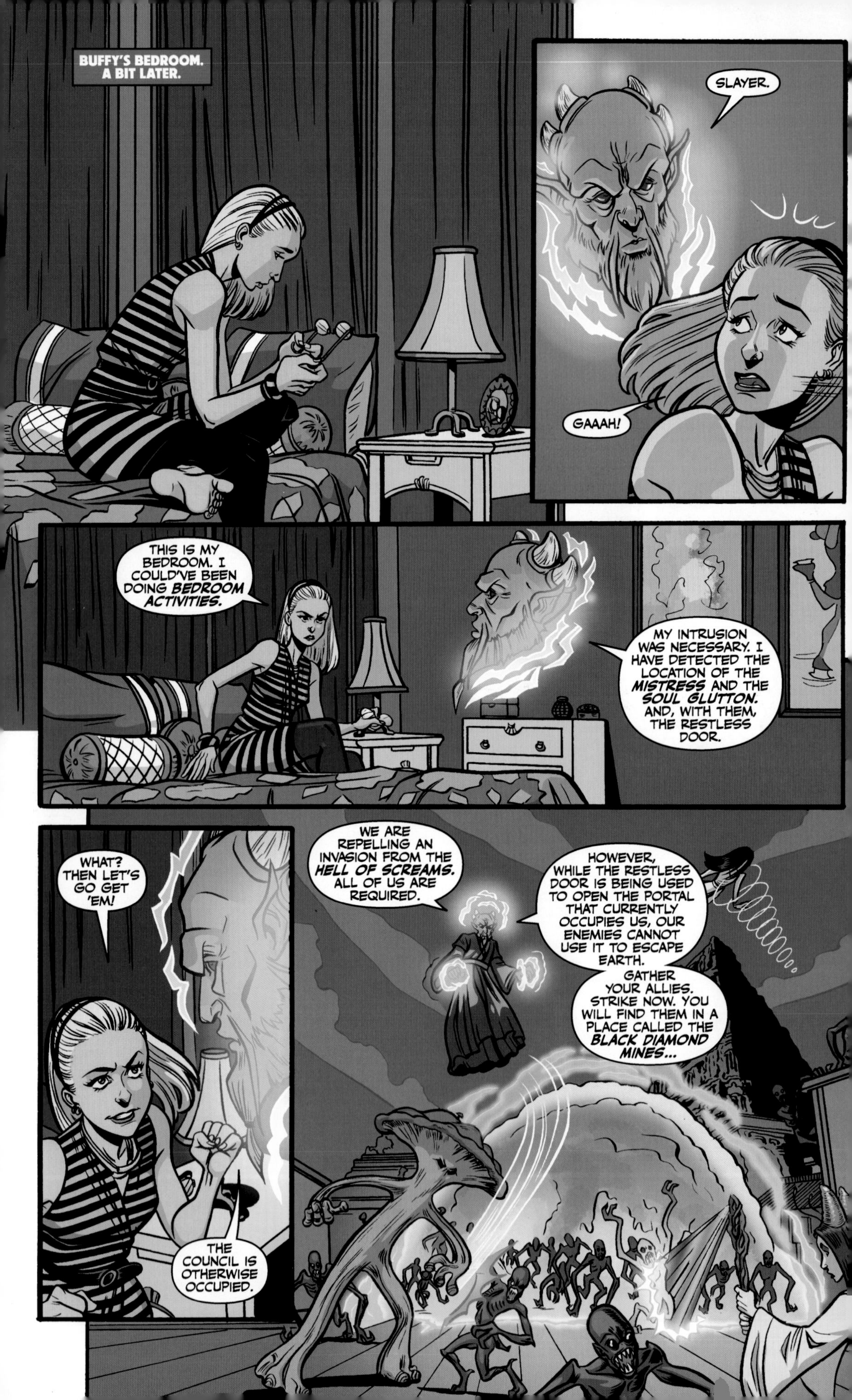
BUFFY'S BEDROOM. A BIT LATER.
SLAYER.
GAAAH!
THIS IS MY BEDROOM. I COULD'VE BEEN DOING BEDROOM ACTIVITIES.
MY INTRUSION WAS NECESSARY. I HAVE DETECTED THE LOCATION OF THE MISTRESS AND THE SOUL GLUTTON. AND, WITH THEM, THE RESTLESS DOOR.
WHAT? THEN LET'S GO GET 'EM!
THE COUNCIL IS OTHERWISE OCCUPIED.
WE ARE REPELLING AN INVASION FROM THE HELL OF SCREAMS. ALL OF US ARE REQUIRED.
HOWEVER, WHILE THE RESTLESS DOOR IS BEING USED TO OPEN THE PORTAL THAT CURRENTLY OCCUPIES US, OUR ENEMIES CANNOT USE IT TO ESCAPE EARTH.
GATHER YOUR ALLIES. STRIKE NOW. YOU WILL FIND THEM IN A PLACE CALLED THE BLACK DIAMOND MINES...

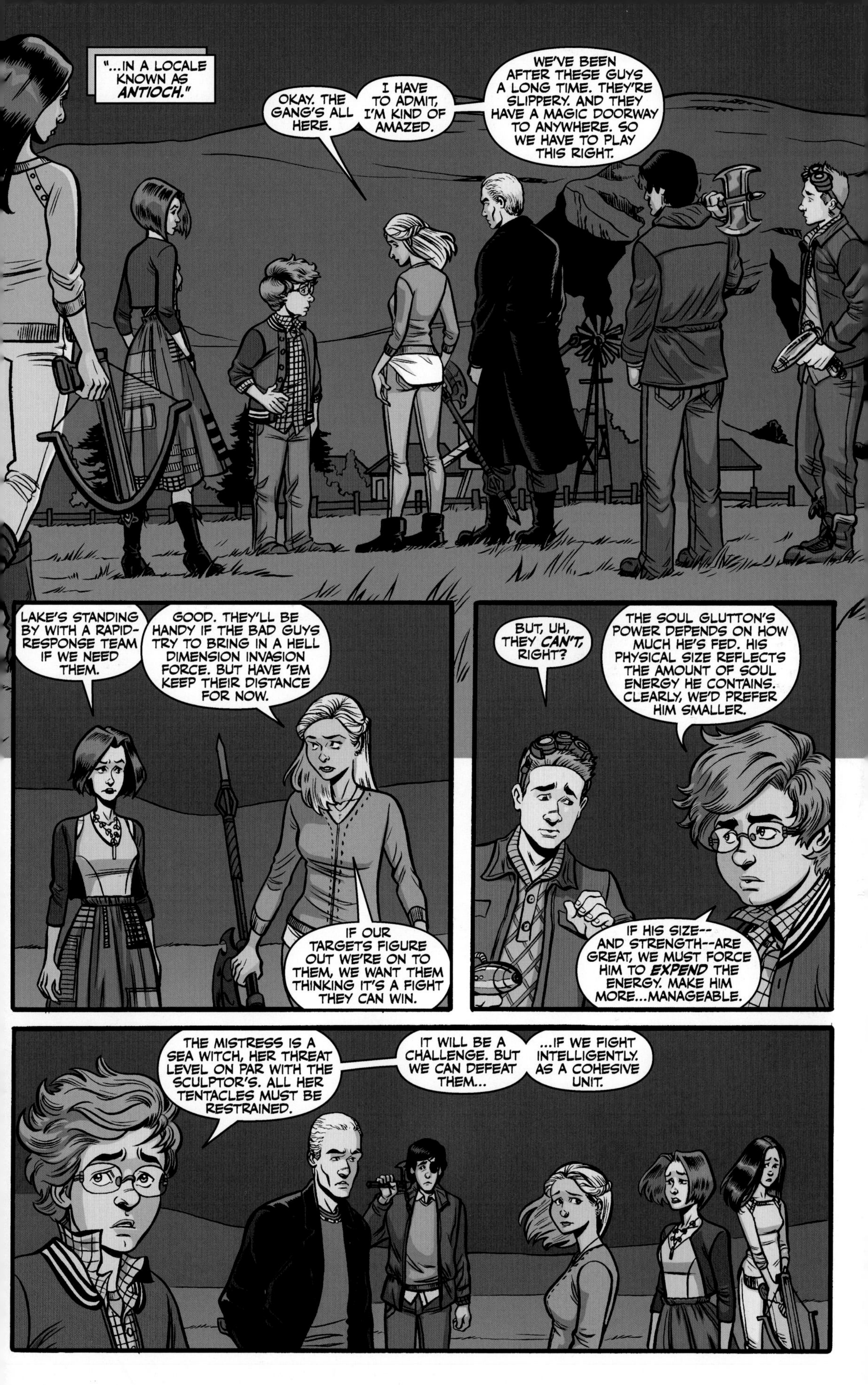
"...IN A LOCALE KNOWN AS *ANTIOCH*."
OKAY. THE GANG'S ALL HERE.
I HAVE TO ADMIT, I'M KIND OF AMAZED.
WE'VE BEEN AFTER THESE GUYS A LONG TIME. THEY'RE SLIPPERY. AND THEY HAVE A MAGIC DOORWAY TO ANYWHERE. SO WE HAVE TO PLAY THIS RIGHT.
LAKE'S STANDING BY WITH A RAPID-RESPONSE TEAM IF WE NEED THEM.
GOOD. THEY'LL BE HANDY IF THE BAD GUYS TRY TO BRING IN A HELL DIMENSION INVASION FORCE. BUT HAVE 'EM KEEP THEIR DISTANCE FOR NOW.
IF OUR TARGETS FIGURE OUT WE'RE ON TO THEM, WE WANT THEM THINKING IT'S A FIGHT THEY CAN WIN.
BUT, UH, THEY *CAN'T*, RIGHT?
THE SOUL GLUTTON'S POWER DEPENDS ON HOW MUCH HE'S FED. HIS PHYSICAL SIZE REFLECTS THE AMOUNT OF SOUL ENERGY HE CONTAINS. CLEARLY, WE'D PREFER HIM SMALLER.
IF HIS SIZE-- AND STRENGTH--ARE GREAT, WE MUST FORCE HIM TO *EXPEND* THE ENERGY. MAKE HIM MORE...MANAGEABLE.
THE MISTRESS IS A SEA WITCH, HER THREAT LEVEL ON PAR WITH THE SCULPTOR'S. ALL HER TENTACLES MUST BE RESTRAINED.
IT WILL BE A CHALLENGE. BUT WE CAN DEFEAT THEM...
...IF WE FIGHT INTELLIGENTLY. AS A COHESIVE UNIT.

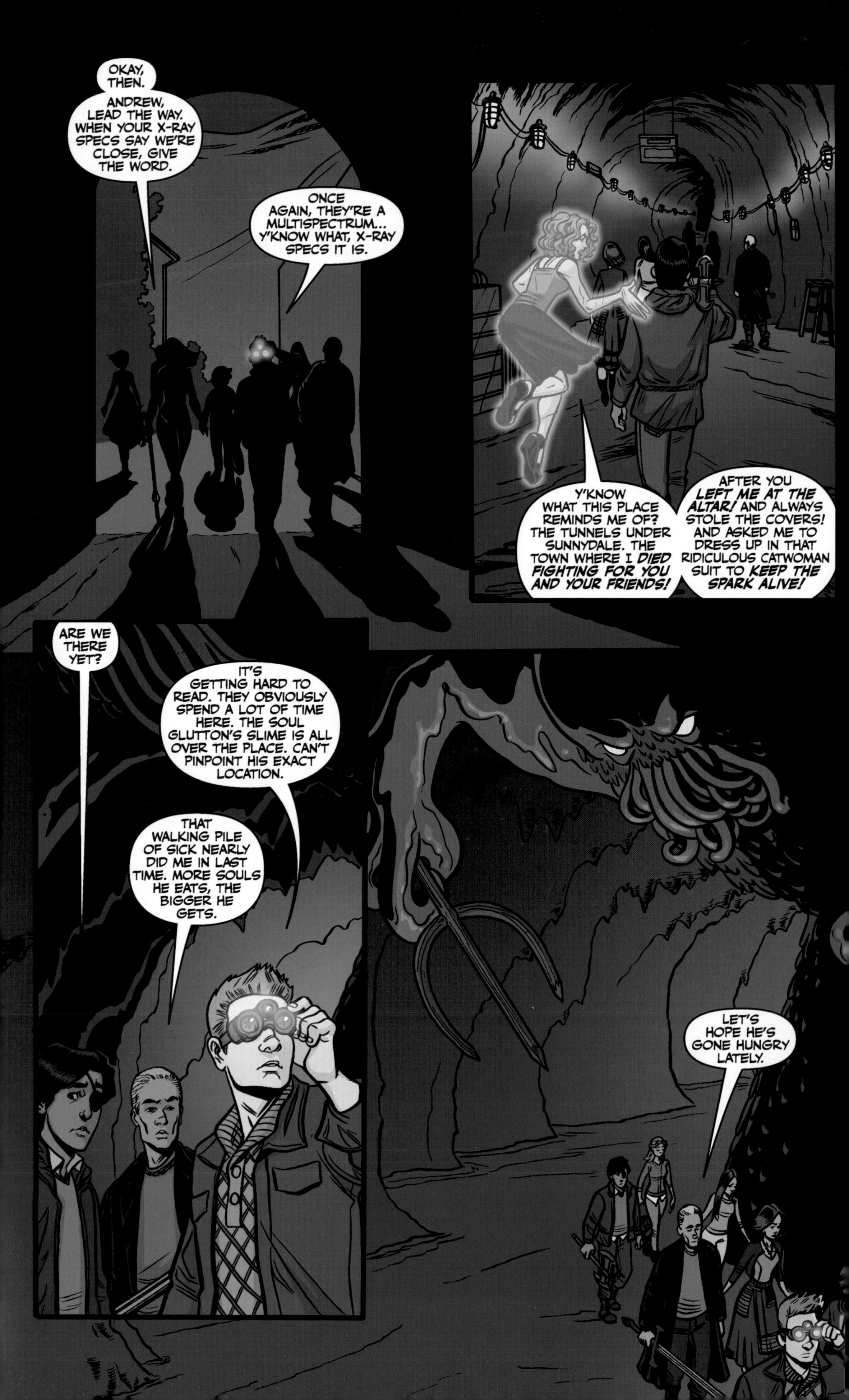
OKAY, THEN. ANDREW, LEAD THE WAY. WHEN YOUR X-RAY SPECS SAY WE'RE CLOSE, GIVE THE WORD.
ONCE AGAIN, THEY'RE A MULTISPECTRUM... Y'KNOW WHAT, X-RAY SPECS IT IS.
Y'KNOW WHAT THIS PLACE REMINDS ME OF? THE TUNNELS UNDER SUNNYDALE. THE TOWN WHERE I *DIED FIGHTING FOR YOU AND YOUR FRIENDS!*
AFTER YOU *LEFT ME AT THE ALTAR!* AND ALWAYS STOLE THE COVERS! AND ASKED ME TO DRESS UP IN THAT RIDICULOUS CATWOMAN SUIT TO *KEEP THE SPARK ALIVE!*
ARE WE THERE YET?
IT'S GETTING HARD TO READ. THEY OBVIOUSLY SPEND A LOT OF TIME HERE. THE SOUL GLUTTON'S SLIME IS ALL OVER THE PLACE. CAN'T PINPOINT HIS EXACT LOCATION.
THAT WALKING PILE OF SICK NEARLY DID ME IN LAST TIME. MORE SOULS HE EATS, THE BIGGER HE GETS.
LET'S HOPE HE'S GONE HUNGRY LATELY.

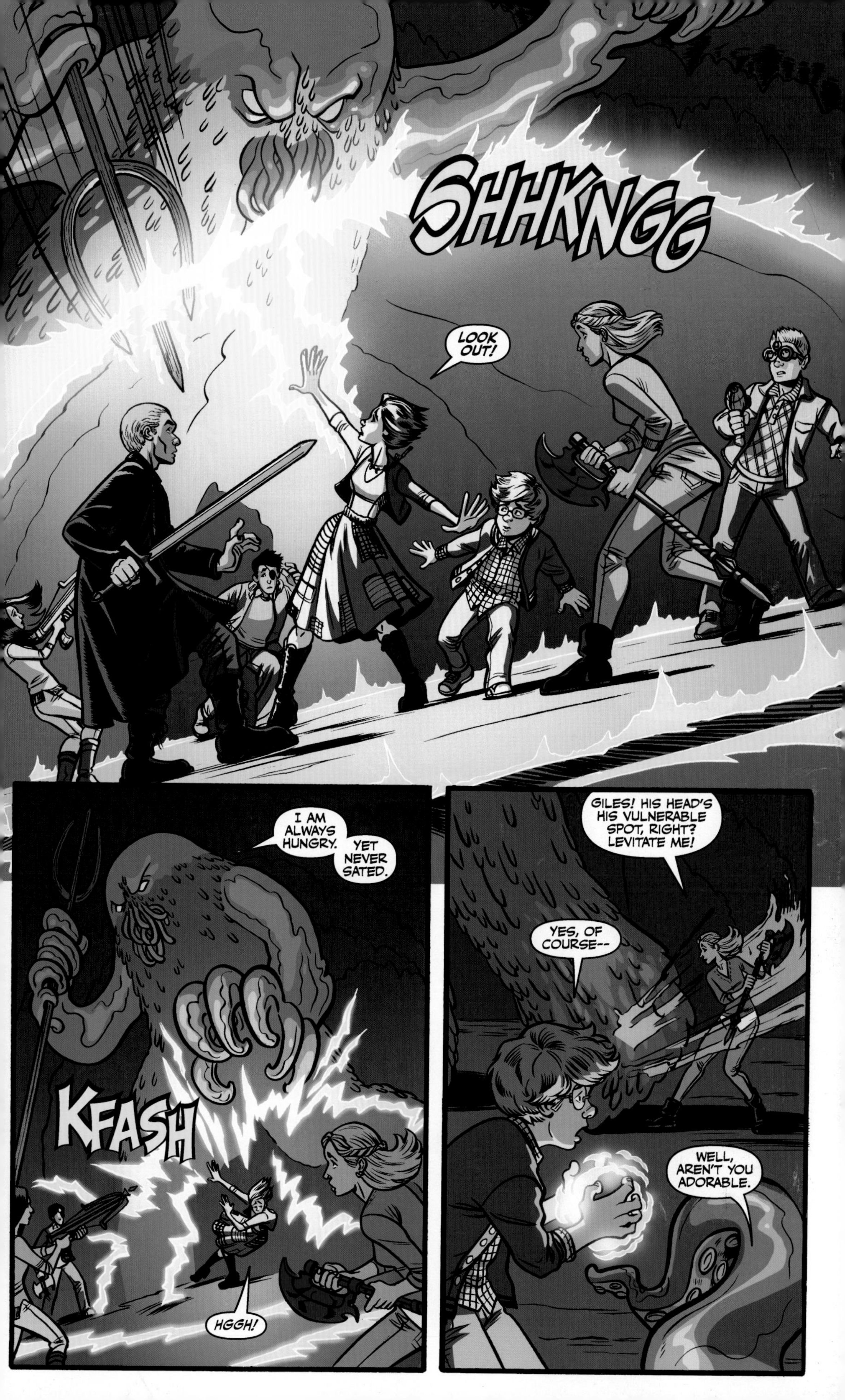
SHHKNGG
LOOK OUT!
I AM ALWAYS HUNGRY.
YET NEVER SATED.
KFASH
HGGH!
GILES! HIS HEAD'S HIS VULNERABLE SPOT, RIGHT? LEVITATE ME!
YES, OF COURSE--
WELL, AREN'T YOU ADORABLE.

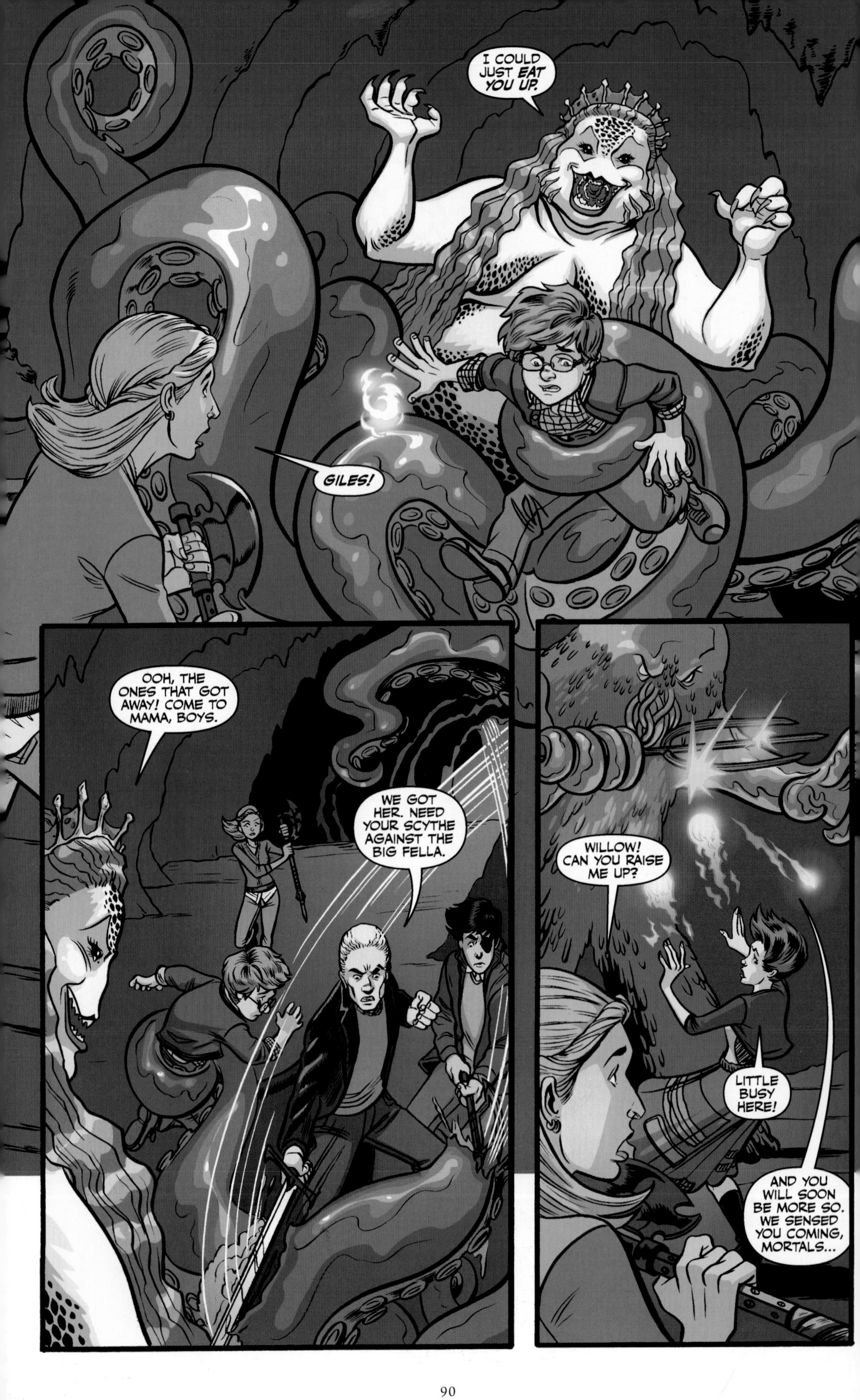
I COULD JUST *EAT* YOU UP.
GILES!
OOH, THE ONES THAT GOT AWAY! COME TO MAMA, BOYS.
WE GOT HER. NEED YOUR SCYTHE AGAINST THE BIG FELLA.
WILLOW! CAN YOU RAISE ME UP?
LITTLE BUSY HERE!
AND YOU WILL SOON BE MORE SO. WE SENSED YOU COMING, MORTALS...

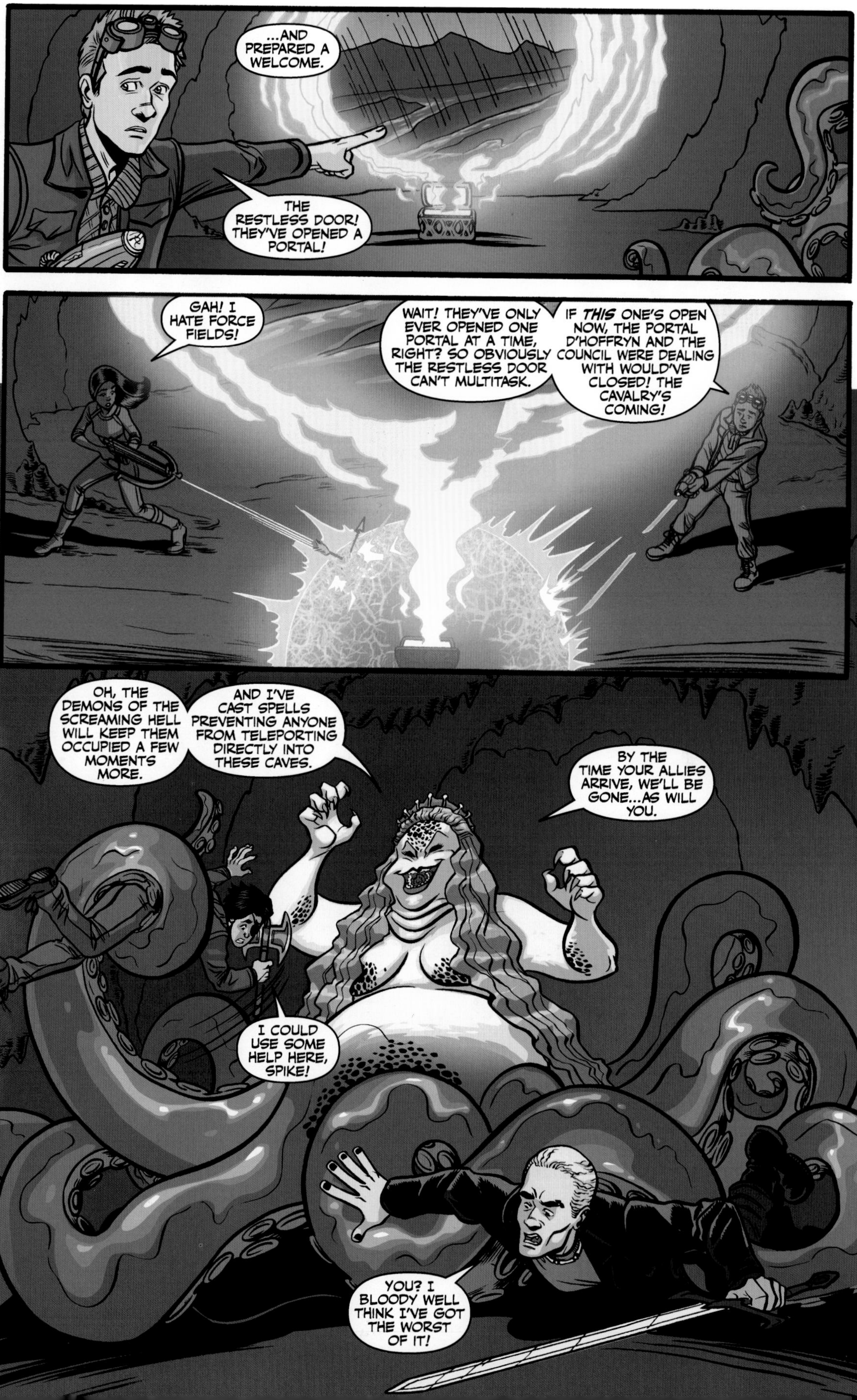
...AND PREPARED A WELCOME.
THE RESTLESS DOOR! THEY'VE OPENED A PORTAL!
GAH! I HATE FORCE FIELDS!
WAIT! THEY'VE ONLY EVER OPENED ONE PORTAL AT A TIME, RIGHT? SO OBVIOUSLY THE RESTLESS DOOR CAN'T MULTITASK.
IF *THIS* ONE'S OPEN NOW, THE PORTAL D'HOFFRYN AND THE COUNCIL WERE DEALING WITH WOULD'VE CLOSED! THE CAVALRY'S COMING!
OH, THE DEMONS OF THE SCREAMING HELL WILL KEEP THEM OCCUPIED A FEW MOMENTS MORE.
AND I'VE CAST SPELLS PREVENTING ANYONE FROM TELEPORTING DIRECTLY INTO THESE CAVES.
BY THE TIME YOUR ALLIES ARRIVE, WE'LL BE GONE...AS WILL YOU.
I COULD USE SOME HELP HERE, SPIKE!
YOU? I BLOODY WELL THINK I'VE GOT THE WORST OF IT!

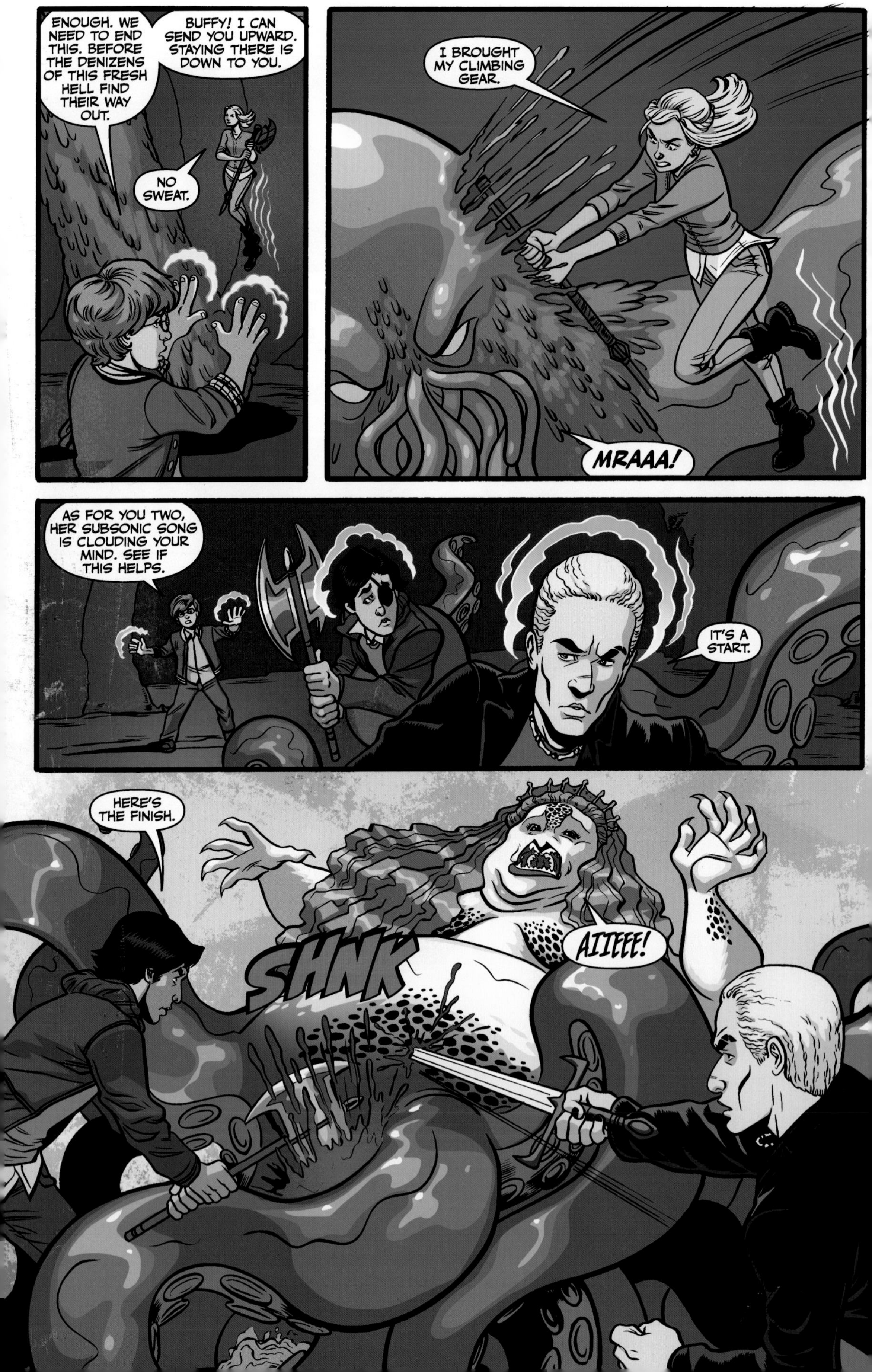

ENOUGH. WE NEED TO END THIS. BEFORE THE DENIZENS OF THIS FRESH HELL FIND THEIR WAY OUT.
BUFFY! I CAN SEND YOU UPWARD. STAYING THERE IS DOWN TO YOU.
NO SWEAT.
I BROUGHT MY CLIMBING GEAR.
MRAAA!
AS FOR YOU TWO, HER SUBSONIC SONG IS CLOUDING YOUR MIND. SEE IF THIS HELPS.
IT'S A START.
HERE'S THE FINISH.
SHNK
AIIEEE!

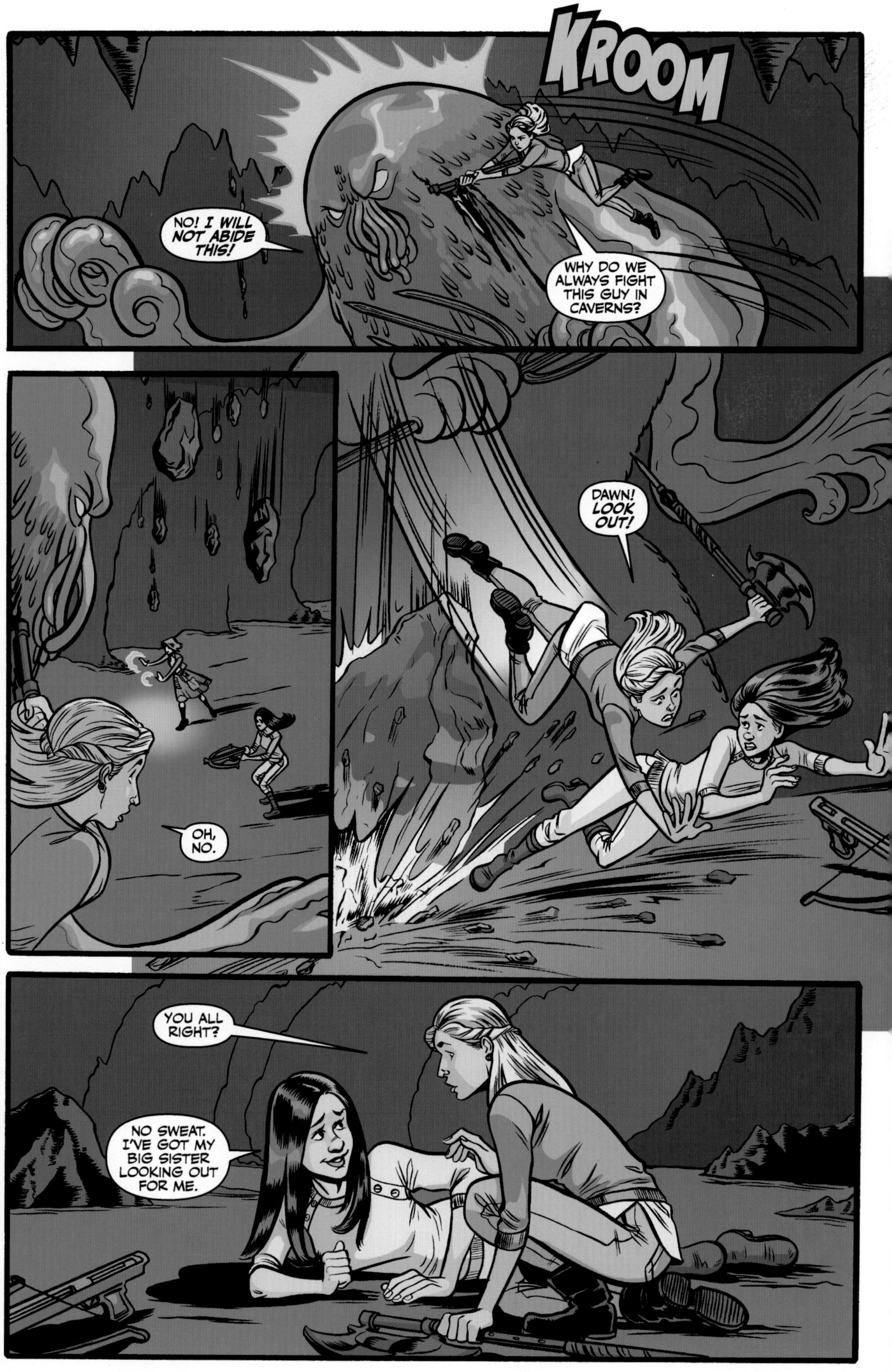
KROOM
NO! I WILL NOT ABIDE THIS!
WHY DO WE ALWAYS FIGHT THIS GUY IN CAVERNS?
OH, NO.
DAWN! LOOK OUT!
YOU ALL RIGHT?
NO SWEAT. I'VE GOT MY BIG SISTER LOOKING OUT FOR ME.

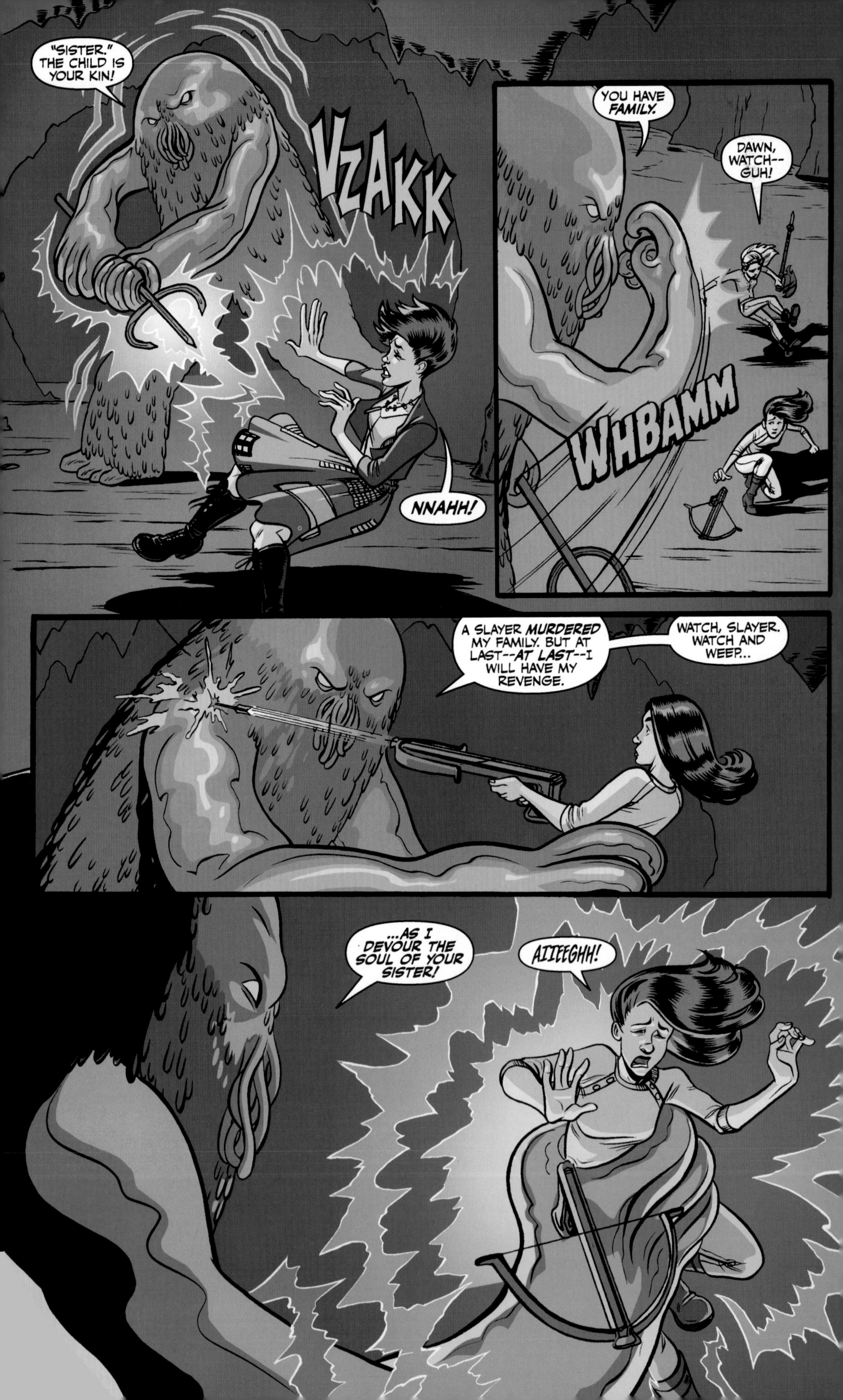
"SISTER." THE CHILD IS YOUR KIN!
VZAKK
NNAHH!
YOU HAVE FAMILY.
DAWN, WATCH-- GUH!
WHBAMM
A SLAYER MURDERED MY FAMILY. BUT AT LAST--AT LAST--I WILL HAVE MY REVENGE.
WATCH, SLAYER. WATCH AND WEEP...
...AS I DEVOUR THE SOUL OF YOUR SISTER!
AIIEEGHH!

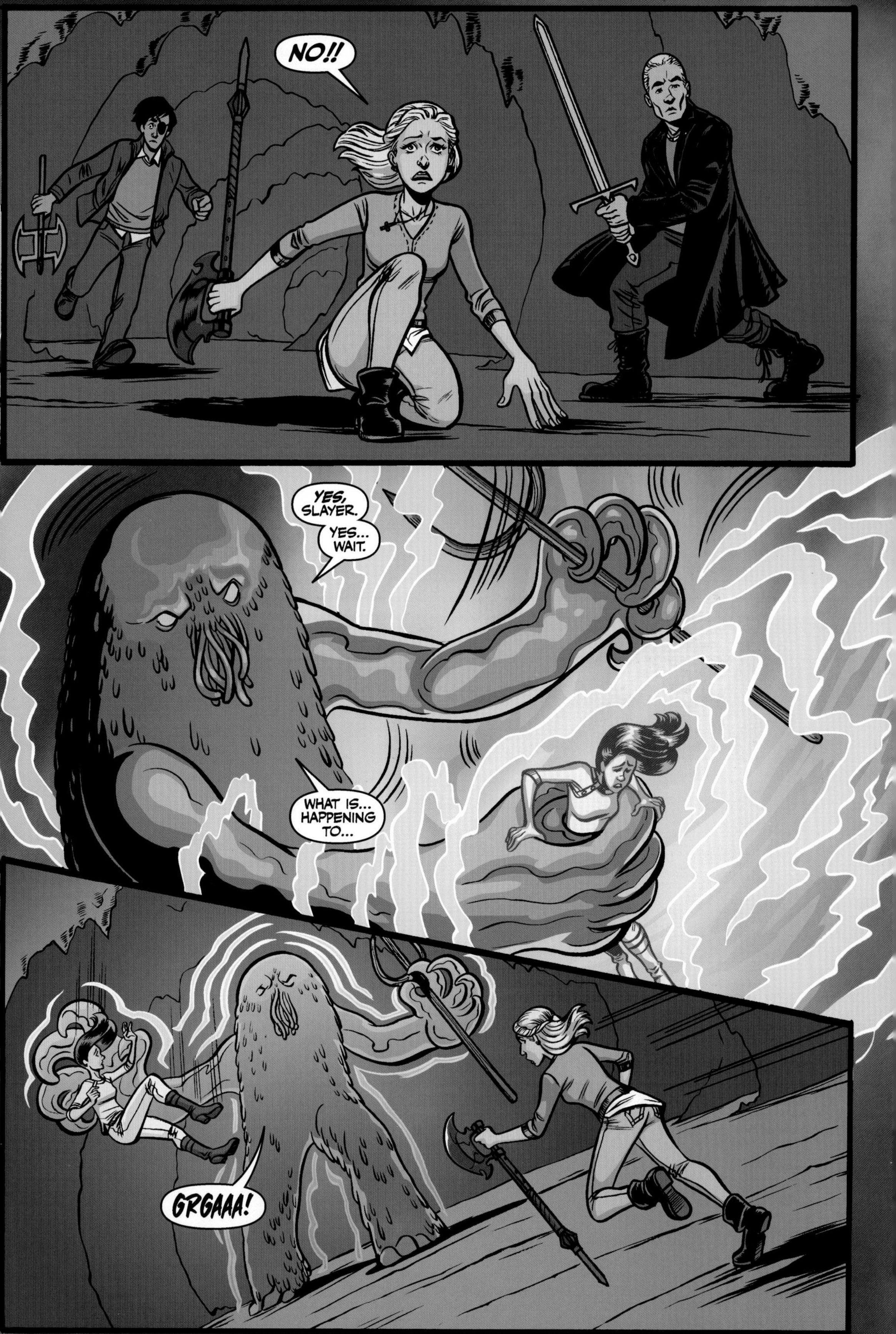
NO!!
YES, SLAYER.
YES... WAIT.
WHAT IS... HAPPENING TO...
GRGAAA!

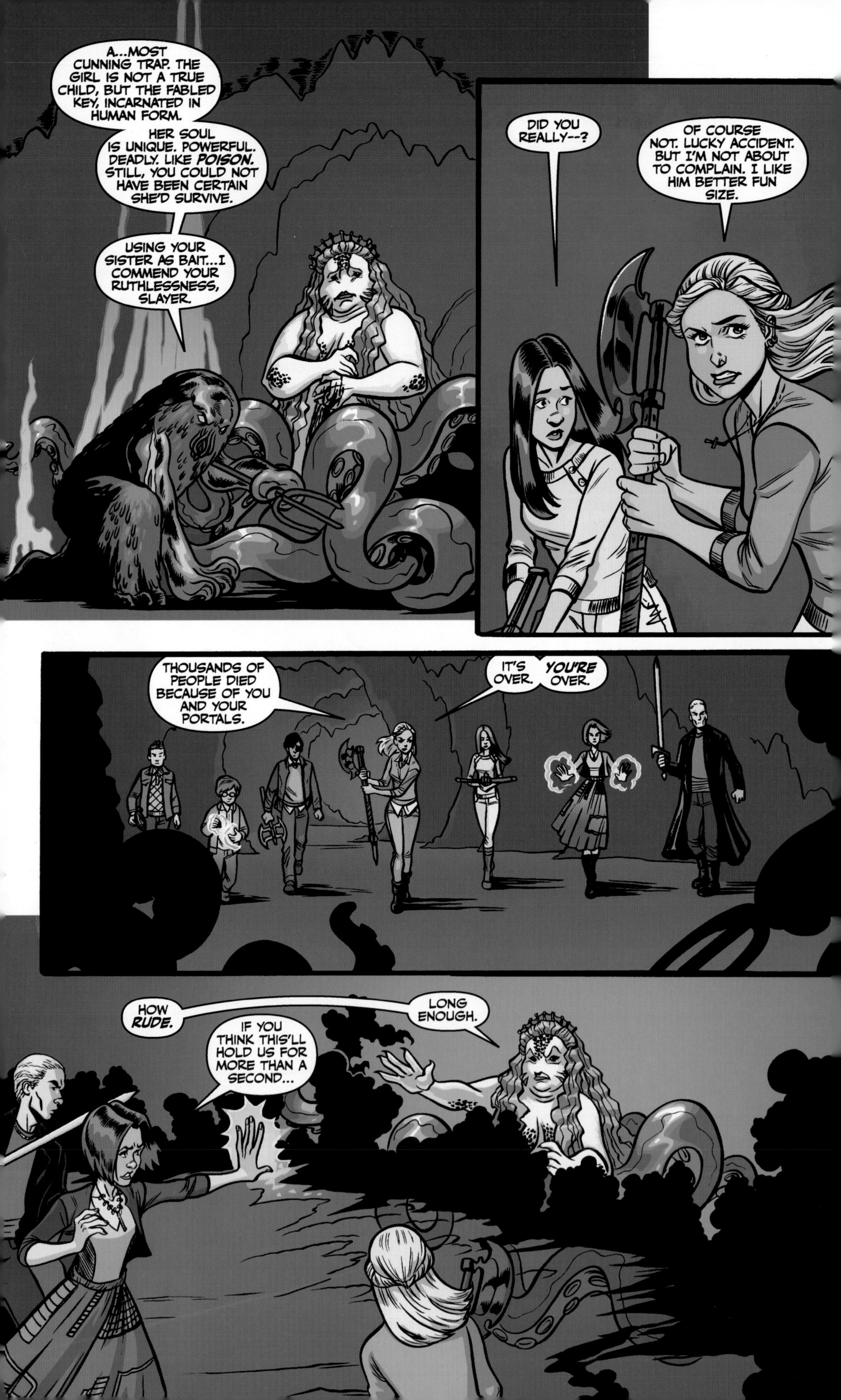
A...MOST CUNNING TRAP. THE GIRL IS NOT A TRUE CHILD, BUT THE FABLED KEY, INCARNATED IN HUMAN FORM.
HER SOUL IS UNIQUE. POWERFUL. DEADLY. LIKE *POISON.* STILL, YOU COULD NOT HAVE BEEN CERTAIN SHE'D SURVIVE.
USING YOUR SISTER AS BAIT...I COMMEND YOUR RUTHLESSNESS, SLAYER.
DID YOU REALLY--?
OF COURSE NOT. LUCKY ACCIDENT. BUT I'M NOT ABOUT TO COMPLAIN. I LIKE HIM BETTER FUN SIZE.
THOUSANDS OF PEOPLE DIED BECAUSE OF YOU AND YOUR PORTALS.
IT'S OVER.
YOU'RE OVER.
HOW *RUDE.*
LONG ENOUGH.
IF YOU THINK THIS'LL HOLD US FOR MORE THAN A SECOND...

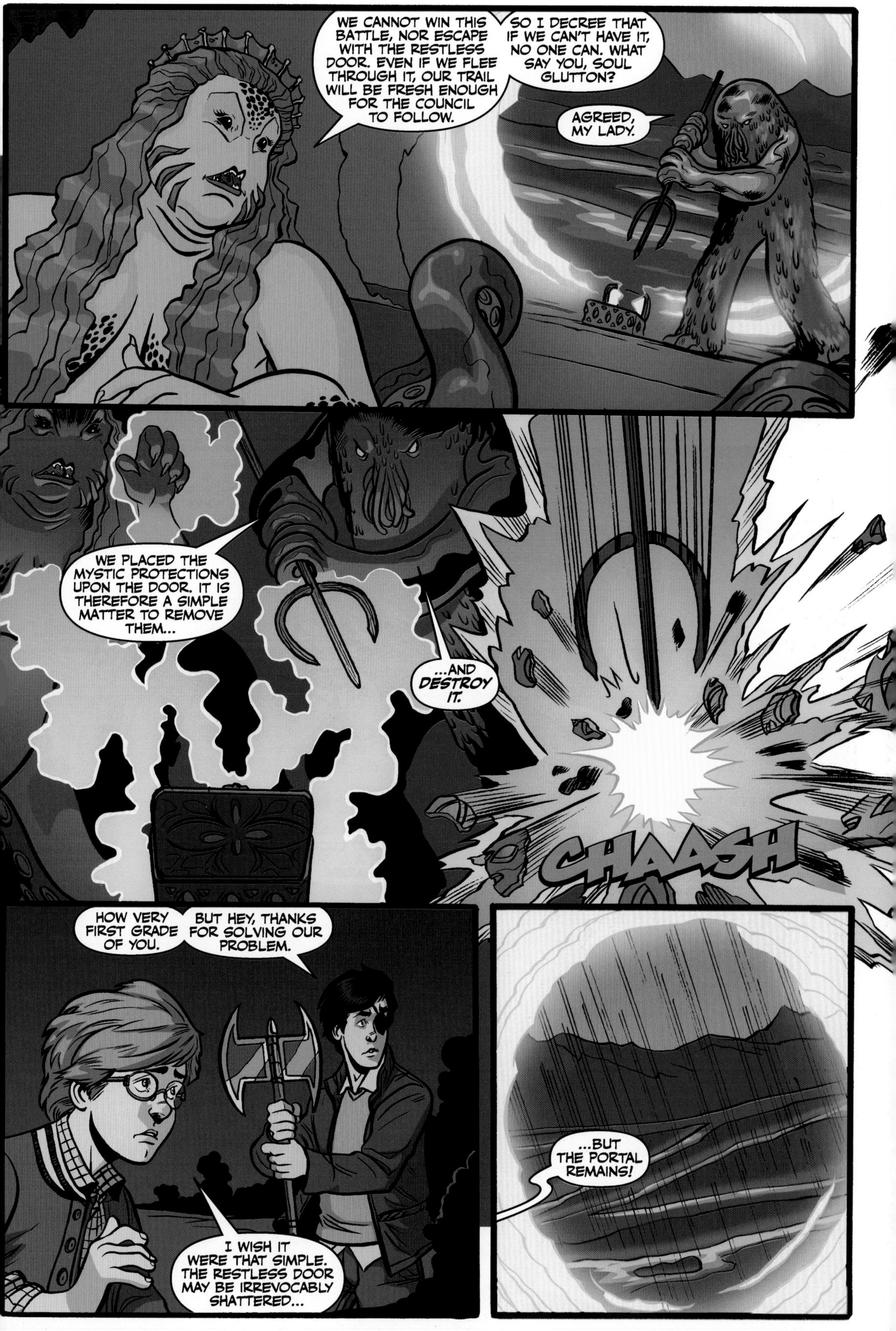
WE CANNOT WIN THIS BATTLE, NOR ESCAPE WITH THE RESTLESS DOOR. EVEN IF WE FLEE THROUGH IT, OUR TRAIL WILL BE FRESH ENOUGH FOR THE COUNCIL TO FOLLOW.
SO I DECREE THAT IF WE CAN'T HAVE IT, NO ONE CAN. WHAT SAY YOU, SOUL GLUTTON?
AGREED, MY LADY.
WE PLACED THE MYSTIC PROTECTIONS UPON THE DOOR. IT IS THEREFORE A SIMPLE MATTER TO REMOVE THEM...
...AND *DESTROY* IT.
CHAASH
HOW VERY FIRST GRADE OF YOU.
BUT HEY, THANKS FOR SOLVING OUR PROBLEM.
I WISH IT WERE THAT SIMPLE. THE RESTLESS DOOR MAY BE IRREVOCABLY SHATTERED...
...BUT THE PORTAL REMAINS!

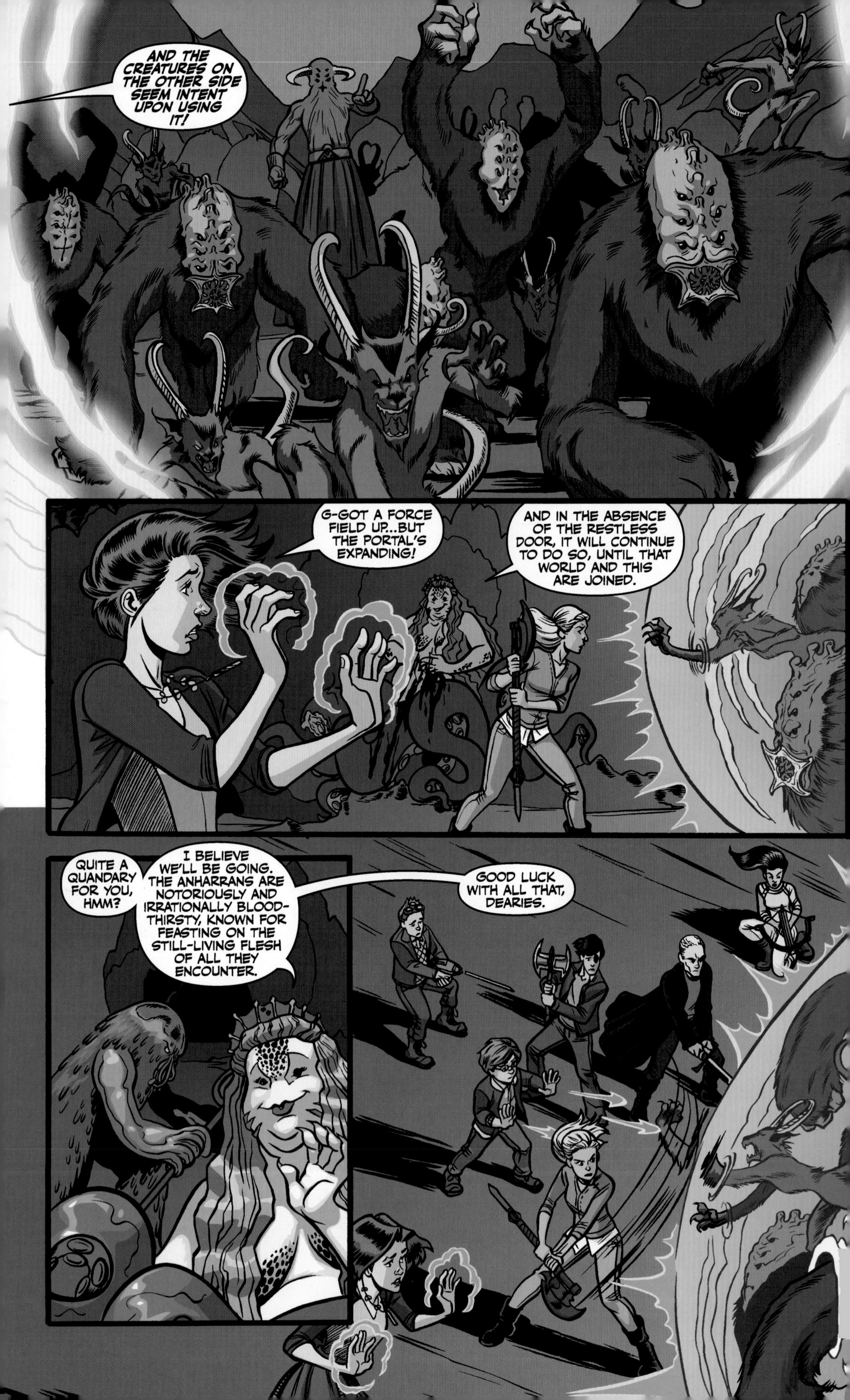
AND THE CREATURES ON THE OTHER SIDE SEEM INTENT UPON USING IT!
G-GOT A FORCE FIELD UP...BUT THE PORTAL'S EXPANDING!
AND IN THE ABSENCE OF THE RESTLESS DOOR, IT WILL CONTINUE TO DO SO, UNTIL THAT WORLD AND THIS ARE JOINED.
QUITE A QUANDARY FOR YOU, HMM?
I BELIEVE WE'LL BE GOING. THE ANHARRANS ARE NOTORIOUSLY AND IRRATIONALLY BLOOD-THIRSTY, KNOWN FOR FEASTING ON THE STILL-LIVING FLESH OF ALL THEY ENCOUNTER.
GOOD LUCK WITH ALL THAT, DEARIES.

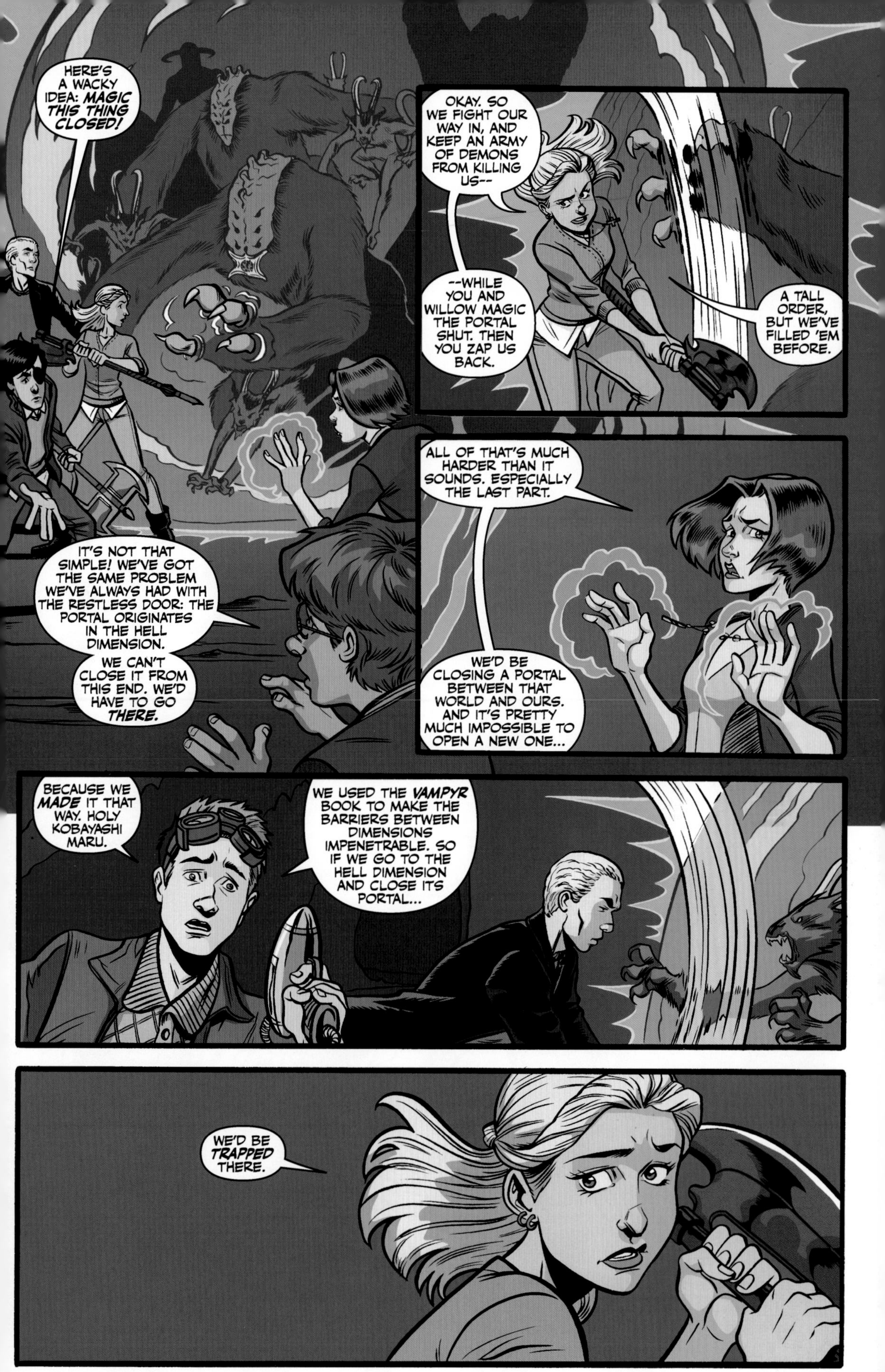
HERE'S A WACKY IDEA: *MAGIC THIS THING CLOSED!*
OKAY. SO WE FIGHT OUR WAY IN, AND KEEP AN ARMY OF DEMONS FROM KILLING US--
--WHILE YOU AND WILLOW MAGIC THE PORTAL SHUT. THEN YOU ZAP US BACK.
A TALL ORDER, BUT WE'VE FILLED 'EM BEFORE.
IT'S NOT THAT SIMPLE! WE'VE GOT THE SAME PROBLEM WE'VE ALWAYS HAD WITH THE RESTLESS DOOR: THE PORTAL ORIGINATES IN THE HELL DIMENSION.
WE CAN'T CLOSE IT FROM THIS END. WE'D HAVE TO GO *THERE.*
ALL OF THAT'S MUCH HARDER THAN IT SOUNDS. ESPECIALLY THE LAST PART.
WE'D BE CLOSING A PORTAL BETWEEN THAT WORLD AND OURS. AND IT'S PRETTY MUCH IMPOSSIBLE TO OPEN A NEW ONE...
BECAUSE WE *MADE* IT THAT WAY. HOLY KOBAYASHI MARU.
WE USED THE *VAMPYR* BOOK TO MAKE THE BARRIERS BETWEEN DIMENSIONS IMPENETRABLE. SO IF WE GO TO THE HELL DIMENSION AND CLOSE ITS PORTAL...
WE'D BE *TRAPPED* THERE.

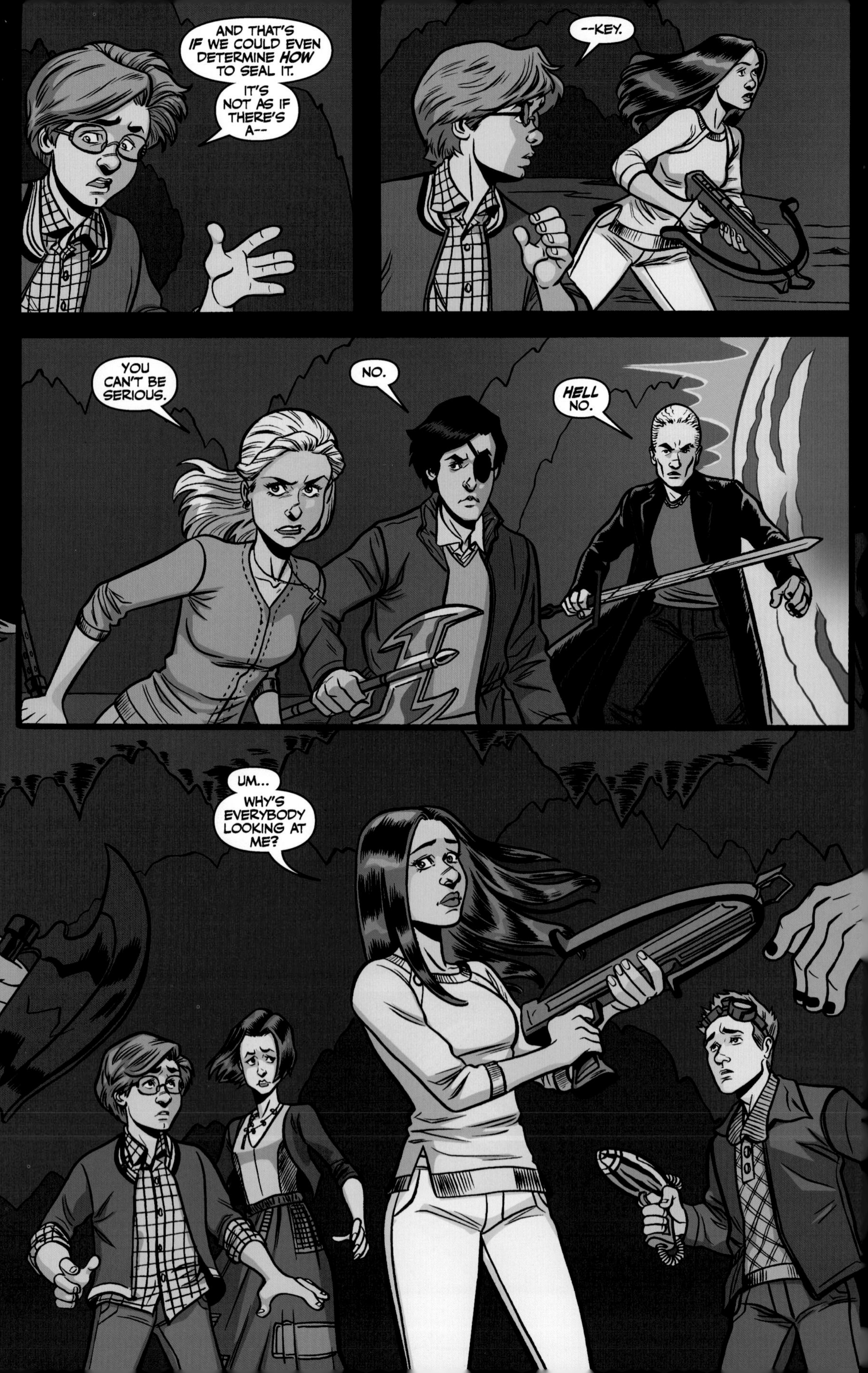

AND THAT'S *IF* WE COULD EVEN DETERMINE *HOW* TO SEAL IT.
IT'S NOT AS IF THERE'S A--
--KEY.
YOU CAN'T BE SERIOUS.
NO.
HELL NO.
UM... WHY'S EVERYBODY LOOKING AT ME?

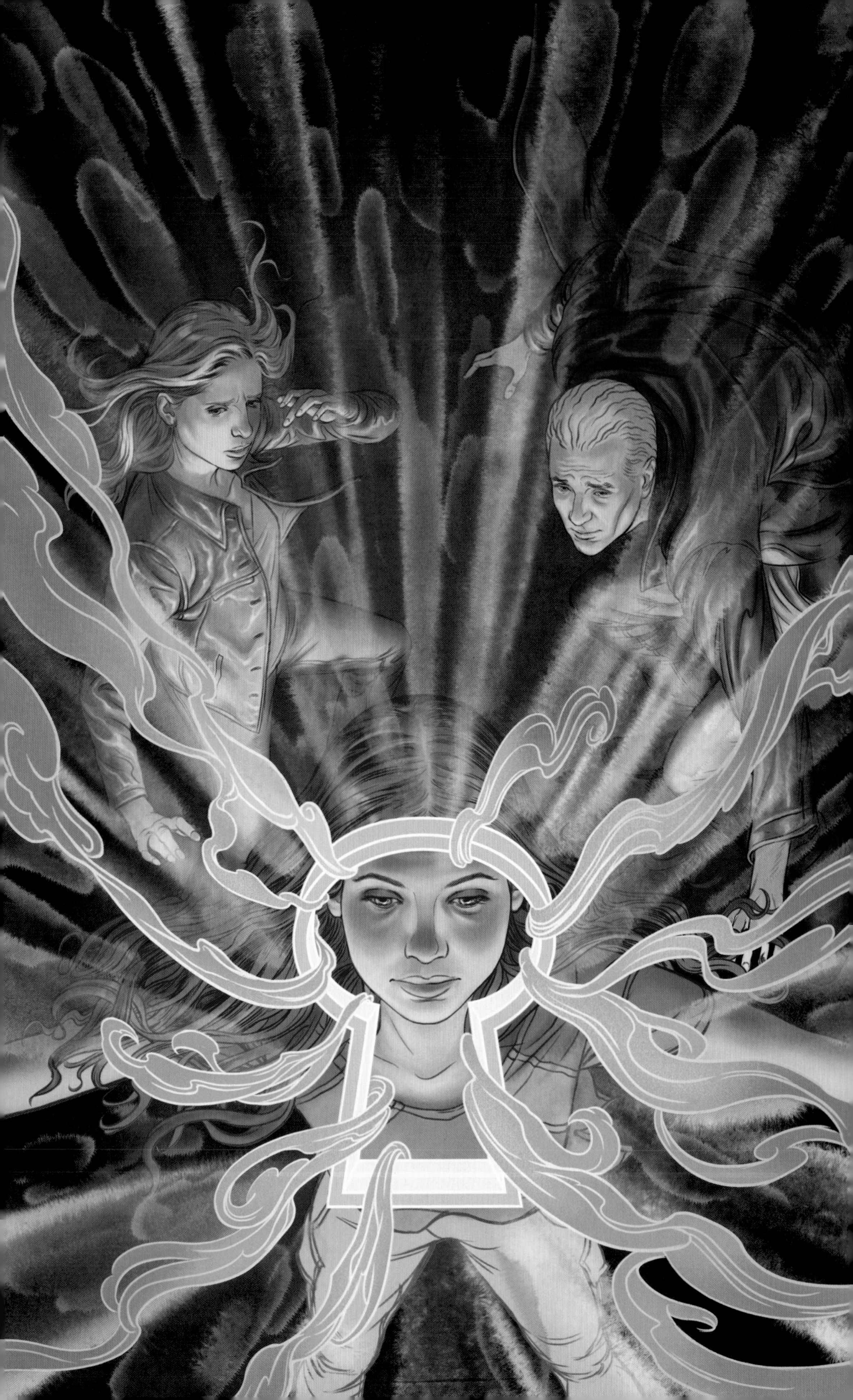

I KEEP FORGETTING I'M NOT A REAL PERSON.

I'M *THE KEY*. A HUNK OF MAGIC ENERGY A BUNCH OF MONKS PUT IN A HUMAN BODY. OPENING AND CLOSING PORTALS IS WHAT I DO...

...I THINK.

DAWN, YOU *ARE* A REAL PERSON. I DON'T CARE WHAT YOU USED TO BE. YOU'RE MY *SISTER*.

AND THERE IS NO WAY I'M LETTING YOU ANYWHERE NEAR *THAT*.

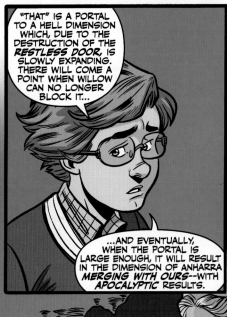

"THAT" IS A PORTAL TO A HELL DIMENSION WHICH, DUE TO THE DESTRUCTION OF THE *RESTLESS DOOR*, IS SLOWLY EXPANDING. THERE WILL COME A POINT WHEN WILLOW CAN NO LONGER BLOCK IT...

...AND EVENTUALLY, WHEN THE PORTAL IS LARGE ENOUGH, IT WILL RESULT IN THE DIMENSION OF ANHARRA *MERGING WITH OURS*--WITH *APOCALYPTIC* RESULTS.

WE MUST PREVENT IT. AND OUR OPTIONS ARE DOWN TO...WELL, *ONE*.

EVEN IF DAWN COULD CLOSE THE PORTAL FROM THE OTHER SIDE, THOSE DEMONS WOULD REND HER TO BITS BEFORE SHE GOT THE CHANCE! WE CAN'T PROTECT HER FROM SO MANY.

...BUT SHE COULDN'T COME BACK.

ACTUALLY, I'M QUITE CONFIDENT THAT, IN AN ENTIRELY MAGIC-BASED REALITY, DAWN WOULD HAVE ACCESS TO HER FULL POWER. SHE'D BE VIRTUALLY *GODLIKE*. NOTHING COULD HURT HER...

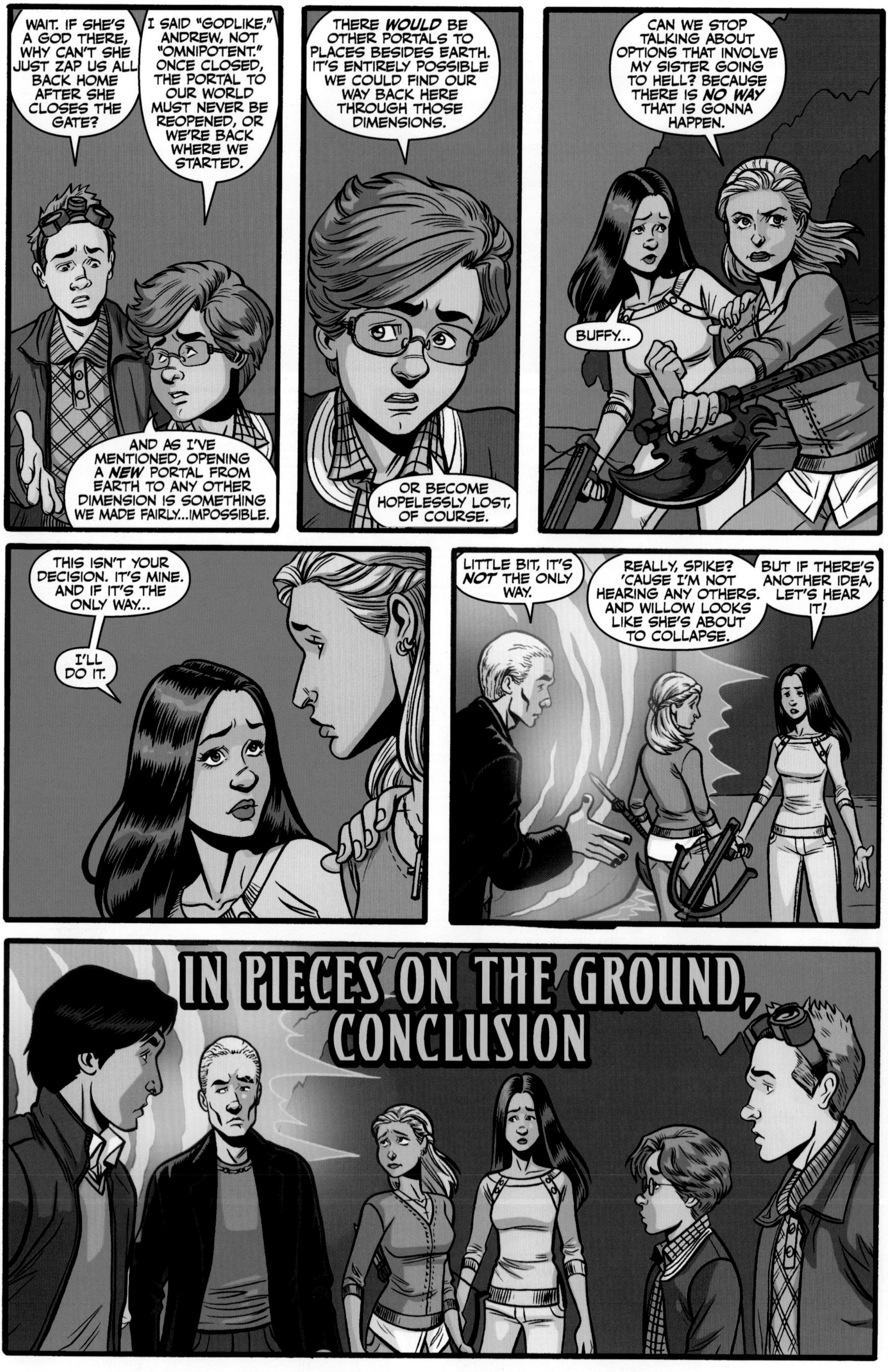
WAIT. IF SHE'S A GOD THERE, WHY CAN'T SHE JUST ZAP US ALL BACK HOME AFTER SHE CLOSES THE GATE?
I SAID "GODLIKE," ANDREW, NOT "OMNIPOTENT." ONCE CLOSED, THE PORTAL TO OUR WORLD MUST NEVER BE REOPENED, OR WE'RE BACK WHERE WE STARTED.
AND AS I'VE MENTIONED, OPENING A *NEW* PORTAL FROM EARTH TO ANY OTHER DIMENSION IS SOMETHING WE MADE FAIRLY...IMPOSSIBLE.
THERE *WOULD* BE OTHER PORTALS TO PLACES BESIDES EARTH. IT'S ENTIRELY POSSIBLE WE COULD FIND OUR WAY BACK HERE THROUGH THOSE DIMENSIONS.
OR BECOME HOPELESSLY LOST, OF COURSE.
CAN WE STOP TALKING ABOUT OPTIONS THAT INVOLVE MY SISTER GOING TO HELL? BECAUSE THERE IS *NO WAY* THAT IS GONNA HAPPEN.
BUFFY...
THIS ISN'T YOUR DECISION. IT'S MINE. AND IF IT'S THE ONLY WAY...
I'LL DO IT.
LITTLE BIT, IT'S *NOT* THE ONLY WAY.
REALLY, SPIKE? 'CAUSE I'M NOT HEARING ANY OTHERS. AND WILLOW LOOKS LIKE SHE'S ABOUT TO COLLAPSE.
BUT IF THERE'S ANOTHER IDEA, LET'S HEAR IT!
IN PIECES ON THE GROUND, CONCLUSION

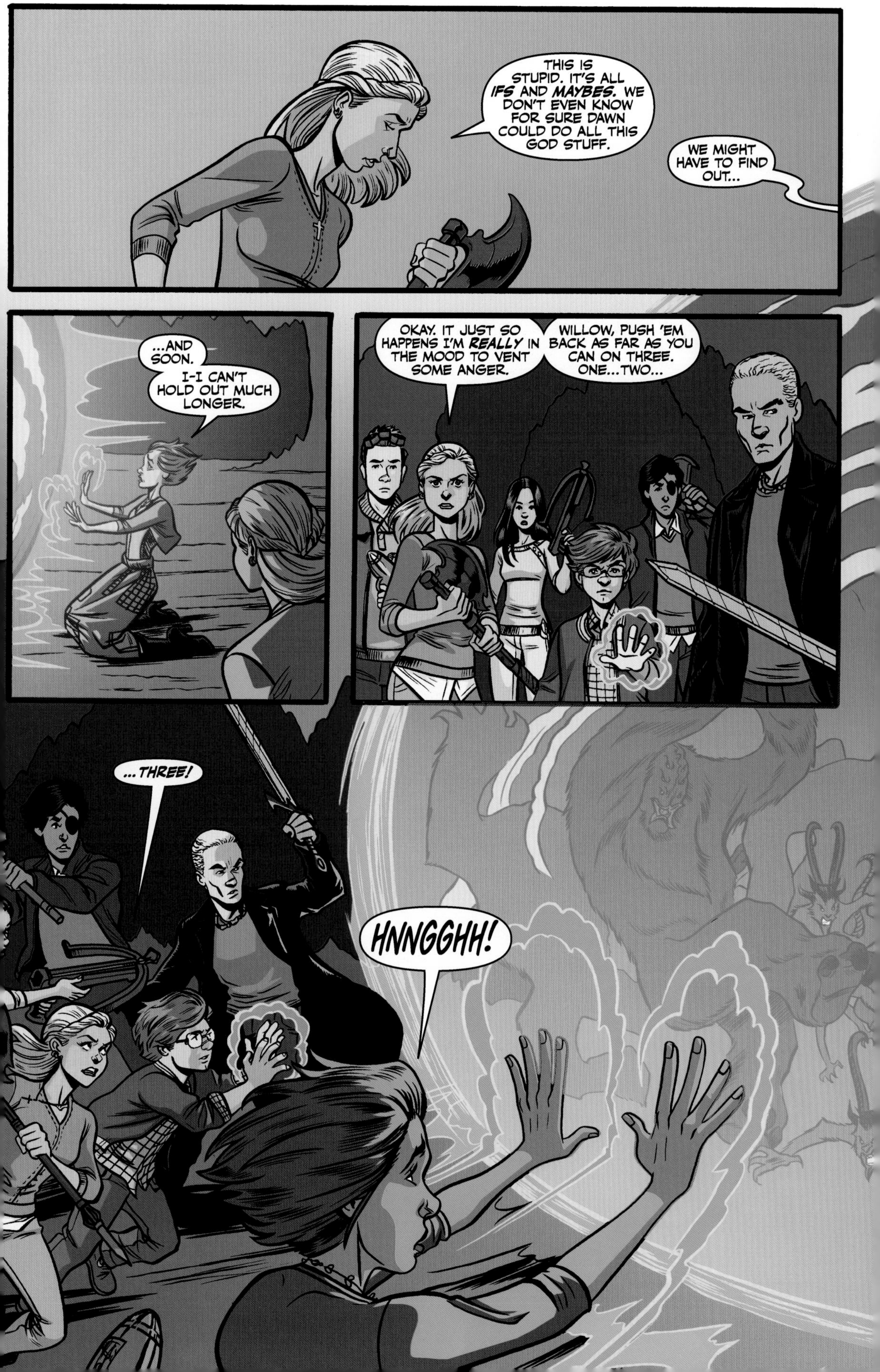
THIS IS STUPID. IT'S ALL *IFS* AND *MAYBES.* WE DON'T EVEN KNOW FOR SURE DAWN COULD DO ALL THIS GOD STUFF.
WE MIGHT HAVE TO FIND OUT...
...AND SOON.
I-I CAN'T HOLD OUT MUCH LONGER.
OKAY. IT JUST SO HAPPENS I'M *REALLY* IN THE MOOD TO VENT SOME ANGER.
WILLOW, PUSH 'EM BACK AS FAR AS YOU CAN ON THREE. ONE...TWO...
...THREE!
HNNGGHH!

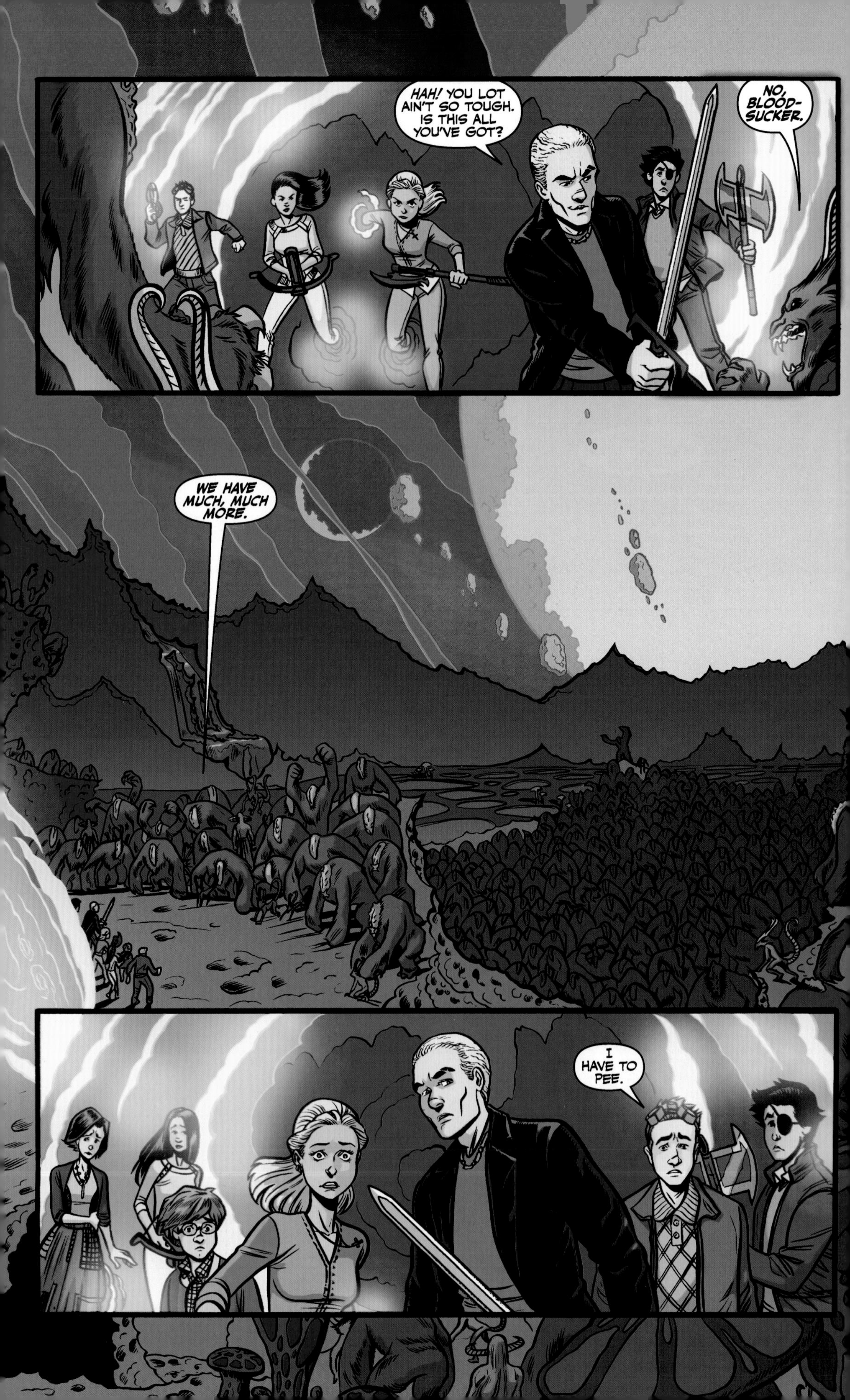
HAH! YOU LOT AIN'T SO TOUGH. IS THIS ALL YOU'VE GOT?
NO, BLOOD-SUCKER.
WE HAVE MUCH, MUCH MORE.
I HAVE TO PEE.

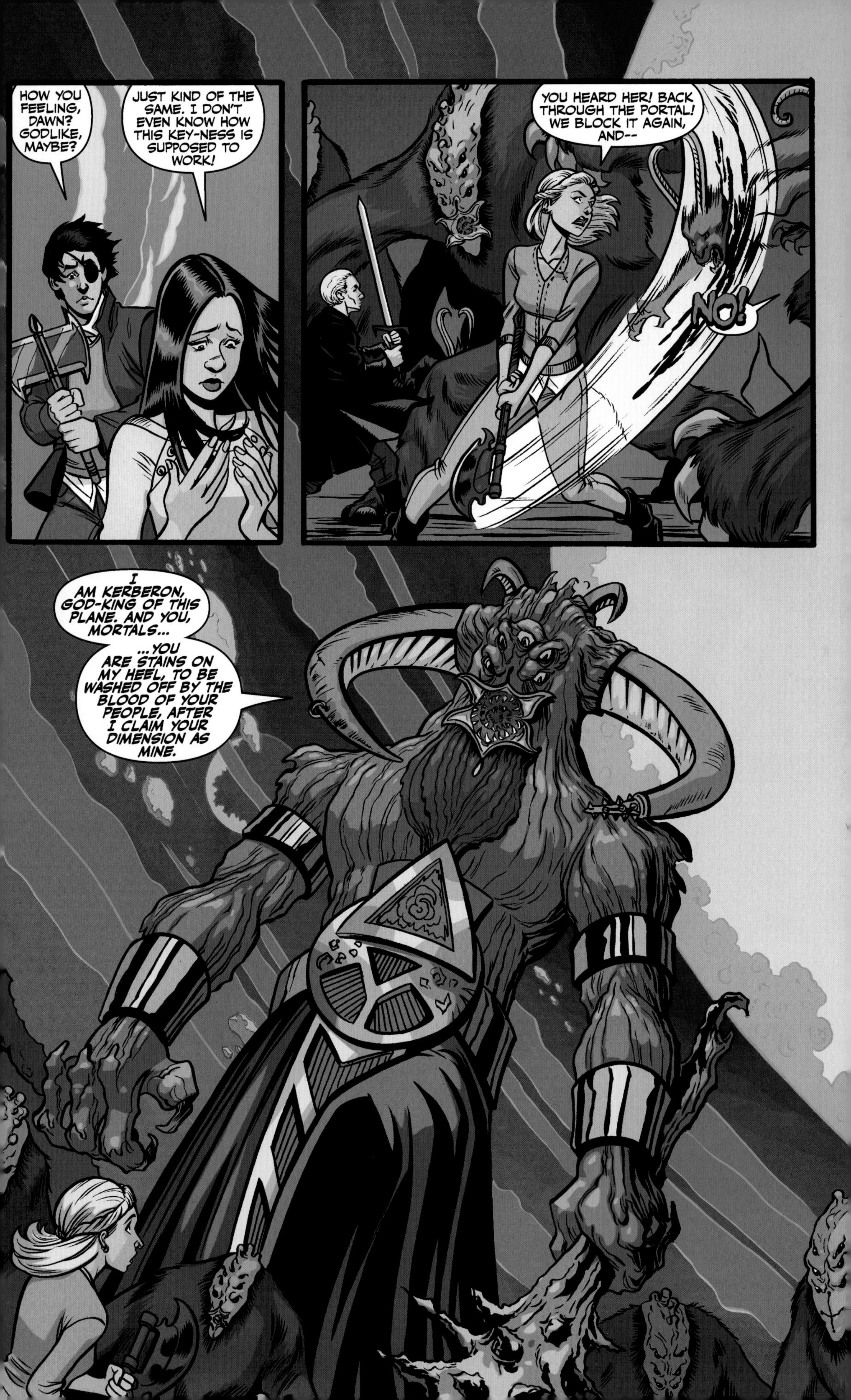
HOW YOU FEELING, DAWN? GODLIKE, MAYBE?
JUST KIND OF THE SAME. I DON'T EVEN KNOW HOW THIS KEY-NESS IS SUPPOSED TO WORK!
YOU HEARD HER! BACK THROUGH THE PORTAL! WE BLOCK IT AGAIN, AND--
NO!
I AM KERBERON, GOD-KING OF THIS PLANE. AND YOU, MORTALS...
...YOU ARE STAINS ON MY HEEL, TO BE WASHED OFF BY THE BLOOD OF YOUR PEOPLE, AFTER I CLAIM YOUR DIMENSION AS MINE.

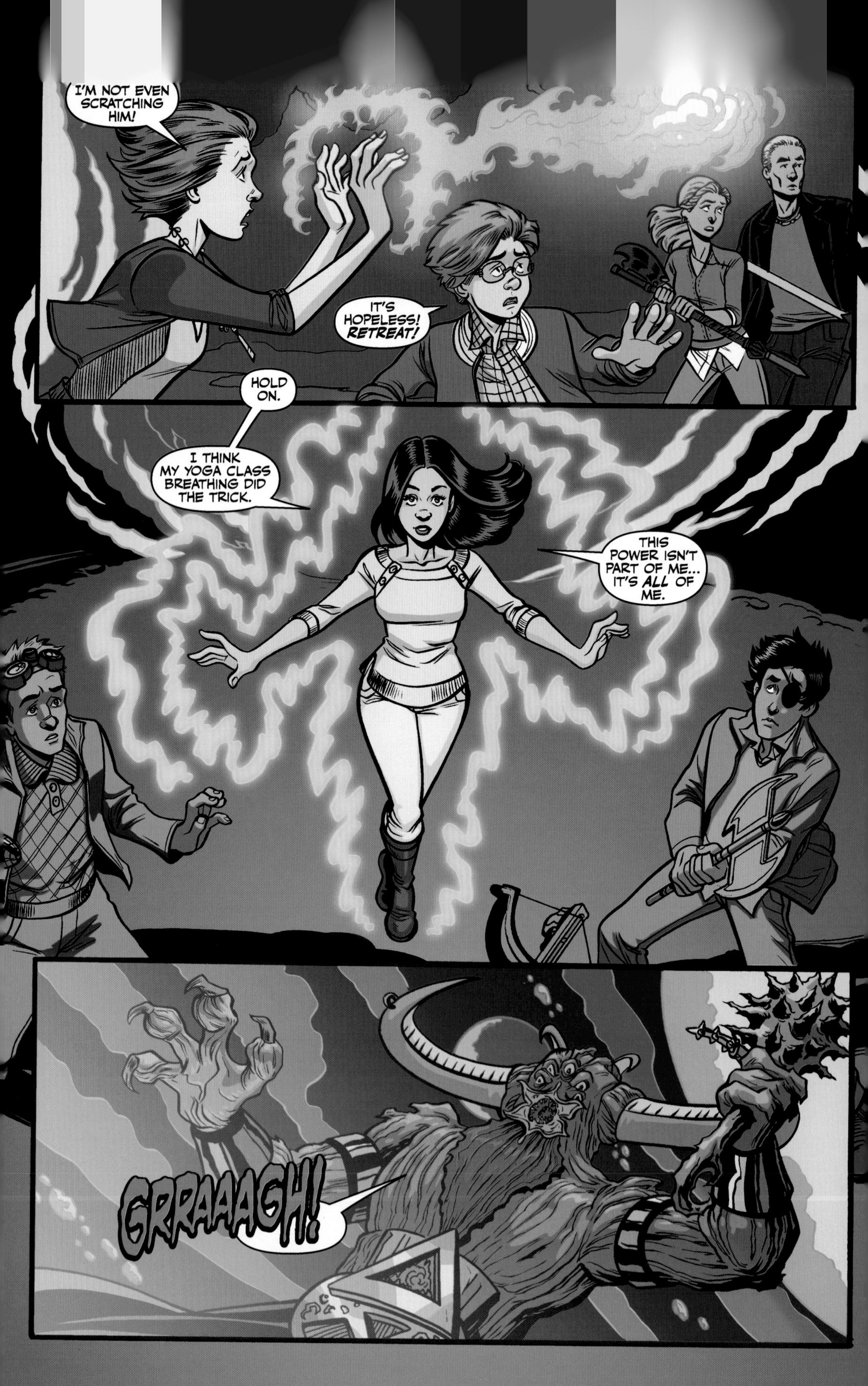
I'M NOT EVEN SCRATCHING HIM!
IT'S HOPELESS! RETREAT!
HOLD ON.
I THINK MY YOGA CLASS BREATHING DID THE TRICK.
THIS POWER ISN'T PART OF ME... IT'S ALL OF ME.
GRRAAAGH!

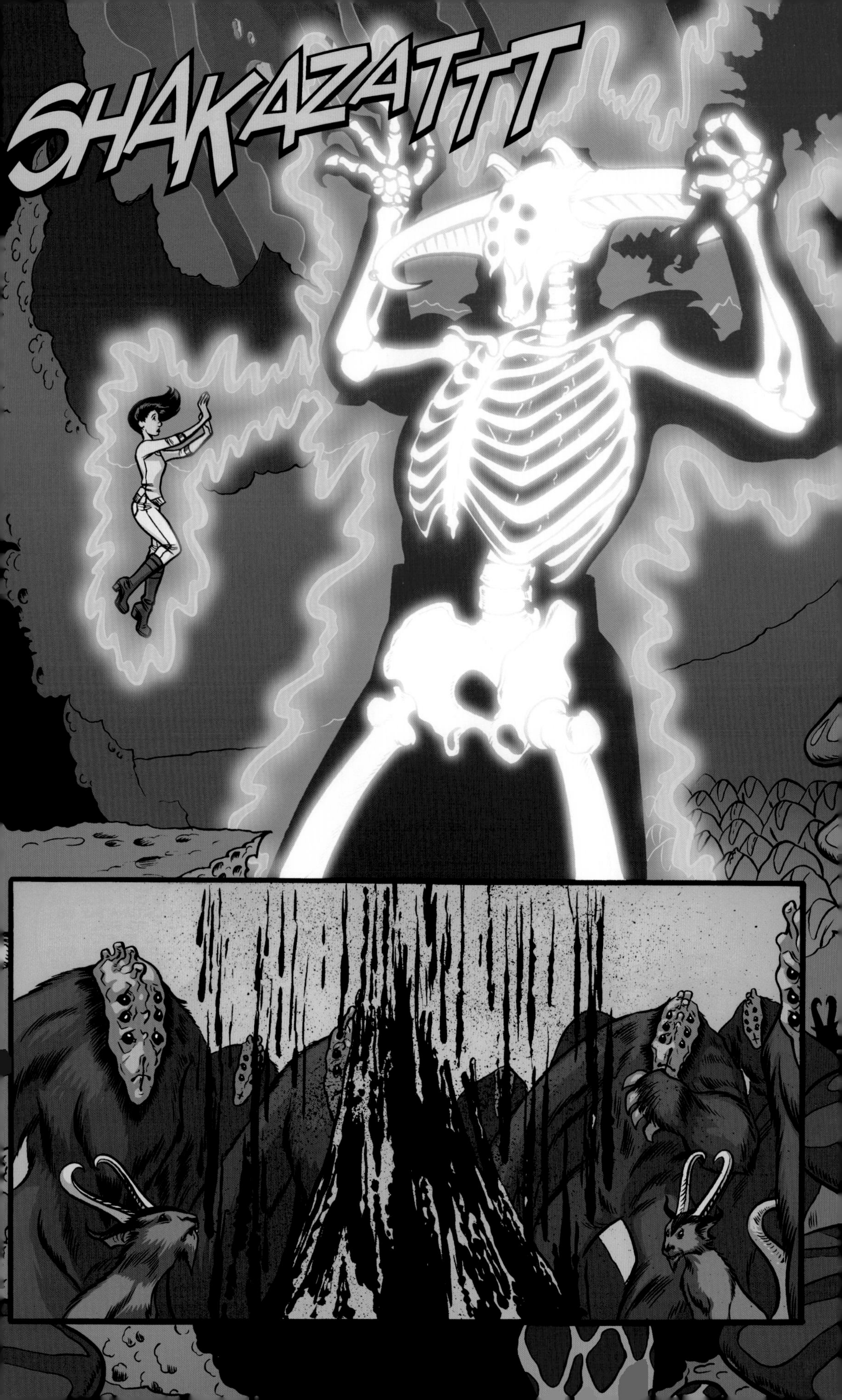
SHAKAZATTT

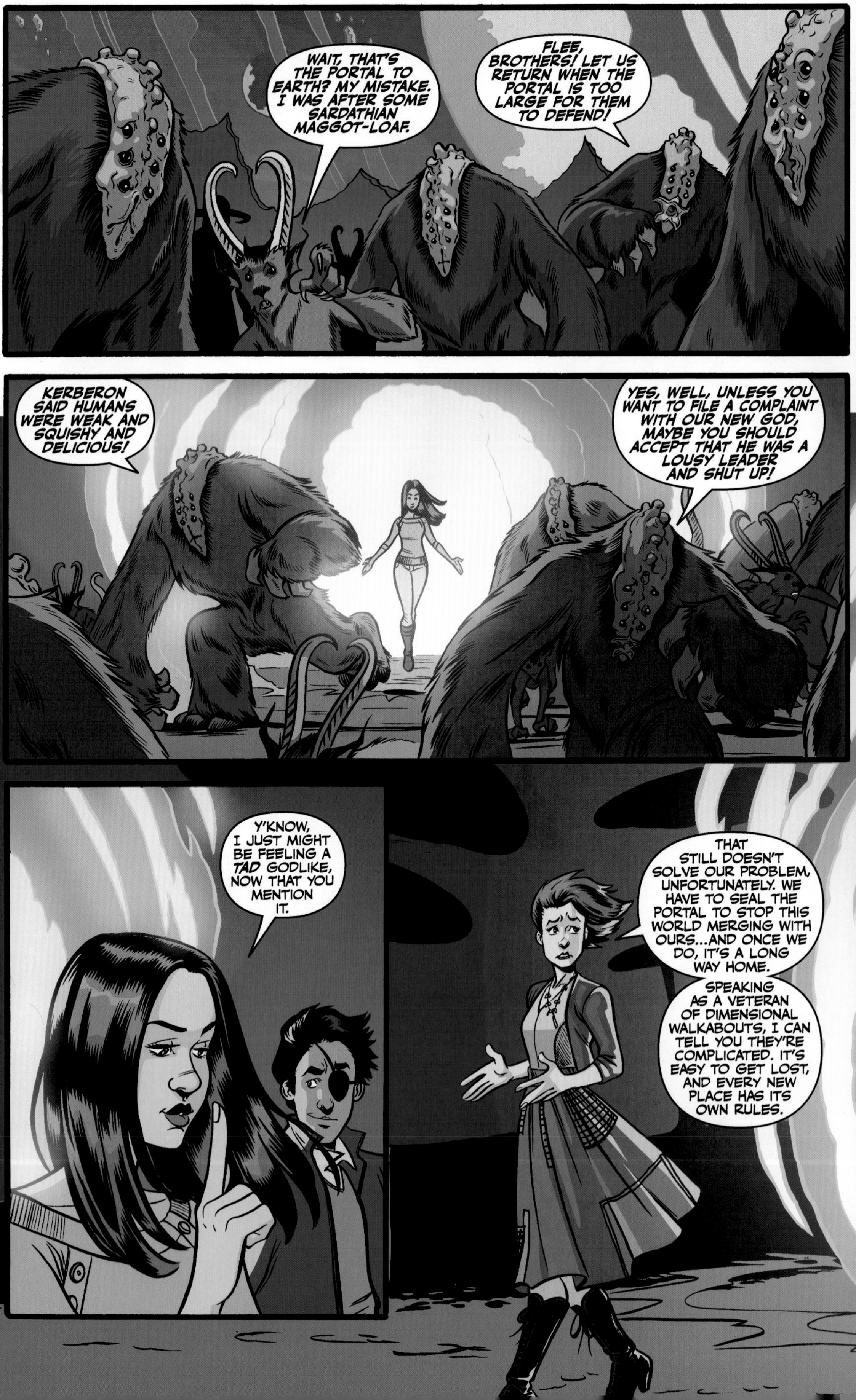
WAIT, THAT'S THE PORTAL TO EARTH? MY MISTAKE. I WAS AFTER SOME SARDATHIAN MAGGOT-LOAF.
FLEE, BROTHERS! LET US RETURN WHEN THE PORTAL IS TOO LARGE FOR THEM TO DEFEND!
KERBERON SAID HUMANS WERE WEAK AND SQUISHY AND DELICIOUS!
YES, WELL, UNLESS YOU WANT TO FILE A COMPLAINT WITH OUR NEW GOD, MAYBE YOU SHOULD ACCEPT THAT HE WAS A LOUSY LEADER AND SHUT UP!
Y'KNOW, I JUST MIGHT BE FEELING A *TAD* GODLIKE, NOW THAT YOU MENTION IT.
THAT STILL DOESN'T SOLVE OUR PROBLEM, UNFORTUNATELY. WE HAVE TO SEAL THE PORTAL TO STOP THIS WORLD MERGING WITH OURS...AND ONCE WE DO, IT'S A LONG WAY HOME.
SPEAKING AS A VETERAN OF DIMENSIONAL WALKABOUTS, I CAN TELL YOU THEY'RE COMPLICATED. IT'S EASY TO GET LOST, AND EVERY NEW PLACE HAS ITS OWN RULES.

I'M ALL FOR A BETTER ALTERNATIVE, BUT SO FAR I HAVEN'T HEARD ONE. WE DON'T HAVE A CHOICE. WE SEAL THE PORTAL, THEN FIND OUR WAY HOME VIA THE SCENIC ROUTE.

WE DON'T *ALL* HAVE TO STAY, THOUGH. ANDREW, XANDER, YOU GUYS CAN HEAD BACK. NO OFFENSE.

I FEEL LIKE I SHOULD PROTEST, BUT I'M RELIEVED. IT TAKES FOREVER TO GET THAT OTHER-DIMENSION SMELL OUT OF MY CLOTHES.

IN POINT OF FACT, BUFFY, *YOU'RE* THE ONE MOST NEEDED ON EARTH.

THE *MISTRESS* AND THE *SOUL GLUTTON* ESCAPED. THEY'RE DESPERATE. THEY'LL MAKE A BID TO RETAIN THEIR POWER AND POSITION.

SO? D'HOFFRYN AND THE MAGIC COUNCIL CAN HANDLE THEM.

I DON'T KNOW THAT THEY CAN. OUR ENEMIES HAVE SPENT MONTHS BRINGING DEMONS TO EARTH, MANY COVERTLY.

THESE DEMONS NOW OWE THEM A DEBT THEY'RE SURE TO CALL IN. THE COUNCIL'S BARELY BEEN ABLE TO KEEP UP WITH THE ONSLAUGHT THUS FAR. AN INCREASE IN HOSTILITIES WILL REQUIRE ALL HANDS ON DECK.

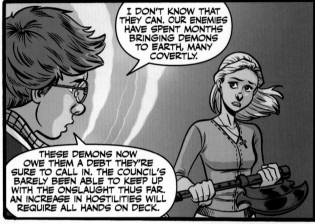

AND WHEN THE SOUL GLUTTON HAS FED WELL, HE BECOMES INCREDIBLY POWERFUL. YOUR SCYTHE IS THE ONLY WEAPON THAT HAS SHOWN AN ABILITY TO TRULY HURT HIM IN THAT STATE.

YOU'RE ASKING ME TO LEAVE DAWN HERE?

IT TURNS MY STOMACH EVEN SAYING IT. BUT YOU SAW WHAT SHE'S CAPABLE OF. SHE'S IN NO DANGER.

DAWN, PLEASE KNOW I WOULD NOT EVEN SUGGEST IT IF INNOCENT LIVES DID NOT HANG IN THE BALANCE.

BUT, OBJECTIVELY SPEAKING, THE WISEST COURSE IS FOR YOU TO REMAIN HERE WHILE WE RETURN TO EARTH AND DEAL WITH THE MORE PRESSING THREAT.

THE MOMENT THAT IS RESOLVED, WE WILL FIND OUR WAY TO YOU AND BRING YOU HOME.

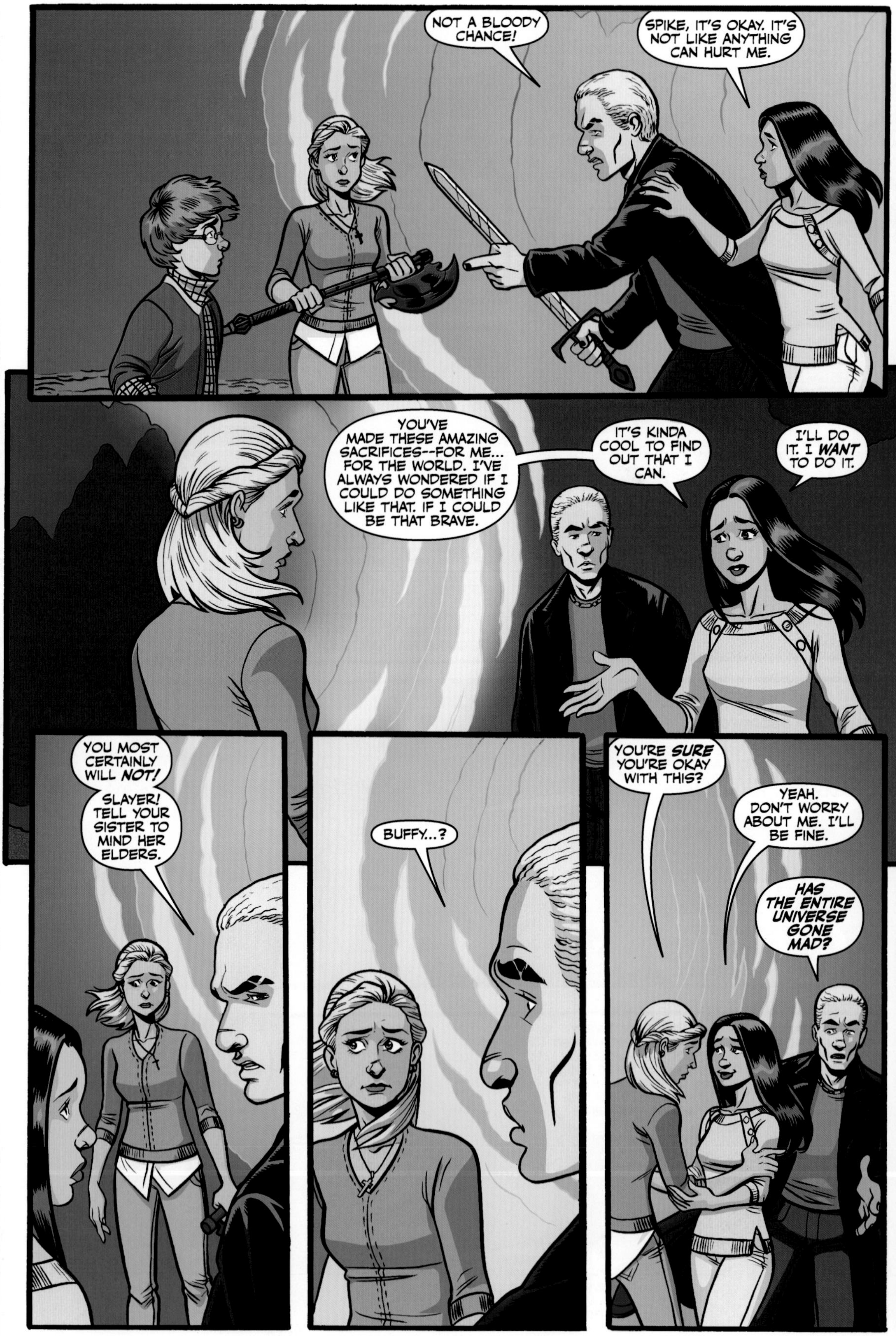
NOT A BLOODY CHANCE!
SPIKE, IT'S OKAY. IT'S NOT LIKE ANYTHING CAN HURT ME.
YOU'VE MADE THESE AMAZING SACRIFICES--FOR ME... FOR THE WORLD. I'VE ALWAYS WONDERED IF I COULD DO SOMETHING LIKE THAT. IF I COULD BE THAT BRAVE.
IT'S KINDA COOL TO FIND OUT THAT I CAN.
I'LL DO IT. I WANT TO DO IT.
YOU MOST CERTAINLY WILL NOT!
SLAYER! TELL YOUR SISTER TO MIND HER ELDERS.
BUFFY...?
YOU'RE SURE YOU'RE OKAY WITH THIS?
YEAH. DON'T WORRY ABOUT ME. I'LL BE FINE.
HAS THE ENTIRE UNIVERSE GONE MAD?

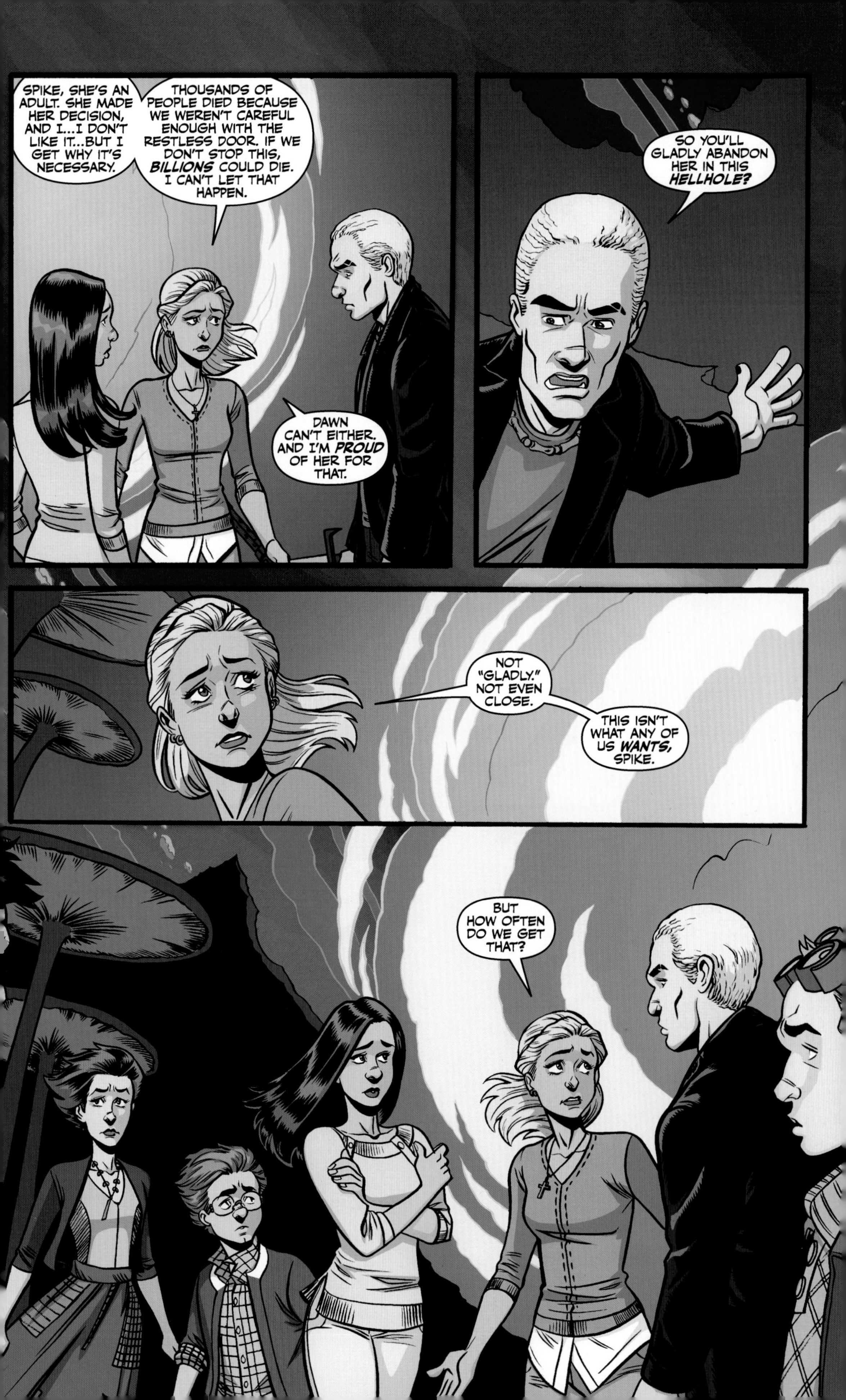
SPIKE, SHE'S AN ADULT. SHE MADE HER DECISION, AND I...I DON'T LIKE IT...BUT I GET WHY IT'S NECESSARY.
THOUSANDS OF PEOPLE DIED BECAUSE WE WEREN'T CAREFUL ENOUGH WITH THE RESTLESS DOOR. IF WE DON'T STOP THIS, BILLIONS COULD DIE. I CAN'T LET THAT HAPPEN.
DAWN CAN'T EITHER. AND I'M PROUD OF HER FOR THAT.
SO YOU'LL GLADLY ABANDON HER IN THIS HELLHOLE?
NOT "GLADLY." NOT EVEN CLOSE.
THIS ISN'T WHAT ANY OF US WANTS, SPIKE.
BUT HOW OFTEN DO WE GET THAT?

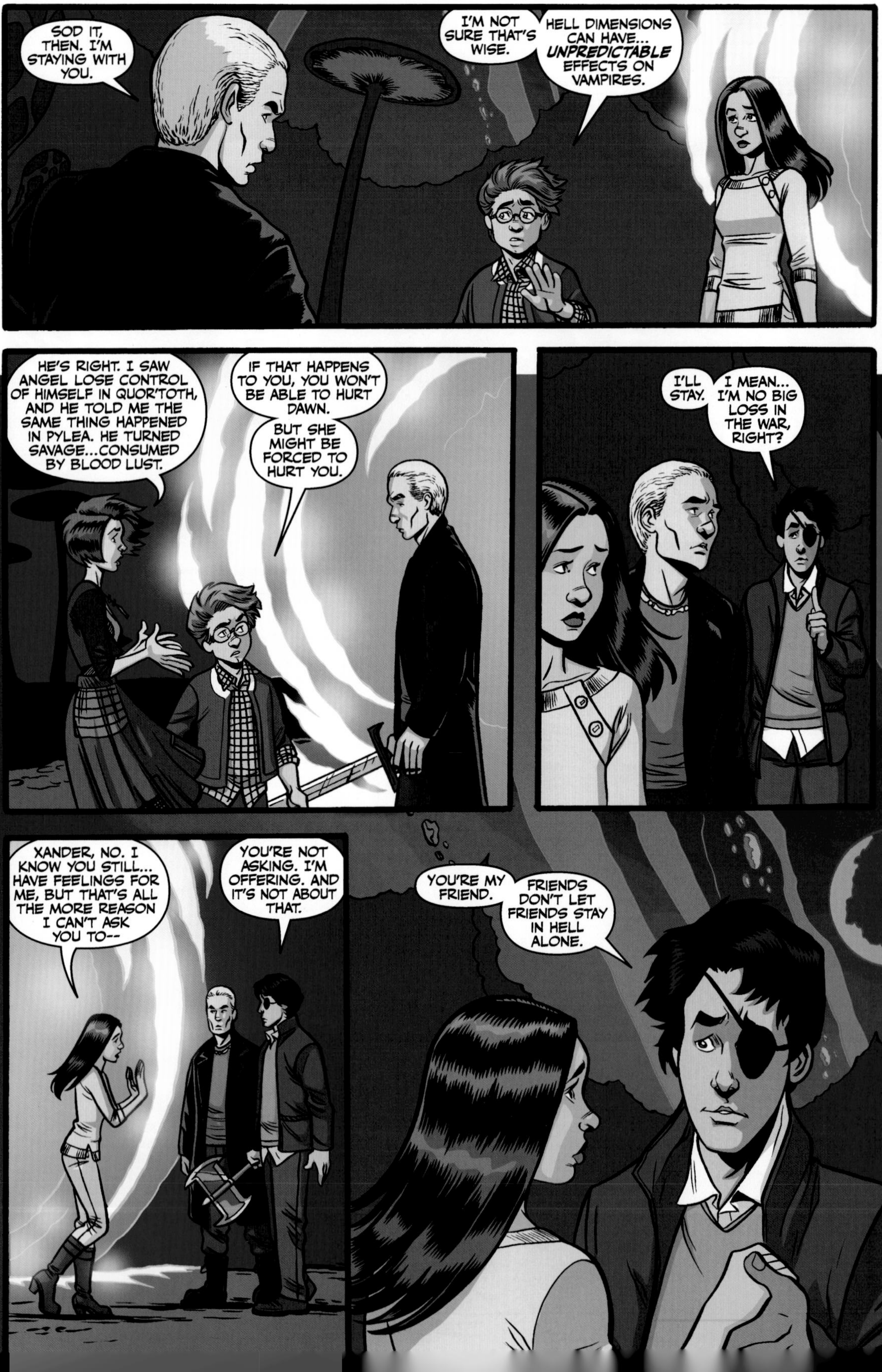
SOD IT, THEN. I'M STAYING WITH YOU.
I'M NOT SURE THAT'S WISE.
HELL DIMENSIONS CAN HAVE... *UNPREDICTABLE* EFFECTS ON VAMPIRES.
HE'S RIGHT. I SAW ANGEL LOSE CONTROL OF HIMSELF IN QUOR'TOTH, AND HE TOLD ME THE SAME THING HAPPENED IN PYLEA. HE TURNED SAVAGE...CONSUMED BY BLOOD LUST.
IF THAT HAPPENS TO YOU, YOU WON'T BE ABLE TO HURT DAWN.
BUT SHE MIGHT BE FORCED TO HURT YOU.
I'LL STAY.
I MEAN... I'M NO BIG LOSS IN THE WAR, RIGHT?
XANDER, NO. I KNOW YOU STILL... HAVE FEELINGS FOR ME, BUT THAT'S ALL THE MORE REASON I CAN'T ASK YOU TO--
YOU'RE NOT ASKING. I'M OFFERING. AND IT'S NOT ABOUT THAT.
YOU'RE MY FRIEND.
FRIENDS DON'T LET FRIENDS STAY IN HELL ALONE.

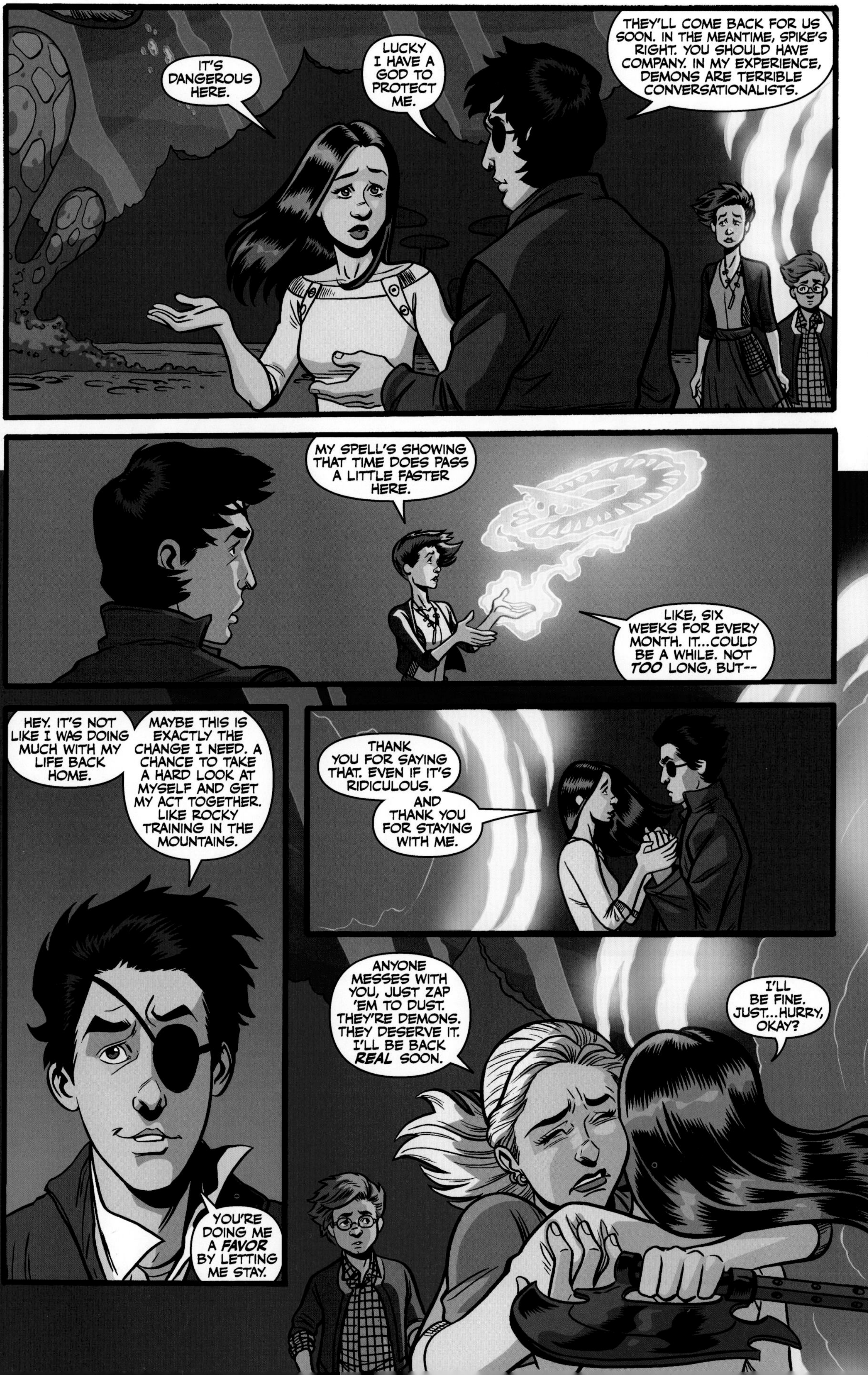
IT'S DANGEROUS HERE.
LUCKY I HAVE A GOD TO PROTECT ME.
THEY'LL COME BACK FOR US SOON. IN THE MEANTIME, SPIKE'S RIGHT. YOU SHOULD HAVE COMPANY. IN MY EXPERIENCE, DEMONS ARE TERRIBLE CONVERSATIONALISTS.
MY SPELL'S SHOWING THAT TIME DOES PASS A LITTLE FASTER HERE.
LIKE, SIX WEEKS FOR EVERY MONTH. IT...COULD BE A WHILE. NOT *TOO* LONG, BUT--
HEY. IT'S NOT LIKE I WAS DOING MUCH WITH MY LIFE BACK HOME.
MAYBE THIS IS EXACTLY THE CHANGE I NEED. A CHANCE TO TAKE A HARD LOOK AT MYSELF AND GET MY ACT TOGETHER. LIKE ROCKY TRAINING IN THE MOUNTAINS.
YOU'RE DOING ME A **FAVOR** BY LETTING ME STAY.
THANK YOU FOR SAYING THAT. EVEN IF IT'S RIDICULOUS.
AND THANK YOU FOR STAYING WITH ME.
ANYONE MESSES WITH YOU, JUST ZAP 'EM TO DUST. THEY'RE DEMONS. THEY DESERVE IT. I'LL BE BACK **REAL** SOON.
I'LL BE FINE. JUST...HURRY, OKAY?

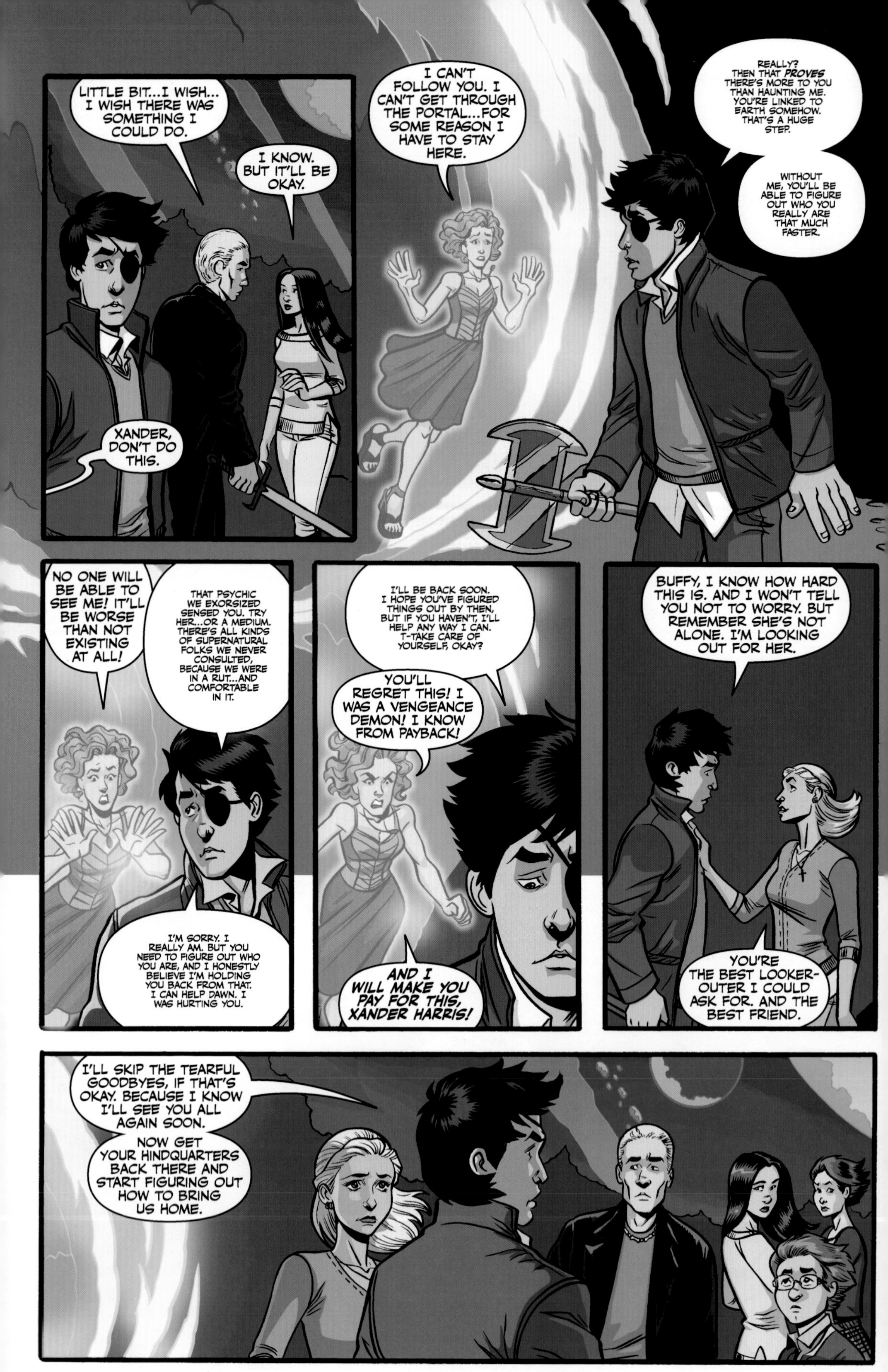
LITTLE BIT...I WISH... I WISH THERE WAS SOMETHING I COULD DO.
I KNOW. BUT IT'LL BE OKAY.
XANDER, DON'T DO THIS.
I CAN'T FOLLOW YOU. I CAN'T GET THROUGH THE PORTAL...FOR SOME REASON I HAVE TO STAY HERE.
REALLY? THEN THAT PROVES THERE'S MORE TO YOU THAN HAUNTING ME. YOU'RE LINKED TO EARTH SOMEHOW. THAT'S A HUGE STEP.
WITHOUT ME, YOU'LL BE ABLE TO FIGURE OUT WHO YOU REALLY ARE THAT MUCH FASTER.
NO ONE WILL BE ABLE TO SEE ME! IT'LL BE WORSE THAN NOT EXISTING AT ALL!
THAT PSYCHIC WE EXORZIZED SENSED YOU. TRY HER...OR A MEDIUM. THERE'S ALL KINDS OF SUPERNATURAL FOLKS WE NEVER CONSULTED, BECAUSE WE WERE IN A RUT...AND COMFORTABLE IN IT.
I'M SORRY. I REALLY AM. BUT YOU NEED TO FIGURE OUT WHO YOU ARE, AND I HONESTLY BELIEVE I'M HOLDING YOU BACK FROM THAT. I CAN HELP DAWN. I WAS HURTING YOU.
I'LL BE BACK SOON. I HOPE YOU'VE FIGURED THINGS OUT BY THEN, BUT IF YOU HAVEN'T, I'LL HELP ANY WAY I CAN. T-TAKE CARE OF YOURSELF, OKAY?
YOU'LL REGRET THIS! I WAS A VENGEANCE DEMON! I KNOW FROM PAYBACK!
AND I WILL MAKE YOU PAY FOR THIS, XANDER HARRIS!
BUFFY, I KNOW HOW HARD THIS IS. AND I WON'T TELL YOU NOT TO WORRY. BUT REMEMBER SHE'S NOT ALONE. I'M LOOKING OUT FOR HER.
YOU'RE THE BEST LOOKER-OUTER I COULD ASK FOR. AND THE BEST FRIEND.
I'LL SKIP THE TEARFUL GOODBYES, IF THAT'S OKAY. BECAUSE I KNOW I'LL SEE YOU ALL AGAIN SOON.
NOW GET YOUR HINDQUARTERS BACK THERE AND START FIGURING OUT HOW TO BRING US HOME.

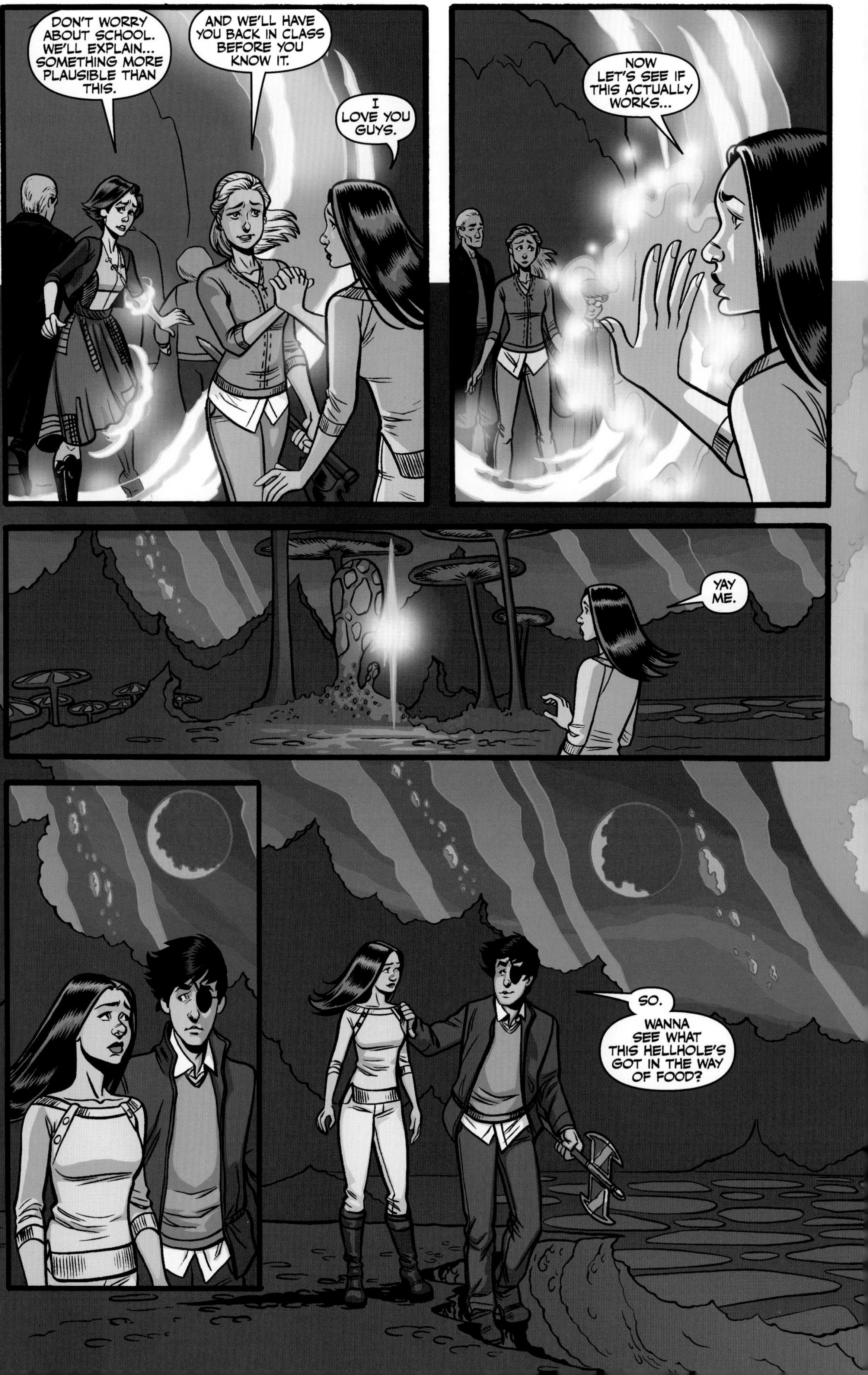
DON'T WORRY ABOUT SCHOOL. WE'LL EXPLAIN... SOMETHING MORE PLAUSIBLE THAN THIS.
AND WE'LL HAVE YOU BACK IN CLASS BEFORE YOU KNOW IT.
I LOVE YOU GUYS.
NOW LET'S SEE IF THIS ACTUALLY WORKS...
YAY ME.
SO.
WANNA SEE WHAT THIS HELLHOLE'S GOT IN THE WAY OF FOOD?

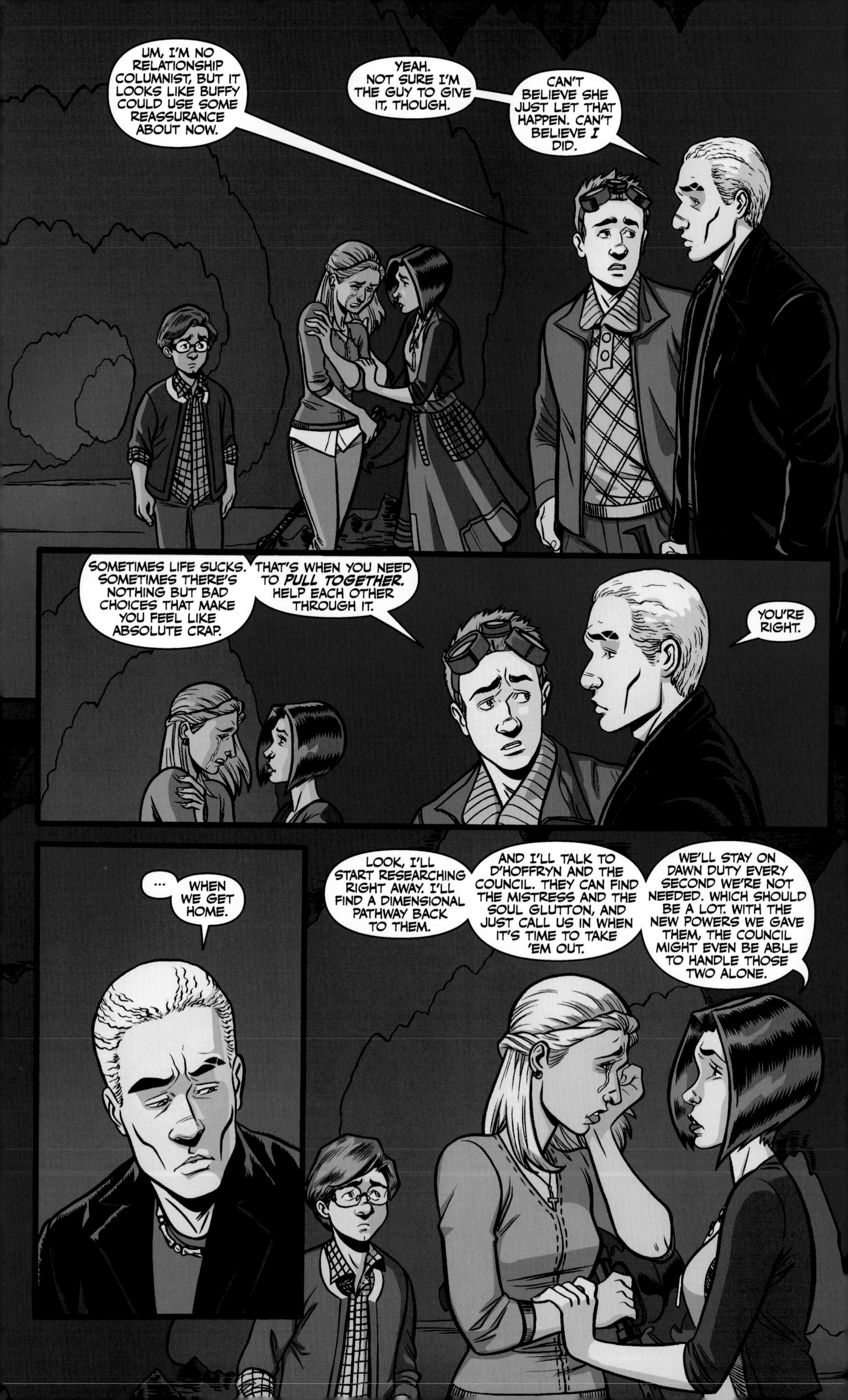
UM, I'M NO RELATIONSHIP COLUMNIST, BUT IT LOOKS LIKE BUFFY COULD USE SOME REASSURANCE ABOUT NOW.
YEAH. NOT SURE I'M THE GUY TO GIVE IT, THOUGH.
CAN'T BELIEVE SHE JUST LET THAT HAPPEN. CAN'T BELIEVE *I* DID.
SOMETIMES LIFE SUCKS. SOMETIMES THERE'S NOTHING BUT BAD CHOICES THAT MAKE YOU FEEL LIKE ABSOLUTE CRAP.
THAT'S WHEN YOU NEED TO ***PULL TOGETHER.*** HELP EACH OTHER THROUGH IT.
YOU'RE RIGHT.
...
WHEN WE GET HOME.
LOOK, I'LL START RESEARCHING RIGHT AWAY. I'LL FIND A DIMENSIONAL PATHWAY BACK TO THEM.
AND I'LL TALK TO D'HOFFRYN AND THE COUNCIL. THEY CAN FIND THE MISTRESS AND THE SOUL GLUTTON, AND JUST CALL US IN WHEN IT'S TIME TO TAKE 'EM OUT.
WE'LL STAY ON DAWN DUTY EVERY SECOND WE'RE NOT NEEDED. WHICH SHOULD BE A LOT. WITH THE NEW POWERS WE GAVE THEM, THE COUNCIL MIGHT EVEN BE ABLE TO HANDLE THOSE TWO ALONE.

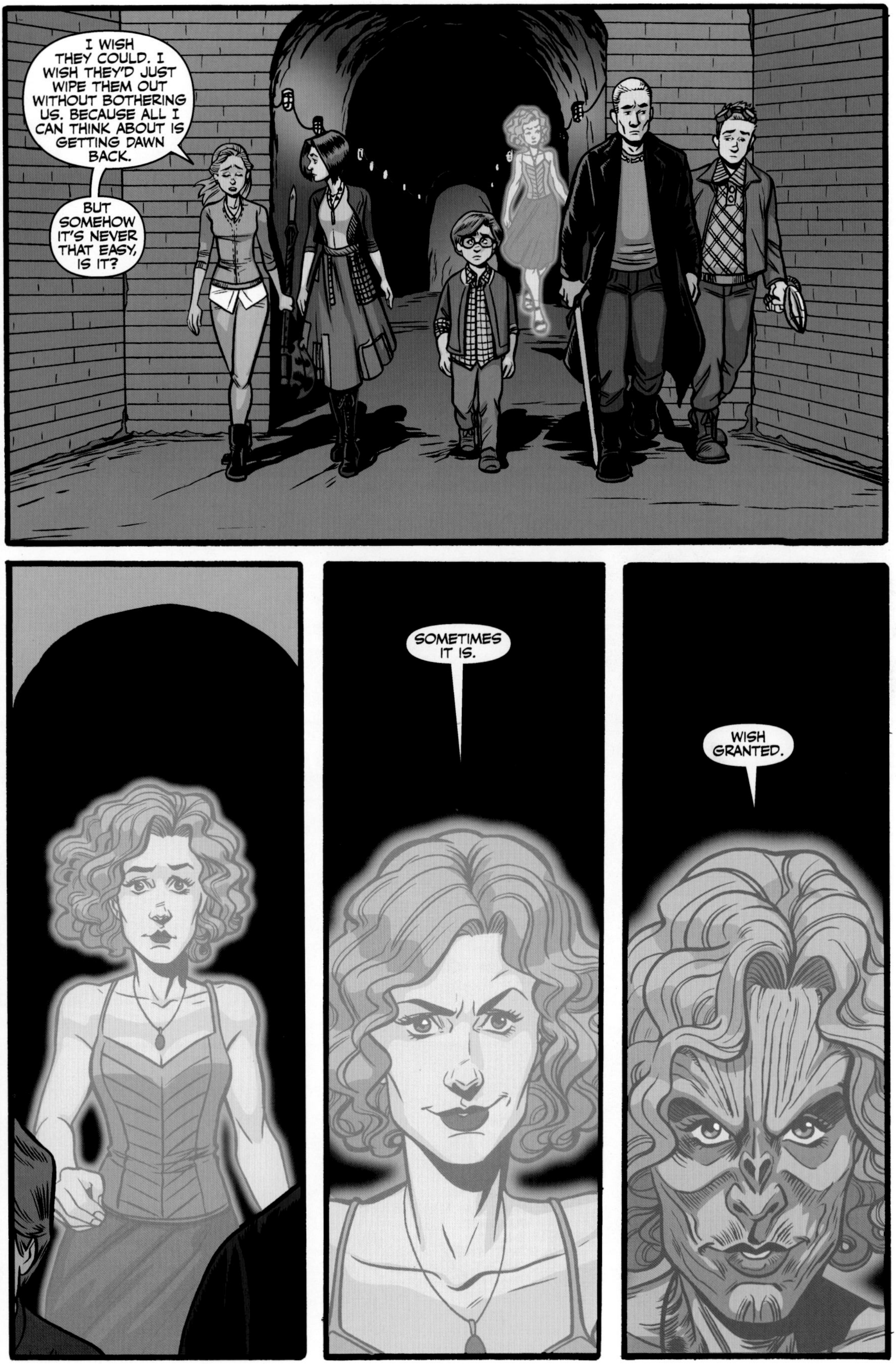
I WISH THEY COULD. I WISH THEY'D JUST WIPE THEM OUT WITHOUT BOTHERING US. BECAUSE ALL I CAN THINK ABOUT IS GETTING DAWN BACK.
BUT SOMEHOW IT'S NEVER THAT EASY, IS IT?
SOMETIMES IT IS.
WISH GRANTED.

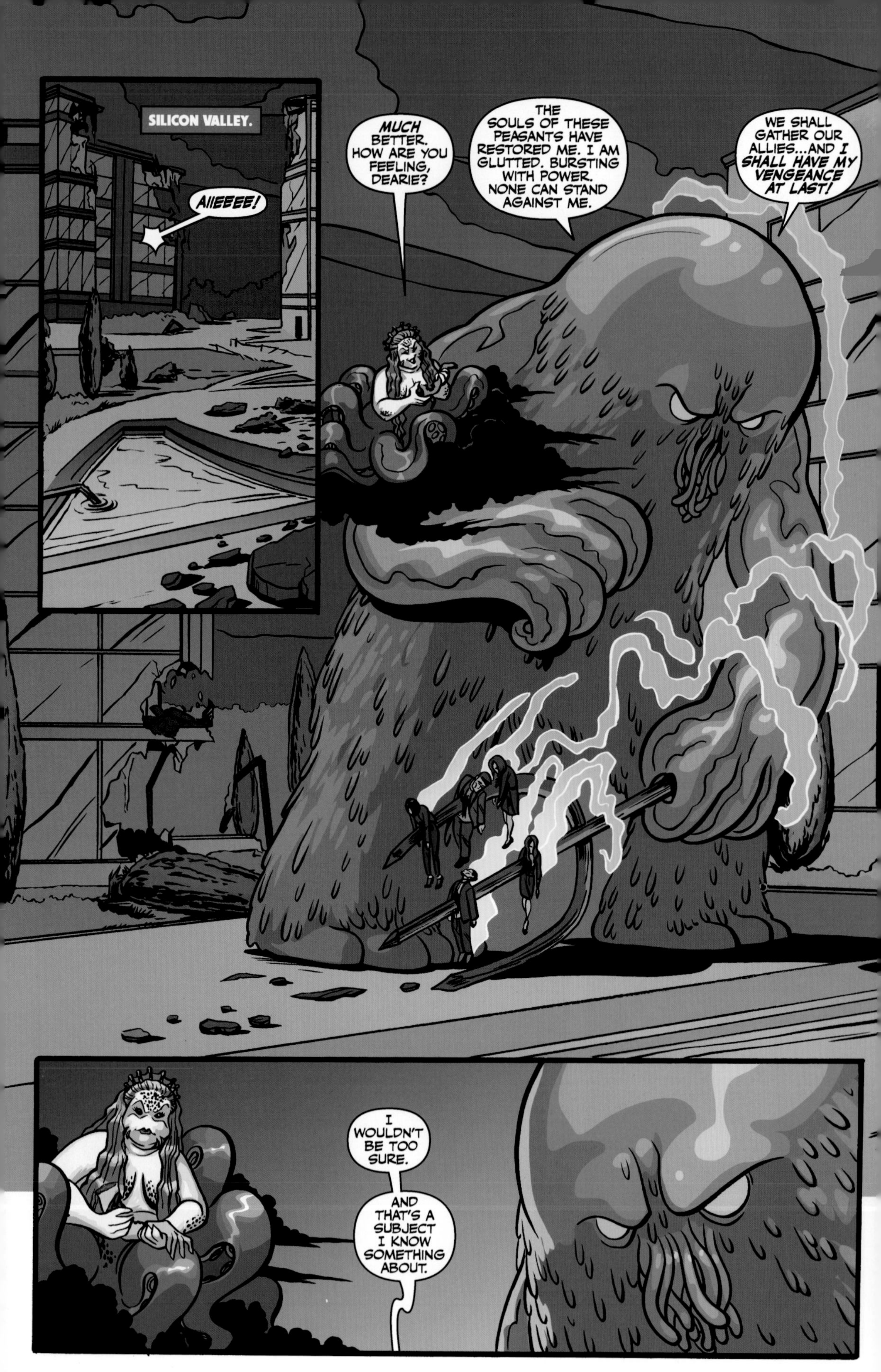
SILICON VALLEY.
AIIEEEE!
MUCH BETTER. HOW ARE YOU FEELING, DEARIE?
THE SOULS OF THESE PEASANTS HAVE RESTORED ME. I AM GLUTTED. BURSTING WITH POWER. NONE CAN STAND AGAINST ME.
WE SHALL GATHER OUR ALLIES...AND I SHALL HAVE MY VENGEANCE AT LAST!
I WOULDN'T BE TOO SURE.
AND THAT'S A SUBJECT I KNOW SOMETHING ABOUT.

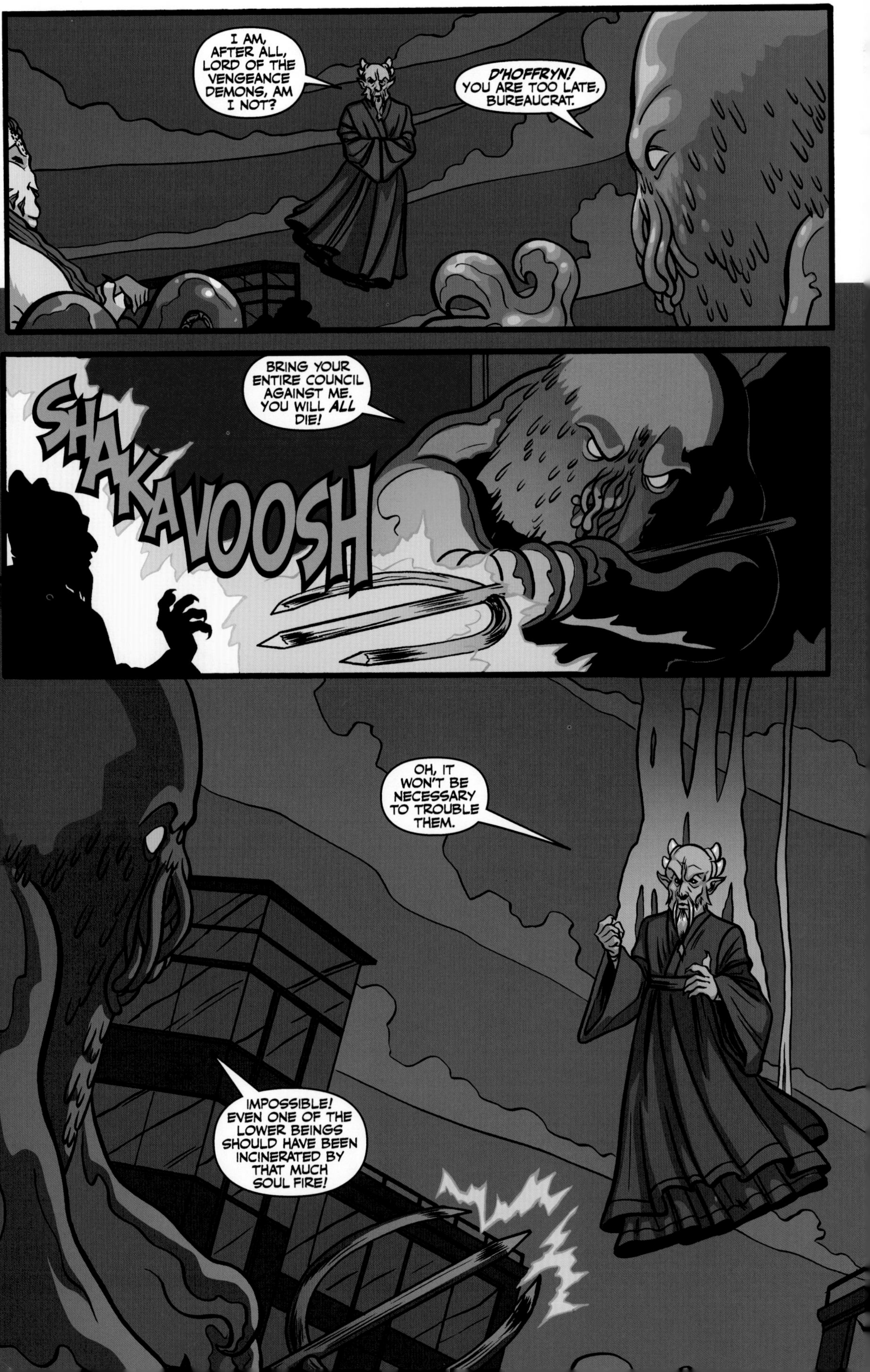
I AM, AFTER ALL, LORD OF THE VENGEANCE DEMONS, AM I NOT?
D'HOFFRYN! YOU ARE TOO LATE, BUREAUCRAT.
BRING YOUR ENTIRE COUNCIL AGAINST ME. YOU WILL ALL DIE!
SHAKAVOOSH
OH, IT WON'T BE NECESSARY TO TROUBLE THEM.
IMPOSSIBLE! EVEN ONE OF THE LOWER BEINGS SHOULD HAVE BEEN INCINERATED BY THAT MUCH SOUL FIRE!

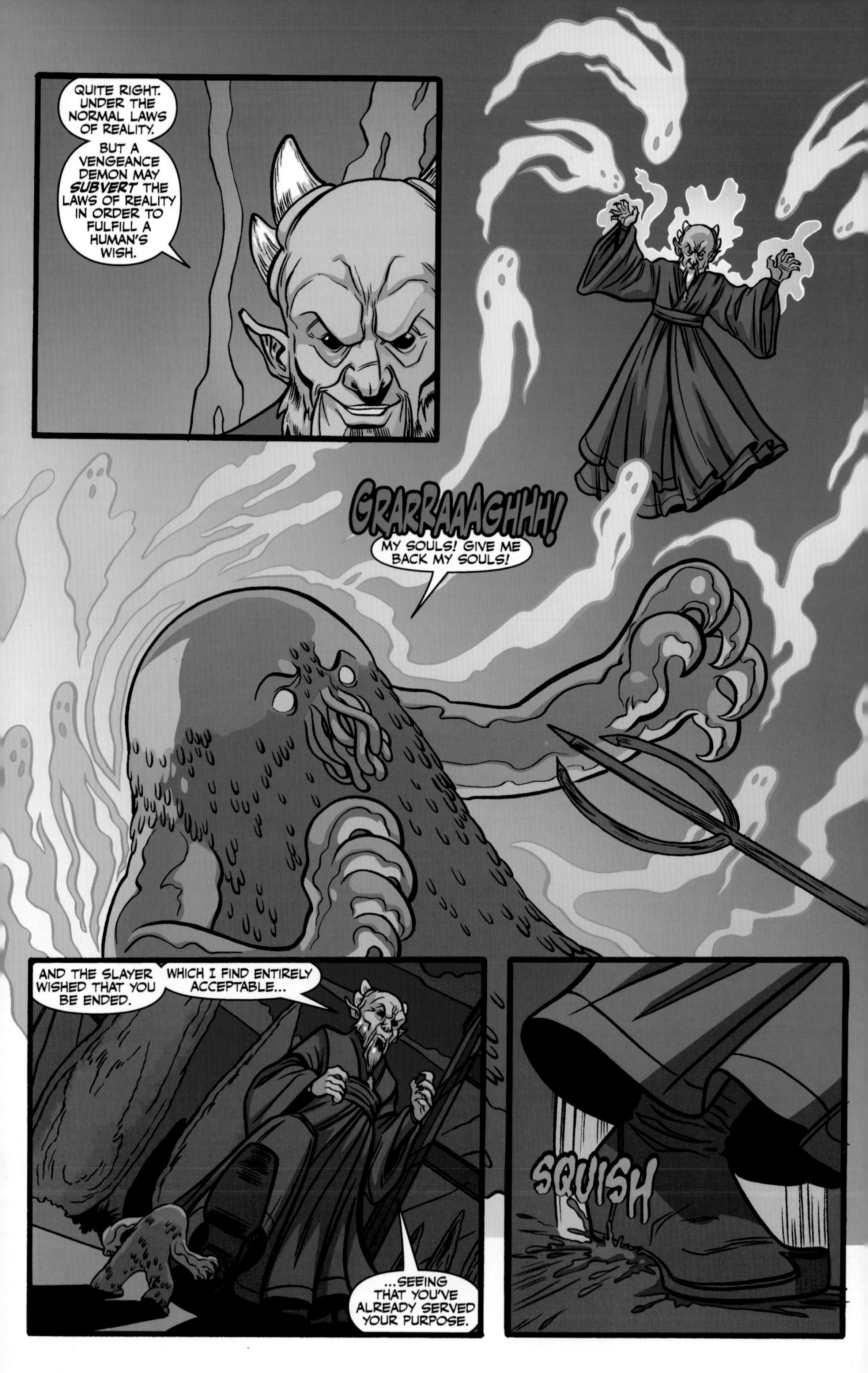
QUITE RIGHT. UNDER THE NORMAL LAWS OF REALITY.
BUT A VENGEANCE DEMON MAY SUBVERT THE LAWS OF REALITY IN ORDER TO FULFILL A HUMAN'S WISH.
GRARRAAAGHHH!
MY SOULS! GIVE ME BACK MY SOULS!
AND THE SLAYER WISHED THAT YOU BE ENDED.
WHICH I FIND ENTIRELY ACCEPTABLE...
...SEEING THAT YOU'VE ALREADY SERVED YOUR PURPOSE.
SQUISH

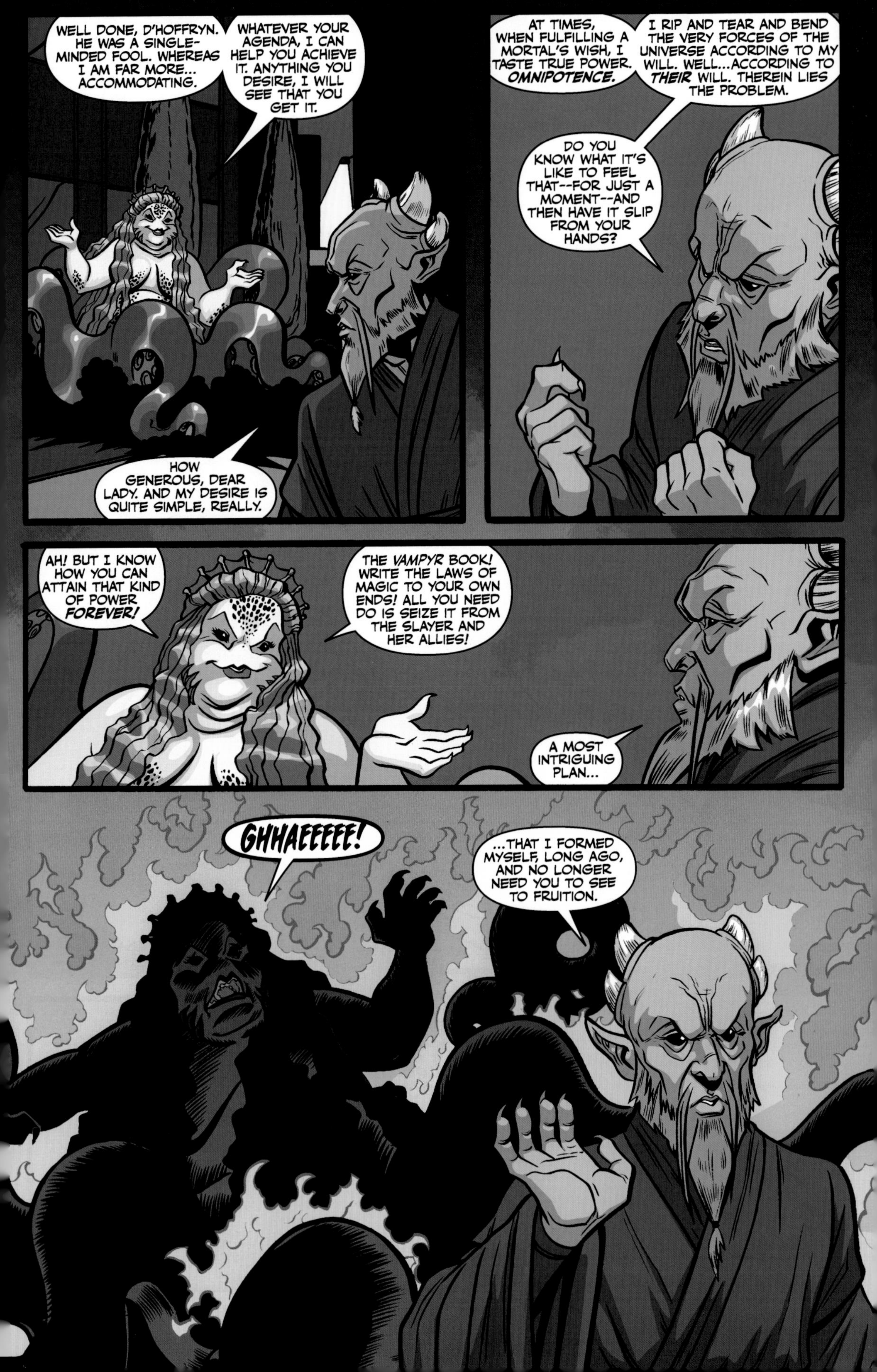
WELL DONE, D'HOFFRYN. HE WAS A SINGLE-MINDED FOOL. WHEREAS I AM FAR MORE... ACCOMMODATING.
WHATEVER YOUR AGENDA, I CAN HELP YOU ACHIEVE IT. ANYTHING YOU DESIRE, I WILL SEE THAT YOU GET IT.
HOW GENEROUS, DEAR LADY. AND MY DESIRE IS QUITE SIMPLE, REALLY.
AT TIMES, WHEN FULFILLING A MORTAL'S WISH, I TASTE TRUE POWER. OMNIPOTENCE.
I RIP AND TEAR AND BEND THE VERY FORCES OF THE UNIVERSE ACCORDING TO MY WILL. WELL...ACCORDING TO THEIR WILL. THEREIN LIES THE PROBLEM.
DO YOU KNOW WHAT IT'S LIKE TO FEEL THAT--FOR JUST A MOMENT--AND THEN HAVE IT SLIP FROM YOUR HANDS?
AH! BUT I KNOW HOW YOU CAN ATTAIN THAT KIND OF POWER FOREVER!
THE VAMPYR BOOK! WRITE THE LAWS OF MAGIC TO YOUR OWN ENDS! ALL YOU NEED DO IS SEIZE IT FROM THE SLAYER AND HER ALLIES!
A MOST INTRIGUING PLAN...
GHHAEEEEE!
...THAT I FORMED MYSELF, LONG AGO, AND NO LONGER NEED YOU TO SEE TO FRUITION.

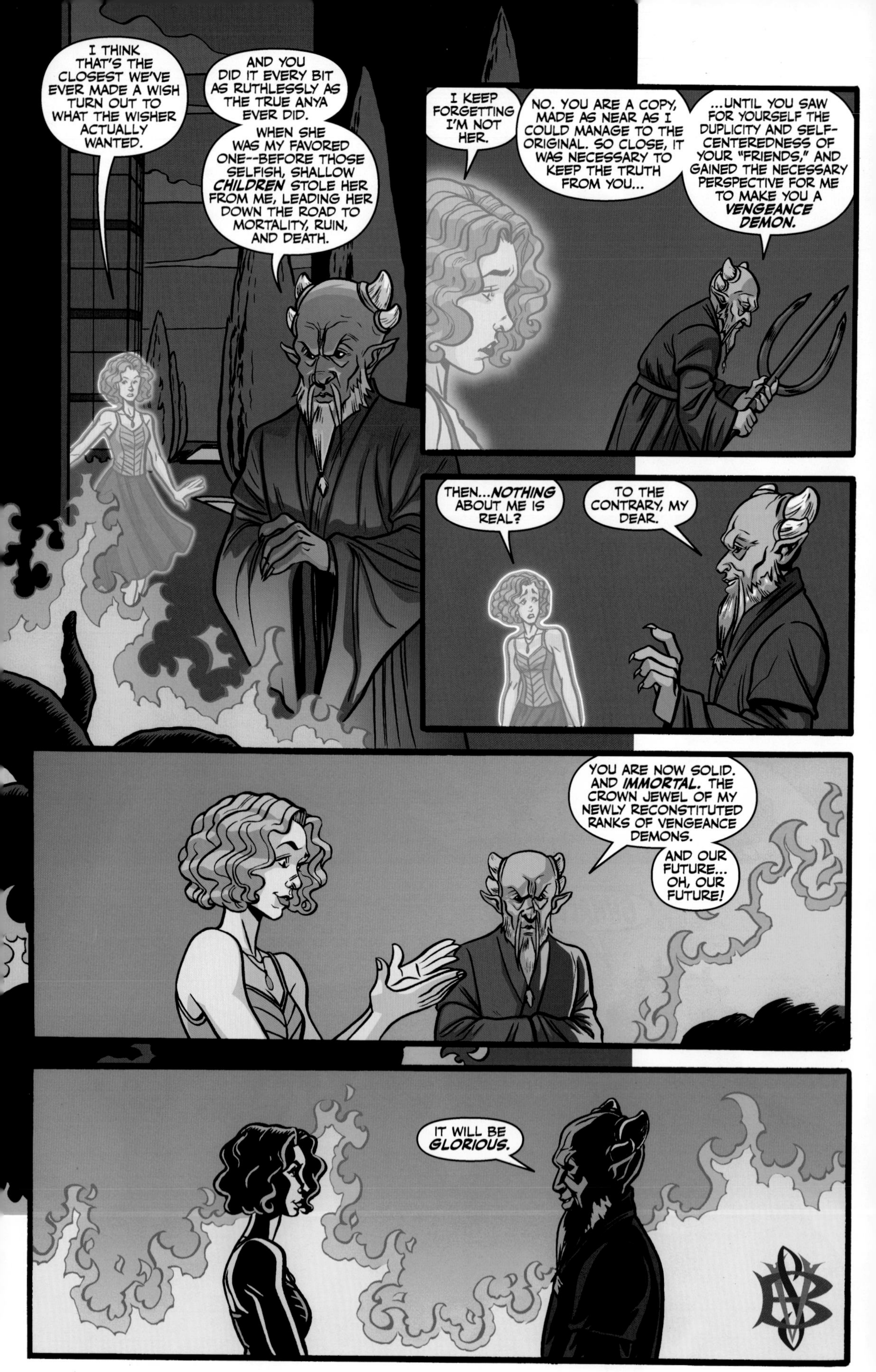
I THINK THAT'S THE CLOSEST WE'VE EVER MADE A WISH TURN OUT TO WHAT THE WISHER ACTUALLY WANTED.
AND YOU DID IT EVERY BIT AS RUTHLESSLY AS THE TRUE ANYA EVER DID.
WHEN SHE WAS MY FAVORED ONE--BEFORE THOSE SELFISH, SHALLOW CHILDREN STOLE HER FROM ME, LEADING HER DOWN THE ROAD TO MORTALITY, RUIN, AND DEATH.
I KEEP FORGETTING I'M NOT HER.
NO. YOU ARE A COPY, MADE AS NEAR AS I COULD MANAGE TO THE ORIGINAL. SO CLOSE, IT WAS NECESSARY TO KEEP THE TRUTH FROM YOU...
...UNTIL YOU SAW FOR YOURSELF THE DUPLICITY AND SELF-CENTEREDNESS OF YOUR "FRIENDS," AND GAINED THE NECESSARY PERSPECTIVE FOR ME TO MAKE YOU A VENGEANCE DEMON.
THEN...NOTHING ABOUT ME IS REAL?
TO THE CONTRARY, MY DEAR.
YOU ARE NOW SOLID. AND IMMORTAL. THE CROWN JEWEL OF MY NEWLY RECONSTITUTED RANKS OF VENGEANCE DEMONS.
AND OUR FUTURE... OH, OUR FUTURE!
IT WILL BE GLORIOUS.

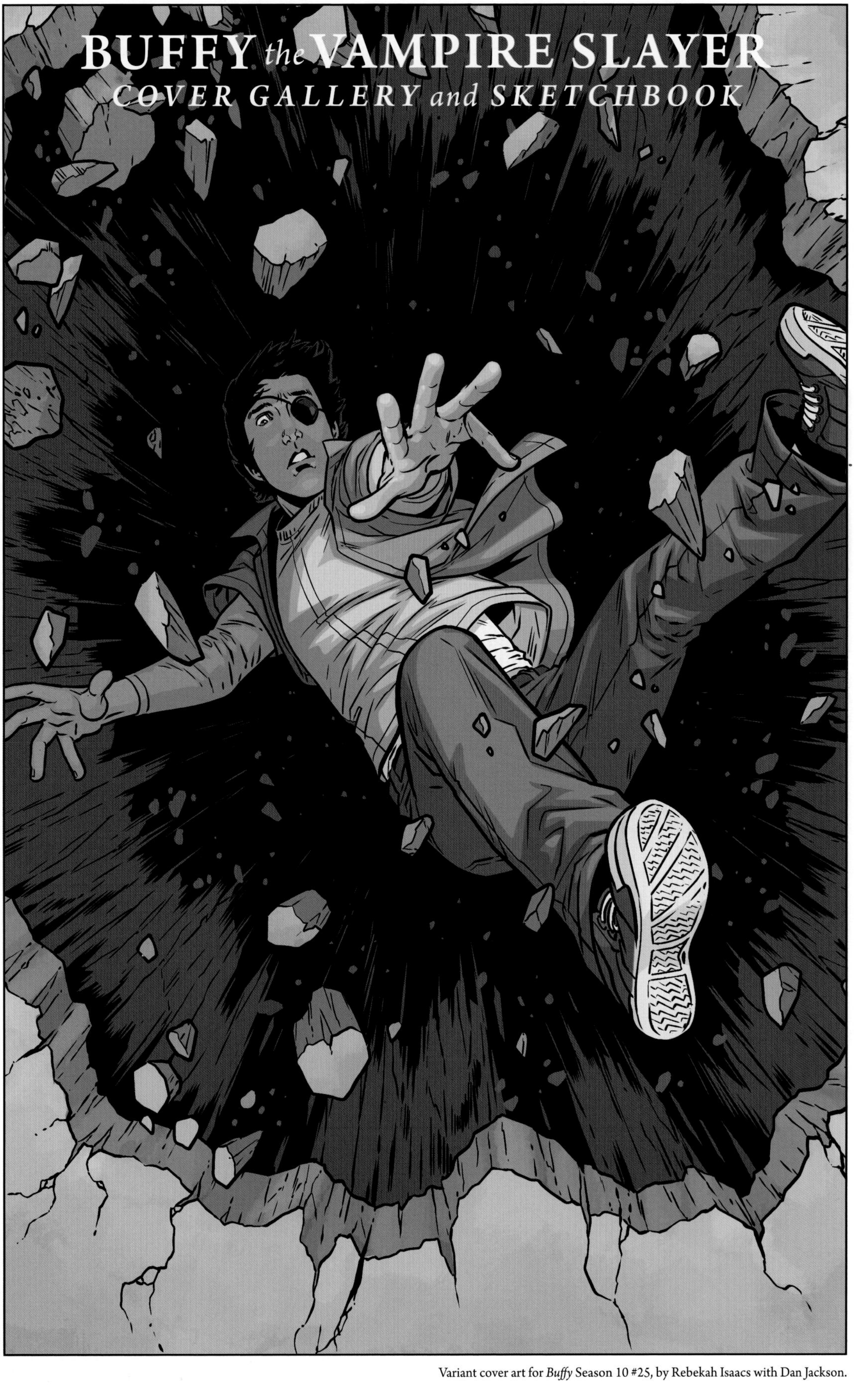
BUFFY the VAMPIRE SLAYER
COVER GALLERY and SKETCHBOOK

Variant cover art for *Buffy* Season 10 #25, by Rebekah Isaacs with Dan Jackson.

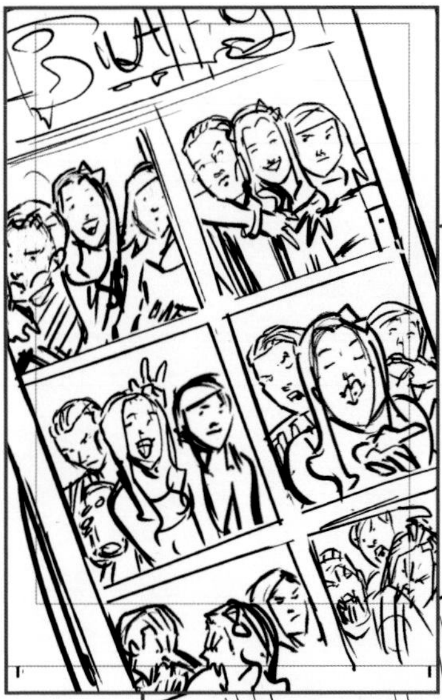

Cover sketch and cover pencils for the issue #21 variant cover, an amazing idea full of so much hilarity from Rebekah.

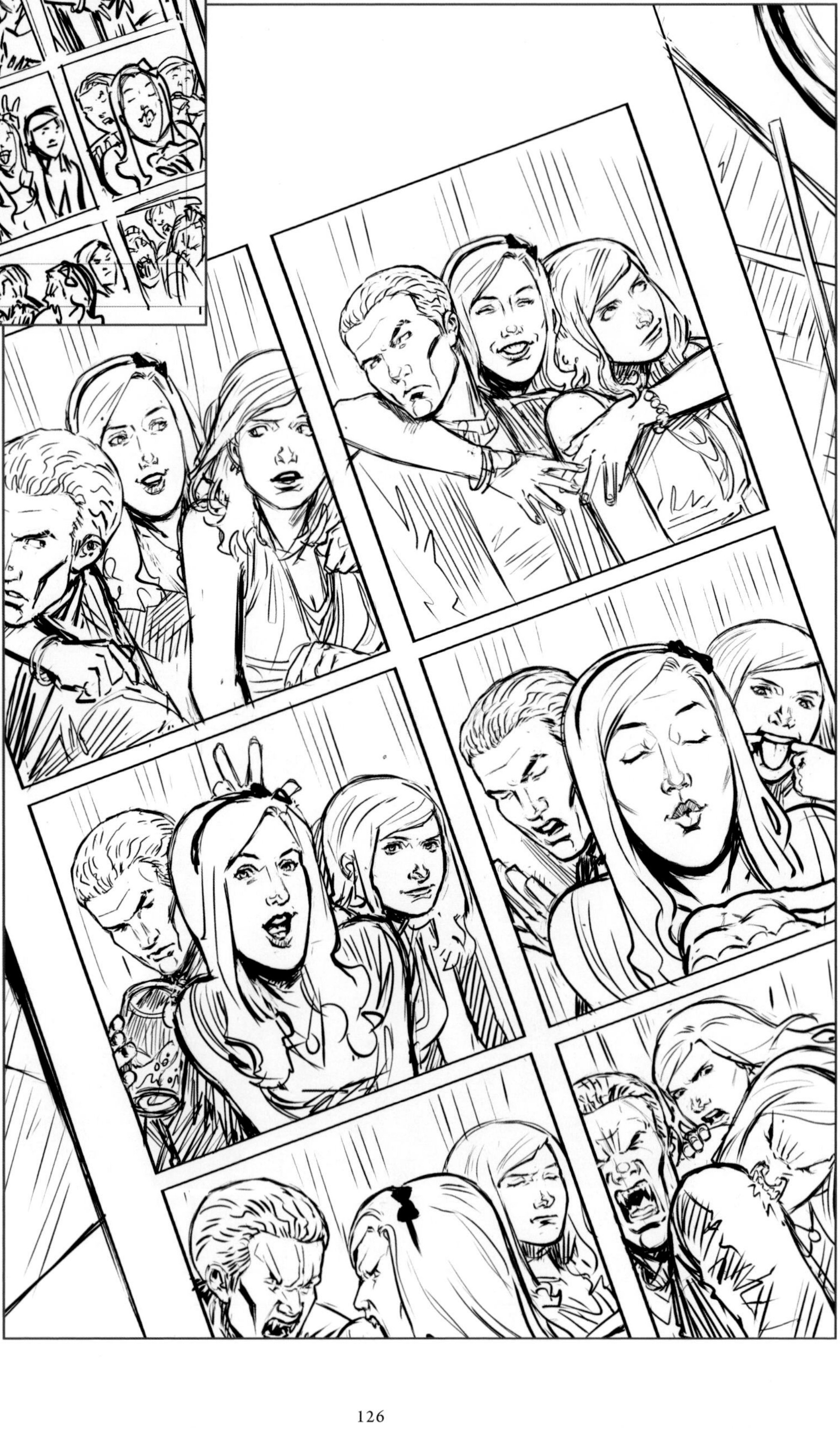

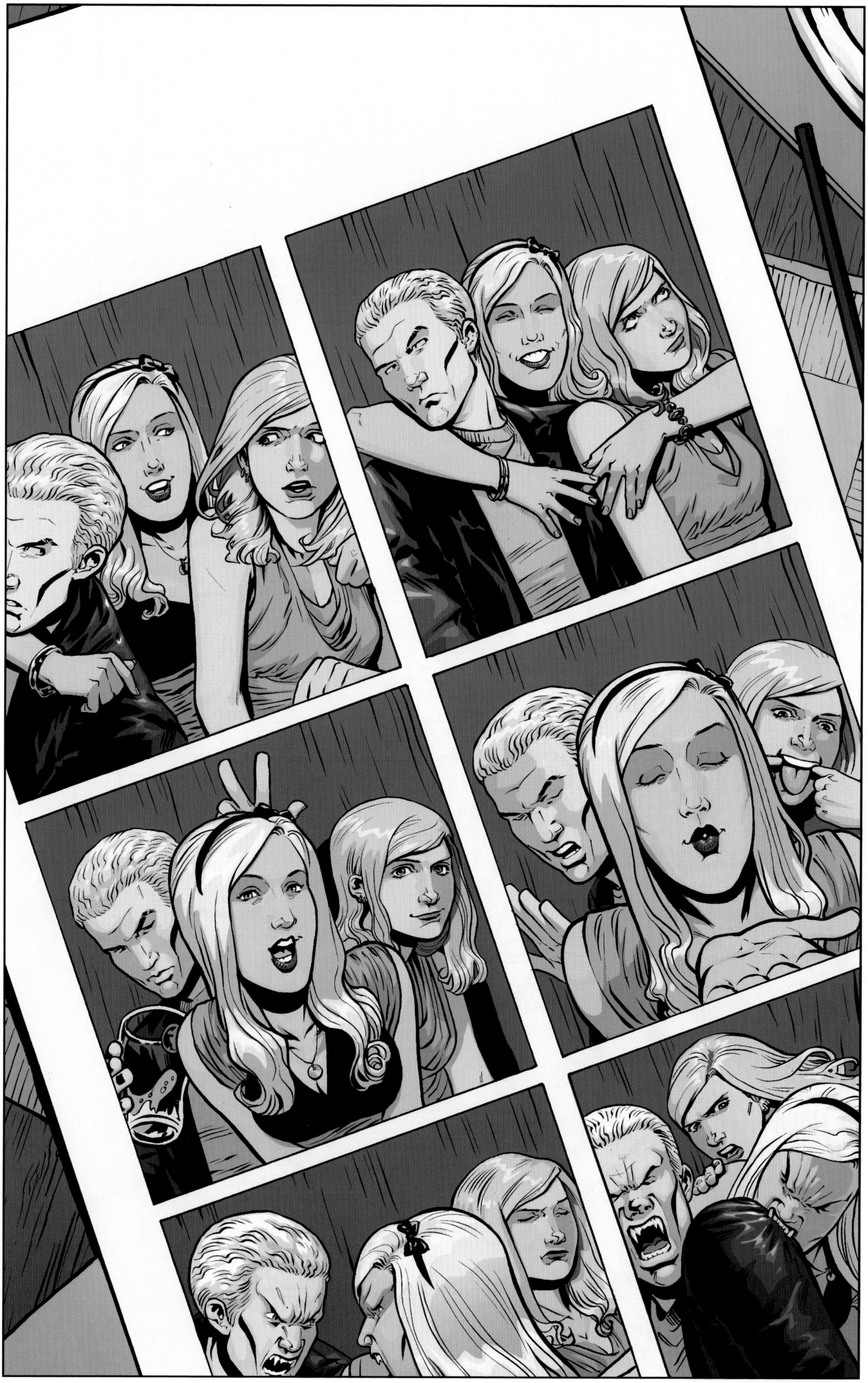

Variant cover art for *Buffy* Season 10 #21, by Rebekah Isaacs with Dan Jackson.

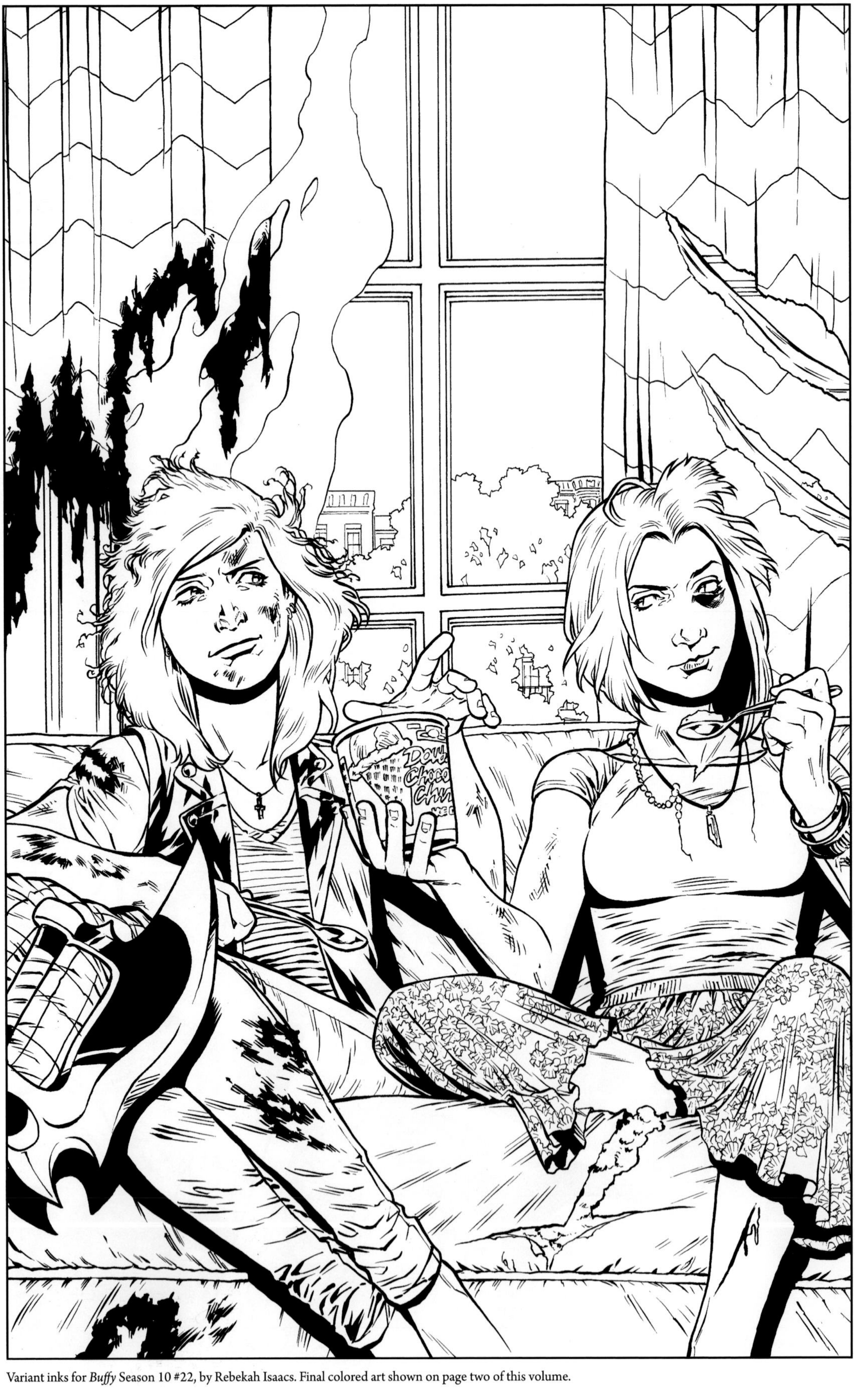

Variant inks for *Buffy* Season 10 #22, by Rebekah Isaacs. Final colored art shown on page two of this volume.

Rebekah's design for Lake Stevens, a new character from the Department of Defense's Unified Supernatural Combatant Command.

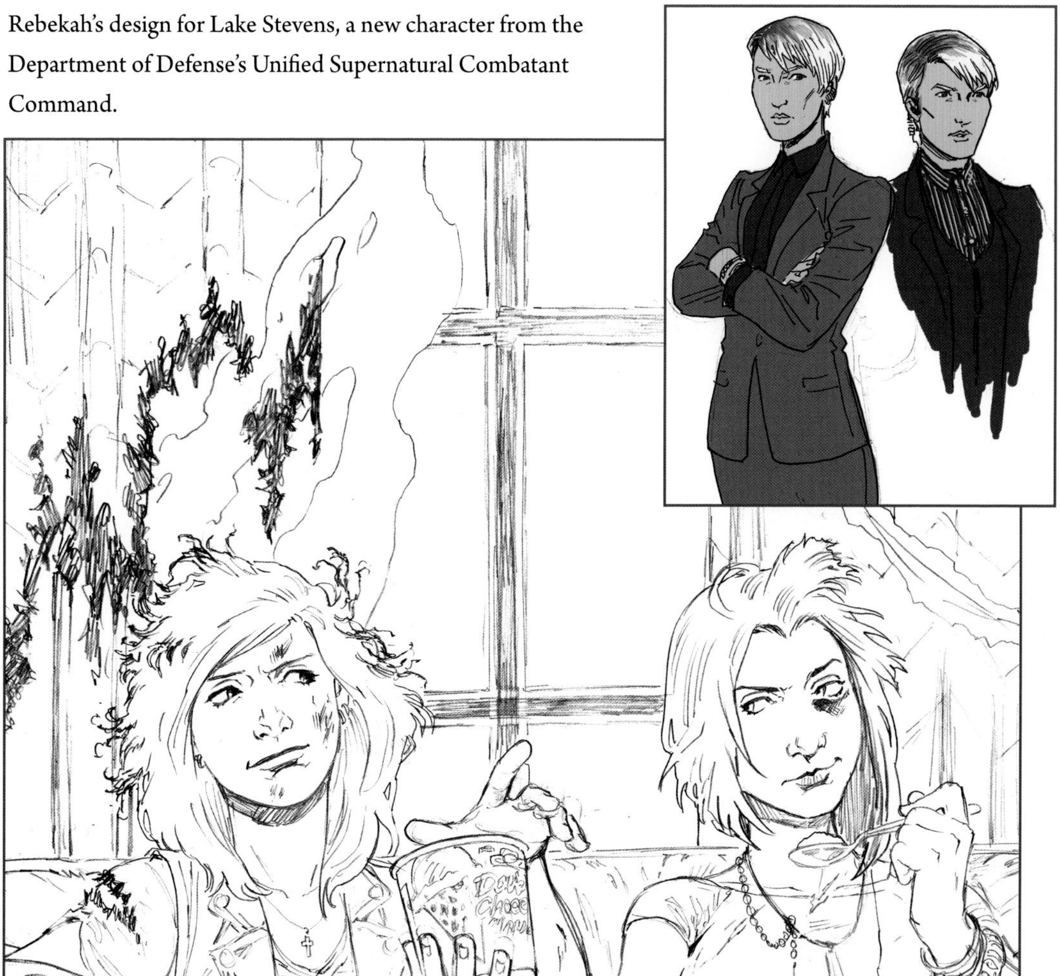

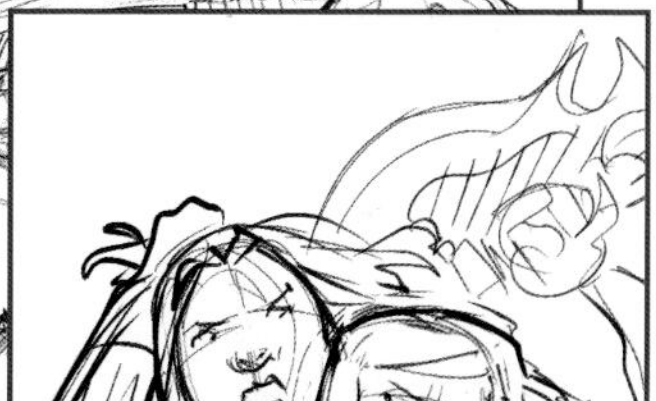

Rebekah's pencils for the issue #22 variant. Also, one of the other sketch options for this cover, representing the argument between Buffy and Willow as an all-out battle.

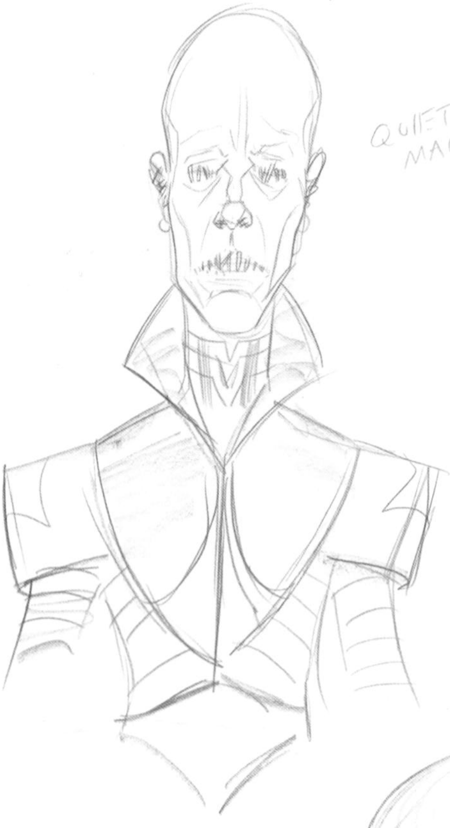

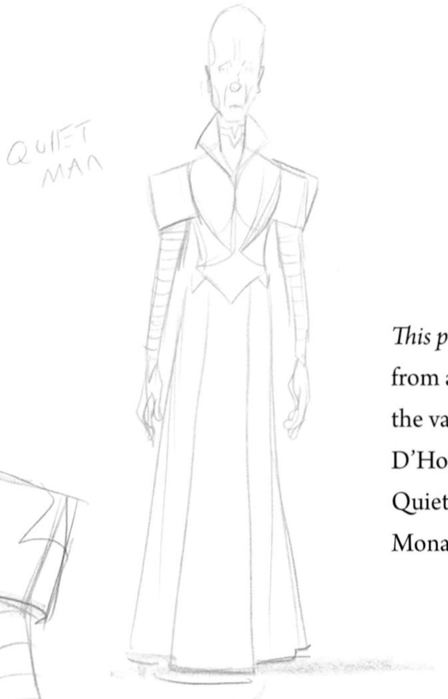
QUIET
MAN

This page and opposite: Designs from artist Megan Levens for the various new members of D'Hoffryn's Magic Council: the Quiet Man, Mushroom Man, Monarch, and Keiko.

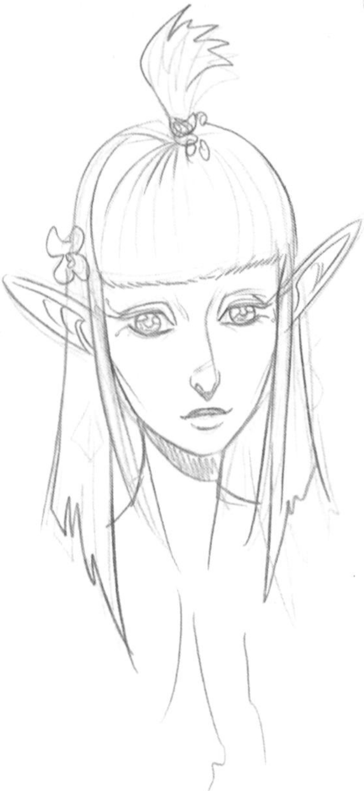

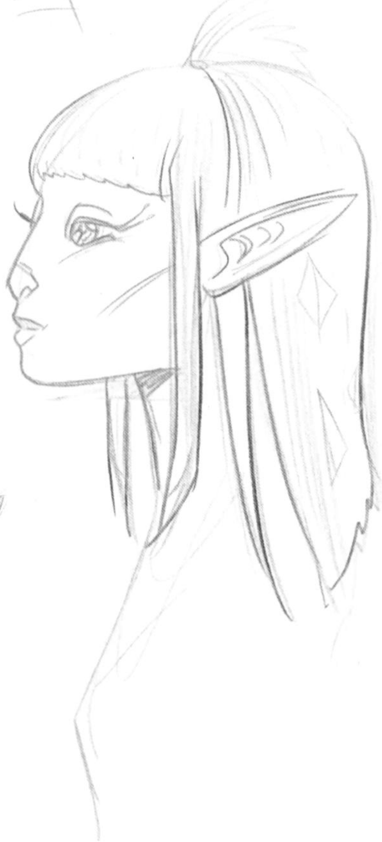

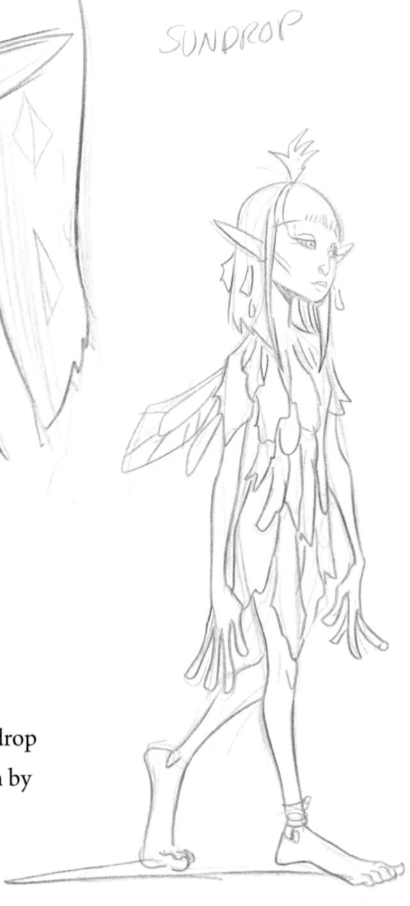
SUNDROP

Young Giles's crush, Sundrop of the Faerie Folk. Design by Megan Levens.

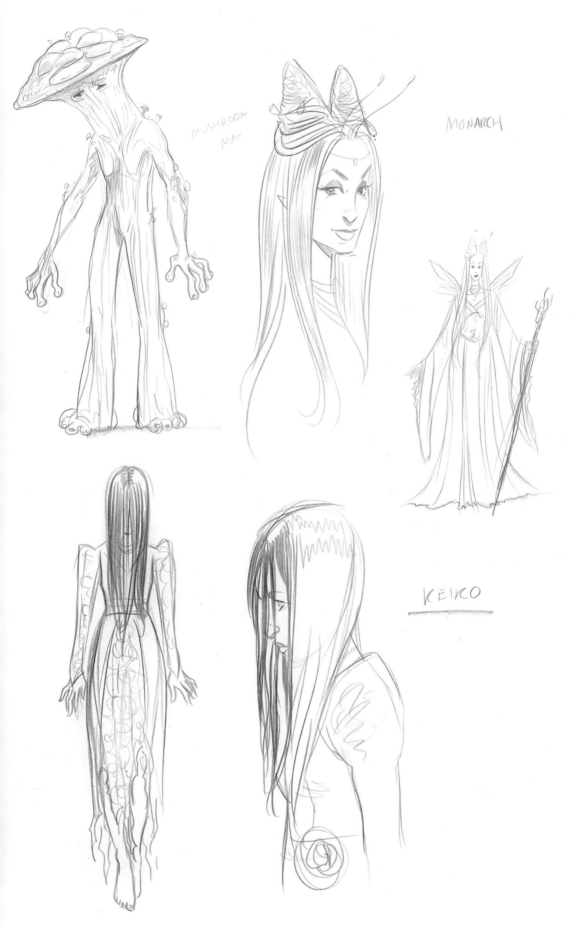

MUSHROOM
MAN

MONARCH

KEIKO

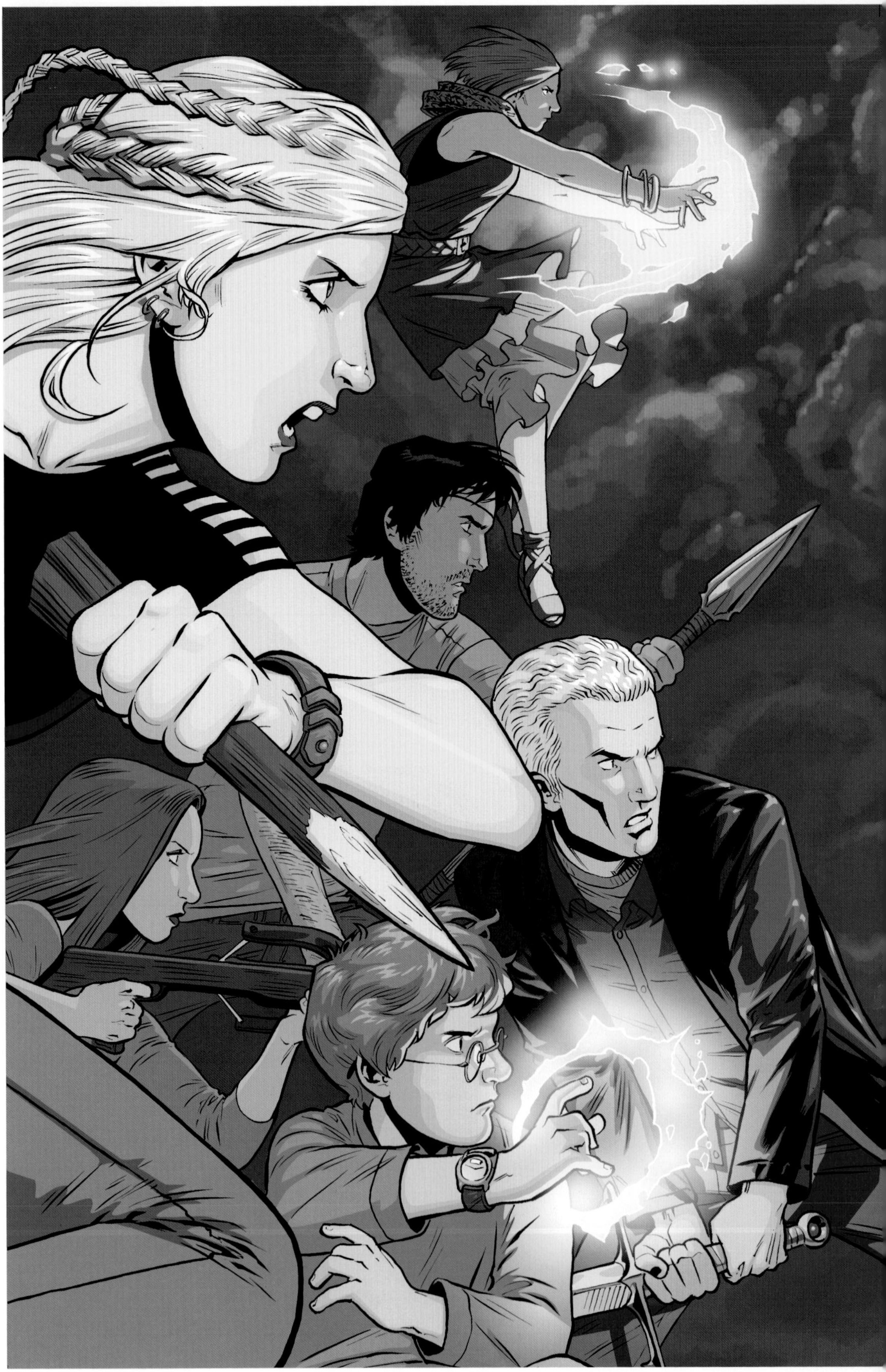

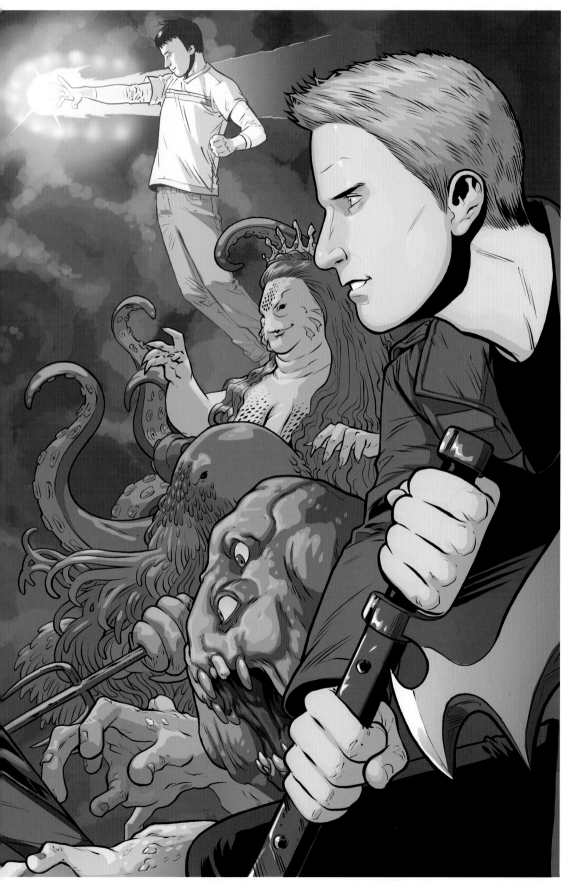

Variant cover art for *Buffy* Season 10 #23 and #24, by Rebekah Isaacs with Dan Jackson. Heroes and villains!

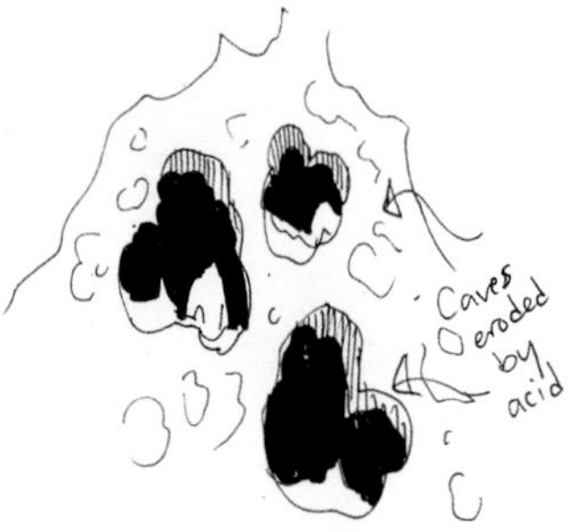
Caves eroded by acid

For the dimension of Anharra, where Dawn and Xander would find themselves trapped at the end of issue #25, Megan and Rebekah were able to coordinate their efforts for the design of Anharra and the Anharrans—as they were drawing them at the same time.

Shown here are Megan Levens's initial designs for the Anharran landscape.

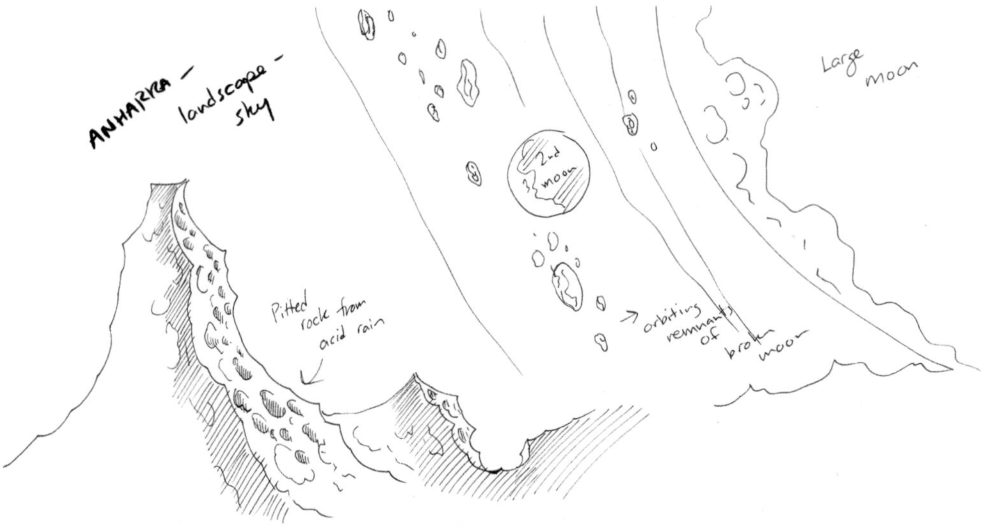
ANHARRA – landscape – sky
Large moon
2nd moon
Pitted rock from acid rain
orbiting remnants of broken moon

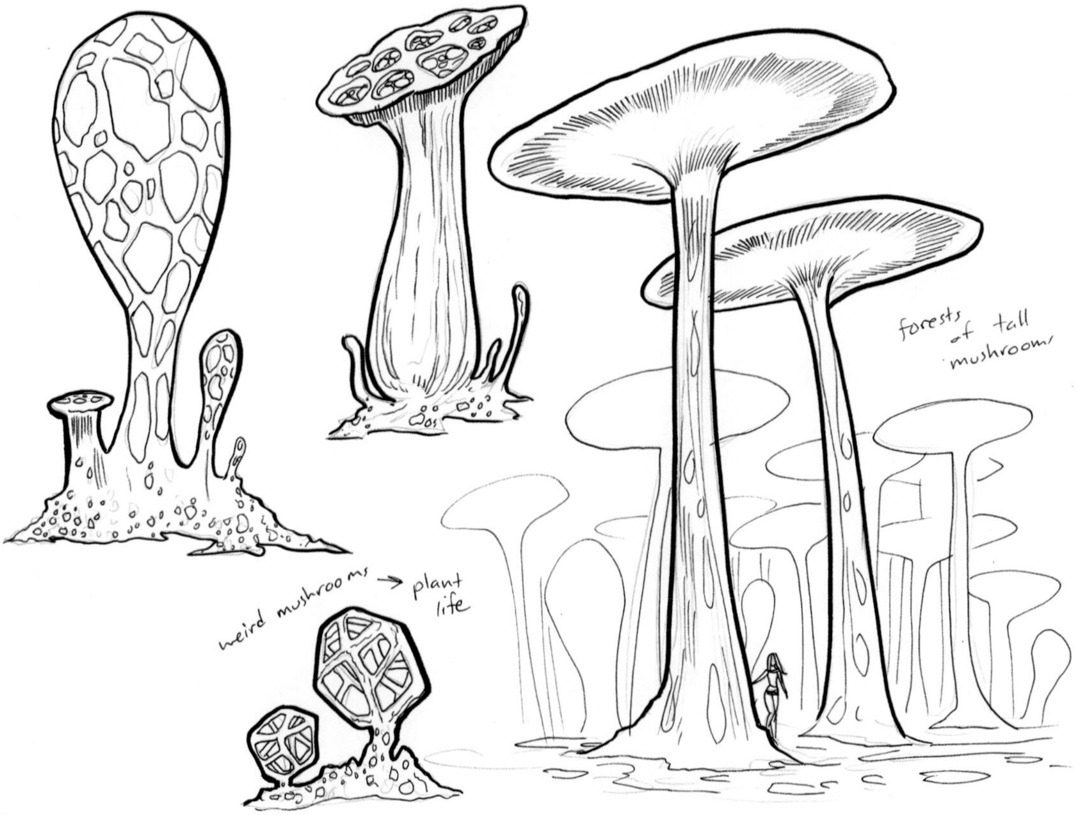
forests of tall mushrooms
weird mushrooms → plant life

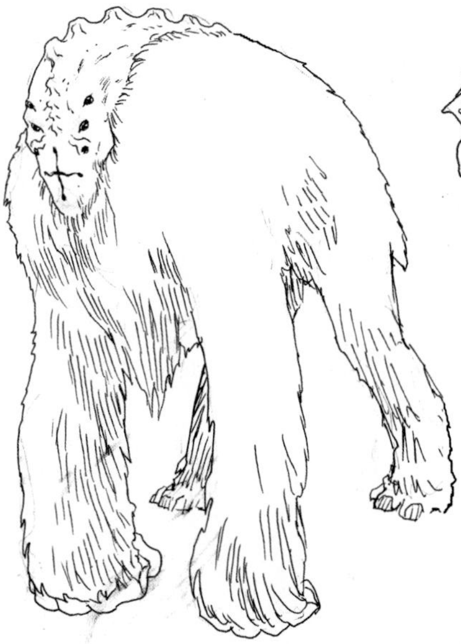
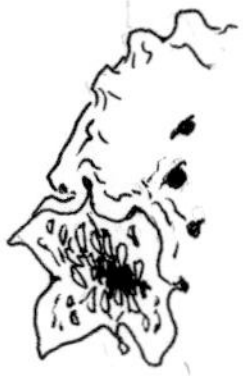
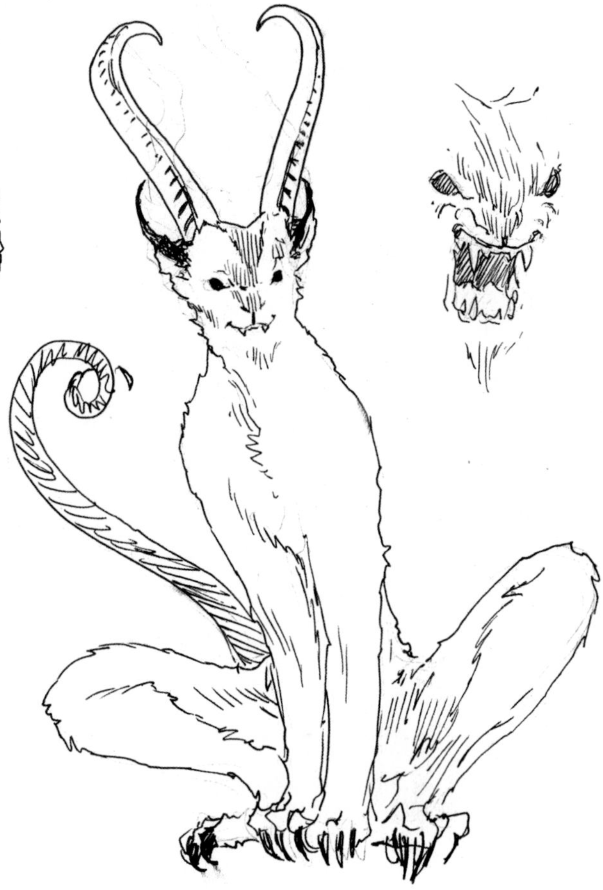
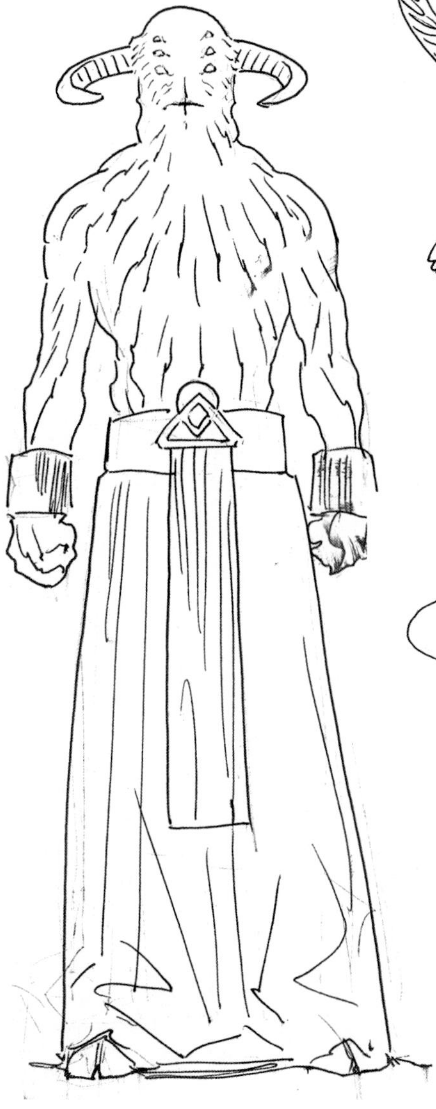
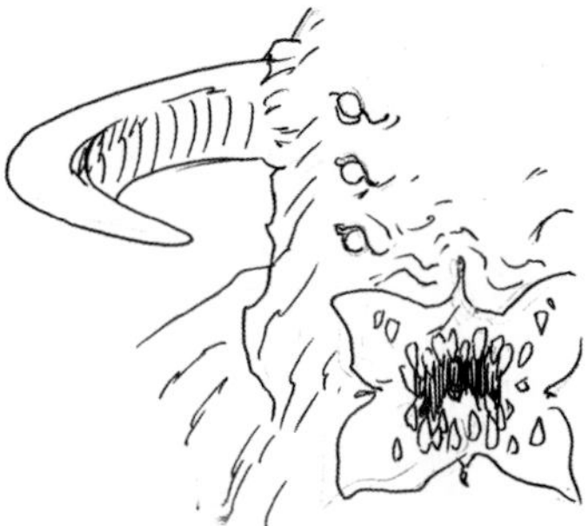

Rebekah's designs for some of the demons of Anharra.

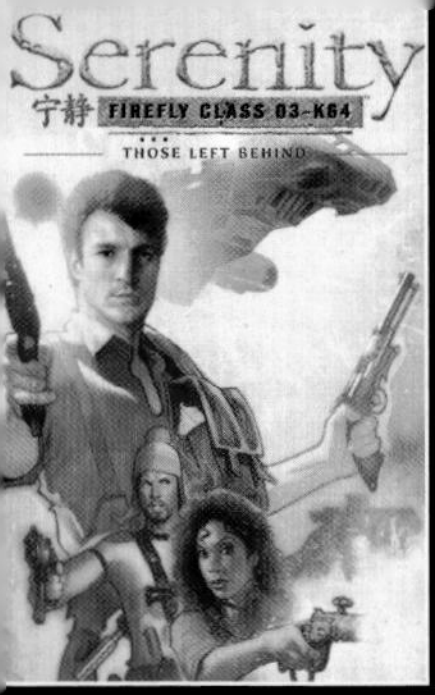
Serenity
FIREFLY CLASS 03-K64
THOSE LEFT BEHIND

SERENITY VOLUME 1: THOSE LEFT BEHIND SECOND EDITION HC
Joss Whedon, Brett Matthews, and Will Conrad
978-1-59582-914-6 | $17.99

SERENITY VOLUME 2: BETTER DAYS AND OTHER STORIES HC
Joss Whedon, Patton Oswalt, Zack Whedon, Patric Reynolds, and others
978-1-59582-739-5 | $19.99

SERENITY VOLUME 3: THE SHEPHERD'S TALE HC
Joss Whedon, Zack Whedon, and Chris Samnee
978-1-59582-561-2 | $14.99

SERENITY VOLUME 4: LEAVES ON THE WIND
Zack Whedon, Georges Jeanty, and Karl Story
978-1-61655-489-7 | $19.99

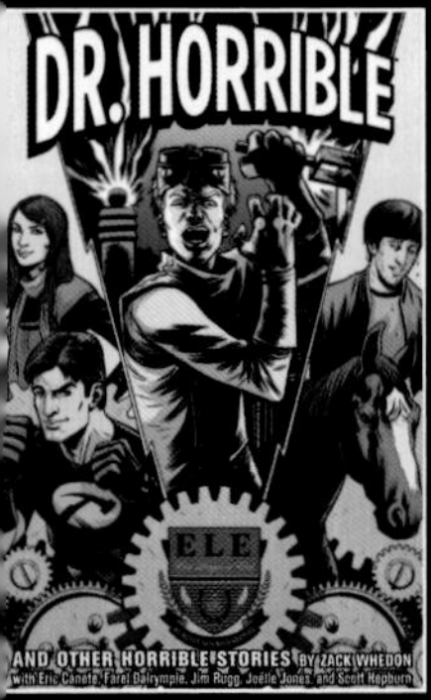
DR. HORRIBLE
AND OTHER HORRIBLE STORIES BY ZACK WHEDON

DR. HORRIBLE AND OTHER HORRIBLE STORIES
Joss Whedon, Zack Whedon, Joëlle Jones, and others
978-1-59582-577-3 | $9.99

DOLLHOUSE: EPITAPHS
Andrew Chambliss, Jed Whedon, Maurissa Tancharoen, and Cliff Richards
978-1-59582-863-7 | $18.99

BUFFY THE VAMPIRE SLAYER: TALES
978-1-59582-644-2 | $29.99

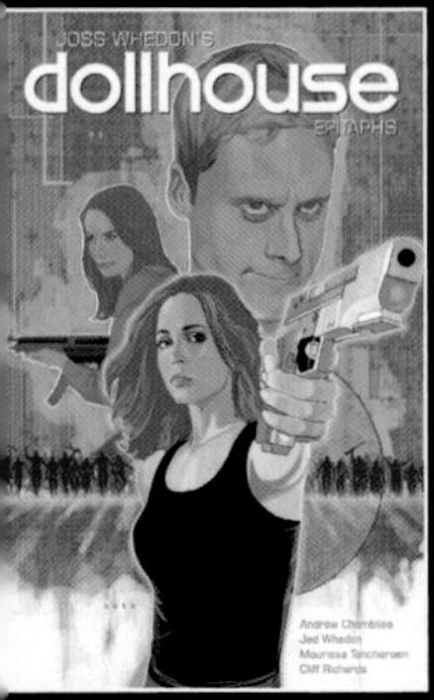
JOSS WHEDON'S
dollhouse
EPITAPHS

ANGEL OMNIBUS
Christopher Golden, Eric Powell, and others
978-1-59582-706-7 | $24.99

BUFFY THE VAMPIRE SLAYER OMNIBUS
Volume 1 978-1-59307-784-6 | $24.99
Volume 2 978-1-59307-826-3 | $24.99
Volume 3 978-1-59307-885-0 | $24.99
Volume 4 978-1-59307-968-0 | $24.99
Volume 5 978-1-59582-225-3 | $24.99
Volume 6 978-1-59582-242-0 | $24.99
Volume 7 978-1-59582-331-1 | $24.99

BUFFY THE VAMPIRE SLAYER: PANEL TO PANEL
978-1-59307-836-2 | $19.99

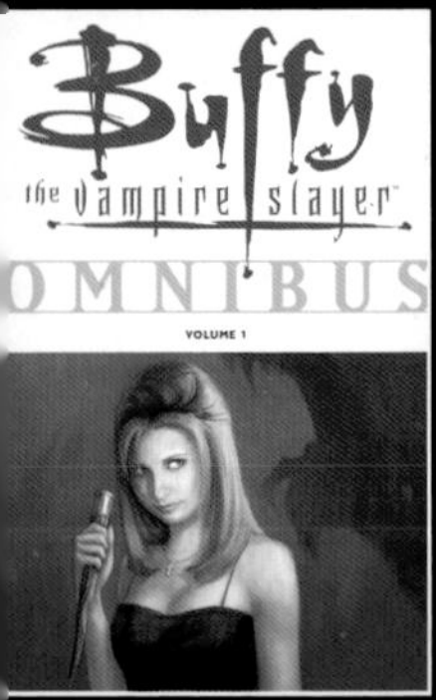
Buffy
the vampire slayer
OMNIBUS
VOLUME 1

BUFFY THE VAMPIRE SLAYER: PANEL TO PANEL—SEASONS 8 & 9
978-1-61655-743-0 | $24.99

SPIKE VOLUME 1: A DARK PLACE
Victor Gischler, Paul Lee, Andy Owens, and Dexter Vines
978-1-61655-109-4 | $17.99

SPIKE: INTO THE LIGHT
James Marsters, Derlis Santacruz, Andy Owens, and Steve Morris
978-1-61655-421-7 | $14.99

WILLOW VOLUME 1: WONDERLAND
Jeff Parker, Christos Gage, Brian Ching, and Jason Gorder
978-1-61655-145-2 | $17.99